Rainer Maria Rilke: Masks and the Man

RAINER MARIA RILKE: MASKS AND THE MAN

By H. F. Peters

GORDIAN PRESS • NEW YORK • 1977

Originally Published 1960
Reprinted 1977

Copyright © 1960 by University of Washington Press
Published by Gordian Press, Inc.
By Arrangement With
University of Washington Press

Library of Congress Cataloging in Publication Data

Peters, Heinz Frederick.
    Rainer Maria Rilke : masks and the man.

    Text in English, poems in English, French, or German.
    Bibliography: p.
    Includes index.
    1. Rilke, Rainer Maria, 1875-1926. 2. Authors,
German--20th century--Biography.
PT2635.I65Z825 1977   831'.9'12 [B]   77-24731
ISBN 0-87752-198-0

To Barry and Emily Cerf

Wer spricht von Siegen? Überstehn ist alles.

Preface

The history of poetry in the first half of the twentieth century is dominated by three major figures: Rainer Maria Rilke, Paul Valéry, and T. S. Eliot. All three are primarily poets' poets in the same sense in which Henry James is primarily a novelist for novelists. They are craftsmen consciously trying to express the human predicament of their age by creating new forms, styles, and myths. As a result they themselves have become legendary, centers of cults to which only the initiated are admitted. This is a pity. For what they have to say has relevance not only to poets and critics but to all who seriously want to understand the human situation in our time.

In writing this book on Rilke it has not been my purpose to add yet another critical study to the already large library of Rilke literature, which has been growing at such an alarming rate that it "threatens to equal that of Shakespeare and Dante." [1] I have written it for two reasons: first, I want to show Rilke's impact on modern poetry; and, second, I want to present Rilke's poetry to the English-speaking reader in such a form that he will be stirred to read it. That, after all, is the only justification for a book of this sort.

"This book is a testimony to a great emotion which, but for Rilke, would never have entered my life. For it arose from contact with one dead who for years had been more alive to me than many of the people around me." [2] These words by the Dutch Rilke scholar F. W. van Heerikhuizen express my sentiments also, and I have written this book chiefly in the hope of arousing interest in Rilke's work among those who do not know it. I realize, of course, that these are not propitious times to advocate the reading of poetry, but I am not resigned to the inevitability of mechanized barbarism. The voice of a genuine poet will be heard even now.

The reader will notice that in addition to my own insights into Rilke's poetry I present the views of many Rilke scholars, critics, commentators, friends, and of Rilke himself. While this method may seem like an arbitrary accumulation of disjointed pieces in a literary jigsaw puzzle, I trust that my own central position provides the unifying theme and that a clear picture of Rilke's poetry and personality emerges. The advantage of this method is that it permits consideration of many facets of Rilke's life and work without trying to prove a thesis, unless, indeed, the reader concludes that this book's underlying thesis is that it is impossible to have a thesis on Rilke. I should not be disturbed if this were the case, for I believe that it is in the nature of Rilke's poetry for every thesis to provoke a counterthesis. This is what the French Rilke scholar Emile Benveniste may have had in mind when he said that it is necessary "to invent a dynamic criticism, suited to such subtle moods as those of Rilke, and able to follow the complex and involved play of forces which rend his remarkable personality." [3]

I do not expect that this book will usher in the age of "dynamic criticism." All I claim is that, while I have listened to what others have said about him, I have turned to Rilke's own words whenever I was in doubt. For the poet's only legitimate interpreter is and always will be—the poem.

❖   ❖

At this point the question arises: How can the testimony of a German poet be conveyed to an English reader? That poems are untranslatable is a truism. Those who have tried to translate Rilke's poems know that even their best efforts are but dull mirrors reflecting an often unrecognizable original. *Traduttore–traditore:* I know of no poet whose work is so much part of the language in which it is written as Rilke's, none that is so greatly betrayed by the translator. And yet such is the challenge of his poetry that efforts to translate it are constantly being made. In his tentative bibliography *Rilke in English*, published in 1946, Richard von Mises lists over sixty translators, a figure that has grown considerably since then.

The translator of poetry must make one fundamental decision spared the translator of prose: he must decide whether to give a prose paraphrase of a given poem or to write a poem around the original. In the foreword of her Rilke translations Miss Herter Norton states the case for the former method. She is quite right in insisting that it is a serious offense to take too great liberty with Rilke's images and symbols for the sake of English meter. On that score her strictures of J. B. Leishman's early translations are just. But she overstates her case for, as Ludwig Lewisohn has pointed out, poems "cannot be split into meaning and form" [4]—least of all Rilke poems. In them "form *is* meaning; and music, message; and rime, revelation." Thus, while Miss Norton's translations are more literal than Leishman's, the latter often approach the spirit of the original more closely. This is particularly true of his later versions of *Sonnets to Orpheus, Duino Elegies* (in collaboration with Stephen Spender), and certain of the *Later Poems.* Indeed, one enthusiastic reviewer has called Leishman's Rilke translations "one of the major achievements of contemporary literature, creative or critical." [5]

The reader will notice that I am heavily indebted to Leishman's translations, which permitted me to make points that I could not easily have made otherwise. He will also notice that I have not hesitated to change Leishman's versions when it seemed to me that a more literal rendering would not hurt a poem's effectiveness. Mr. Leishman's permission to make these changes is gratefully acknowledged. Before deciding on which English translations to include I consulted as many different versions as I could find with the result that in some instances I was forced to make a translation of my own.

While I thus hope that even the reader who does not know German will get some impression of Rilke's incomparable music, I am quite aware that "poems are, with the best knowledge and intention, not to be translated without losses." [6] My endeavor has been to keep these losses at a minimum. The reader may judge whether I have succeeded by comparing the English versions with Rilke's originals immediately following them.

In writing this book the counsel and encouragement of many

of my colleagues has been a great comfort to me. I remember with special gratitude the late Curtis D. Vail of the University of Washington who spared neither time nor effort to suggest improvements during the writing of the first draft. My thanks are due also to Professors Victor Lange of Princeton University, Howard Mumford Jones of Harvard, Karl Aschenbrenner of the University of California at Berkeley, and Heinz Politzer of Oberlin College. To Miss Bonnie Huddart, a former student of mine at Reed College, I am beholden for a last minute checking of the manuscript, and to Miss Barclay Ball of Portland State College for preparing the index.

Finally, I wish to thank a number of publishers for their kind permission to quote from books for which they hold the copyright: The Insel-Verlag, Wiesbaden, for permission to quote from Rilke's *Sämtliche Werke, Gesammelte Werke,* and *Die Aufzeichnungen des Malte Laurids Brigge;* The Hogarth Press, London, for permission to quote from Rilke's *Poems, Later Poems, Requiem, Sonnets to Orpheus,* and *Selected Poems* translated by J. B. Leishman, and from John Linton's translation of *The Notebook of Malte Laurids Brigge;* New Directions, Norfolk, Conn., for permission to quote from *Poems from the Book of Hours,* translated by Babette Deutsch, and from *Rainer Maria Rilke: Poems 1906–1926,* translated by J. B. Leishman; W. W. Norton & Co., New York, for permission to quote from *Rainer Maria Rilke; Duino Elegies,* translated by J. B. Leishman and Stephen Spender and from *Rilke and Benvenuta,* translated by Cyrus Brooks; Macmillan & Co., London, for permission to quote from *Selected Letters of Rainer Maria Rilke,* translated by F. C. Hull; Random House, Inc., New York, for permission to quote from W. H. Auden's *In Time of War,* from *Journey to a War* by W. H. Auden and Christopher Isherwood; Routledge & Kegan Paul Ltd., London, for permission to quote from *The Foreign Gate,* by Sidney Keyes. The bust of Rilke by Fritz Huf is reproduced by courtesy of the Kunstverein Winterthur, Switzerland.

H. F. P.

Neahkahnie, Oregon

Contents

1   *Tonight in China*

> The dangers and the punishments grew greater;
> And the way back by angels was defended
> Against the poet and the legislator.
>   W. H. Auden, *In Time of War*

From the reception accorded to a poet by his contemporaries certain conclusions can be drawn about the direction in which the *Zeitgeist* moves. It goes without saying that by "contemporaries" I do not mean the general public, for the general public does not read poetry—it probably never has—I mean the "happy few" who do. Randall Jarrell thinks they "grow fewer and unhappier day by day"; [1] and there is no doubt that the spirit of the present age is particularly unfavorable to the poet. Amidst a "war haunted, machine-driven multitude" whose preoccupation with the prosaic problems of life leaves them neither time, leisure, nor inclination to cultivate their spiritual potentialities, the modern poet finds himself isolated. The sight of the self-destructive forces let loose in his age fills him with despair. He responds to it, according to his temperament and experience, either by taking part in the political and social conflicts that rage around him, by detaching himself completely from his fellow men and becoming more and more eccentric, cynical, and obscure, by seeking refuge in the Church or by trying to generate new spiritual values.

Between the two world wars many of the younger poets thought that world revolution was the road to salvation and became champions of communist utopias, only to find that they had served a God who failed; others drifted into a waste land of despair, scorned the

1

cheapness and hollowness of modern life, and ended up by returning to the faith of their fathers; yet others played a complex game of hide-and-seek with their readers by deliberately concealing their meanings behind an esoteric pattern of private symbols. Styles changed in quick succession: symbolists, impressionists, expressionists, imagists, dadaists, surrealists, existentialists vied with each other to revive the poetic spirit but failed to convince anyone except a few "thin-lipped academic critics." [2]

In the midst of this poetic Tower of Babel the voice of a genuine poet arose, quietly at first but more and more commanding. It was noticed in Germany around the turn of the century, but was not really heard until many years later. It attracted attention in France in the twenties, in England in the thirties, in America in the forties. By now its sound is familiar to lovers of poetry everywhere in the world.

The growth of this voice, the universality of its appeal, is one of the most amazing cultural phenomena of our age. It is difficult to account for it, although a number of reasons will be given in the course of this inquiry. To begin with let us look at the facts: How did this voice grow and what impact has it had on modern poetry? Our first witness is W. H. Auden.

When Auden and Isherwood set out to visit China in January, 1938, their purpose was to write a travel book about the East, but the outbreak of the Sino-Japanese war caused them to change their plans. The travelers became war correspondents and the book in which they report their impressions and reflections became a *Journey to a War*. It is no literary masterpiece and is mainly interesting today because it reflects the temper of young writers in the thirties: their passionate political convictions, their hatred of war and fascism, their sympathy with left-wing causes, and their faith in Russia. Read in the context of the nineteen-fifties it seems naïve at times and unrealistic, but then, who knows what people twenty years hence will say about our own attitudes and convictions.

The book's most permanent part is undoubtedly the epilogue: a sonnet sequence written by Auden and entitled *In Time of War*. Its main theme is the condition of man which is contrasted with that of the animals and plants:

> Fish swam as fish, peach settled into peach . . .
> And knew their station and were good for ever . . .
> Till finally there came a childish creature
> On whom the years could model any feature,
> And fake with ease a leopard or a dove . . .[3]

Mention is made of the fate of the poet: "some say he was blind" who "mistook for song/ The little tremors of his mind and heart/ At each domestic wrong";[4] and life is praised: "life as it blossoms out in a jar or a face";[5] and the conclusion reached:

> The life of man is never quite completed . . .
> Some saw too clearly all that man was born for.
> Loss is their shadow-wife, Anxiety
> Receives them like a grand hotel . . .[6]

The reader who is familiar with modern poetry will have no difficulty in noticing that these poems, although they are unmistakably Auden, reflect sentiments and use imagery reminiscent of another voice which in the thirties began to be heard in England: the voice of Rainer Maria Rilke. If there were any doubt about Auden's debt to Rilke, the *Twenty-third Sonnet* would dispel it. It evokes Rilke's memory by reminding the reader of the lonely vigil in the tower of Muzot that preceded the creation of the *Duino Elegies*:

> When all the apparatus of report
> Confirms the triumph of our enemies;
> Our bastion pierced, our army in retreat,
> Violence successful like a new disease,
>
> And Wrong a charmer everywhere invited;
> When we regret that we were ever born:
> Let us remember all who seemed deserted.
> Tonight in China let me think of one,
>
> Who through ten years of silence worked and waited,
> Until in Muzot all his powers spoke,
> And everything was given once for all:
>
> And with the gratitude of the Completed
> He went out in the winter night to stroke
> That little tower like a great animal.[7]

This is a remarkable poem for a number of reasons. That Auden, amidst the turmoil of the Chinese scene, thought of Rilke—one of the most unpolitical of poets—is perhaps indicative of the change which was to come over most of the young English and American poets who had stood in the vanguard of social protest. They learned that their responsibility was to write poetry, not political tracts, and that the really important question was not a change of the economic system but a change of the human heart. From a preoccupation with revolutionary ideas they returned to the basic problems of human existence. Rilke had said: "You must change your life," [8] and now Auden echoes: "Nothing is given: we must find our law." [9]

It is noteworthy that Auden does not consider Rilke a poet of despair. On the contrary, he exhorts the reader to learn from Rilke's example that patient and persistent endeavor can turn despair into fulfillment. The spirit of the *Duino Elegies* has triumphed over the despair of *The Waste Land*.

Finally, the poem shows Auden's familiarity with Rilke and the Rilke myth. For it is a myth that Rilke waited "ten years of silence" before he was able to finish the *Elegies* although, like most myths, it contains a psychological truth. This will be discussed in its proper place. Here it must suffice to point out that Auden's sonnet is in part an almost literal paraphrase of Rilke's words in a letter to Lou Andreas-Salomé, written in Muzot on February 11, 1922, in which he tells her of the completion of the *Elegies:* "I have gone out and stroked my little Muzot for having guarded all this for me and at last granted it to me, stroked it like a great, old animal." [10] This letter was first published in 1935 in the volume *Briefe aus Muzot,* where Auden may have come across it.

Corroboration that Rilke's impact on English poetry begins about that time is further furnished by Auden's review of Leishman and Spender's translation of *Duino Elegies* which appeared in the *New Republic* on September 6, 1939. In this review Auden says that "not the least interesting phenomenon of the last four years has been the growing influence of Rilke upon English poetry." He notes that Rilke's technique as well as his way of looking at life are finding English imitators:

Rilke's most immediate and obvious influence has been upon diction and imagery. One of the constant problems of the poet is how to express abstract ideas in concrete terms . . . Rilke is almost the first poet since the 17th century to find a fresh solution. His method is the direct opposite to that of the Elizabethans, but like them and unlike the Metaphysicals, he thinks in physical rather than intellectual symbols. While Shakespeare, for example, thought of the non-human world in terms of the human, Rilke thinks of the human in terms of the non-human, of what he calls Things (Dinge), a way of thought which, as he himself pointed out, is more characteristic of the child than the adult. To the former, tables, dolls, houses, trees, dogs etc. have a life which is just as real as their own or that of their parents. . . . It is this kind of imagery which is already beginning to appear in English poetry (e.g. Stephen Spender's "Napoleon in 1814") and is likely, I think, to become commoner.[11]

This proved to be a correct estimate. For as their lives became entangled in the confusion of the age many of the younger English poets turned to Rilke for solace and inspiration. Sidney Keyes, for example, a promising young poet who was killed in Tunisia in 1943 at the age of twenty, considered Rilke one of the "greatest and most influential poets in the last 100 years." [12] There is a passage in *The Foreign Gate*, one of the best poems Keyes left, which reads almost like a translation of the *First Duino Elegy:*

> Once a man cried and the great Orders heard him:
> Pacing upon a windy wall at night
> A pale unlearned poet out of Europe's
> Erratic heart cried and was filled with speech.
> Were I to cry, who in that proud hierarchy
> Of the illustrious would pity me?
> What should I cry, how should I learn their language?
> The cold wind takes my words.[13]

Rilke, who had a strong sense for mysterious spiritual correspondences, would have been moved if he had known this poem and the fate of the youth who wrote it. It was one of the last poems Keyes wrote before he was drafted and shipped to Africa where he died. As if he had known that it would be his epitaph he prefaced this poem with three lines from Rilke's *Sixth Elegy:*

> Strangely close to the youthfully-dead is the hero.
> . . . Fate, enraptured all of a sudden,
> sings him into the storm of her roaring world.[14]

Wunderlich nah ist der Held doch den jugendlich Toten. . . .
das plötzlich begeisterte Schicksal
singt ihn hinein in den Sturm seiner aufrauschenden Welt.[15]

It is apparent that by the end of the thirties Rilke's influence on English poetry was considerable. Auden and Isherwood felt it in China, it was dominant in Keyes and his Oxford friends, it impelled Leishman and Spender to translate *Duino Elegies* and aroused Professor Butler's critical curiosity. Nor were these the only ones: The indefatigable B. J. Morse, who had started translating Rilke in the twenties (bibliophiles treasure copies of Morse's translations of the *Second* and *Sixth Elegies* published in Trieste in 1926) continued to bring out translations of the *Elegies* in Welsh journals.

During the forties Rilke's name appeared more and more frequently in American scholarly journals and in the little magazines. Jessie Lemont, Herter Norton, Babette Deutsch, Ludwig Lewisohn, C. F. MacIntyre, all of them Rilke admirers of long standing, tried to attract the attention of American readers to the work of the German poet by publishing translations, reviews and commentaries. At a time when everything German was suspect, when such representatives figures of German thought as Nietzsche and Wagner were held responsible by many people in England and America for yet another outbreak of the *furor teutonicus*, a poet of the German tongue invaded the English-speaking world. This is but one of the many Rilkean paradoxes.

Miss Butler's book is easily the most important critical study that has appeared in English on Rilke's life and work, although it received a mixed reception when it came out in 1941. The poet Edward Sackville-West, himself a Rilke translator, reviewed it favorably in the *New Statesman*. He called it a "most able and sensitive study" and liked both Miss Butler's treatment of Rilke's life and her critical appraisal of Rilke's poetry: "the sustained brilliance of her exposition would be . . . difficult to overestimate." [16] This, however, was not the prevailing opinion. Stephen Spender, writing in the *Dublin Review*, was much more reserved. He granted Miss Butler scholarly competence but chided her for her "schoolmistress attitude." She combines, he said, "a gnawing passion for Rilke and his works with a deep contempt for his inferiority in the life of action and sex to other men." [17] Even more outspoken is J. L. Trausil in a letter to the *Saturday Review of Literature*. Miss Butler is said to display a "curiously nagging animosity towards her hero": "Rilke is drawn as an ass—a silly, affected Laforgue-cum-Wilde young man who developed into a kind of inhibited Daddy Browning, amateur of young girls and sexless angels and death, sadist, onanist, rose obsessed and finally rose murdered." Trausil doubts Miss Butler's ability to be objective "even in the handling of objective matter" and concludes that "in spite of a great deal of writing around the poems there is a strange unawareness of the poems themselves. It would have been better, one almost feels, if they did not exist at all." [18]

It is only fair to say that Miss Butler admitted in her introduction that the subject of her study was still a mystery to her which she would never fathom. Since she devoted a great deal of time and energy to it, it is understandable that Rilke's elusiveness irritated her. Her main trouble was that instead of trying to understand Rilke's poetry she set out to "explode" the Rilke legend. This is a pity, for the Rilke legend does not really matter, and his poetry matters a great deal. In any case, when all the exploding is done and Rilke's "human-all-too-human"—or as Miss Butler would say "inhuman"—side has been thoroughly exposed, there still remains an extraordinary man, certainly not a weak man. What strikes the objective observer most forcefully is exactly the opposite: Rilke's tenacity to live his life according to his concept of what a poet's life should be, regardless of the consequences to himself or to others, giving undivided attention to the major problems of existence and wrestling with his angel until he was blessed.

It is quite true that such a life falls outside the human norm. The normal person is not able or willing to live a life of such intense devotion; nor would Rilke wish him to do so. He repeatedly warned against being taken as a model and deplored the tendency to interpret his poetry by relating it to his life: "It is false to deduce the artist from his personal relationships, if for no other reason than that he cannot be deduced from anything. He is and remains the miracle." [19]

And yet Miss Butler is not the only critic who relates Rilke's work to his life. In his very thoughtful study Eudo C. Mason says "it is impossible to disregard the personal and biographical, indeed the psychological, element in Rilke's poetry, even though this meets with Rilke's violent opposition." [20] Peter Demetz calls Rilke's life "his most significant creation" [21] and Heerikhuizen says "the life of Rainer Maria Rilke has not the appearance of a twentieth century life; it was lived in Biblical and Dantesque proportions." [22] Miss Butler would take issue with such statements. To her, Rilke was a neurotic weakling who indulged in "much private hypocritical patter . . . about the cosmic functions of art." [23] But no sooner has she penned the word "hypocritical" when she admits that it is "probably inaccurate."

Rilke's American translator MacIntyre is caught in the same dilemma. He says he was surprised to discover that Rilke "seems to have been all things to all critics," whereupon he boldly sets out to isolate his own Rilke: "a man who during a certain period of his life rode the twin fillies of the wing'd horse, sculpture and painting, keeping a firm foot on each, and singing, as he went, his beautifully formed and colored sonnets, or polishing small concert and salon pieces, sonatas in miniature." [24] So far so good. Unfortunately, MacIntyre is carried away by his metaphor and makes Rilke gallop "out of the tent into the night of the soul in the *Duineser Elegien* and into the foggy obfuscations of *Die Sonette an Orpheus*." [25] A few pages later, however, he regrets the "unfortunate sentence" and announces that he has translated *Duino Elegies* three times.

This is all rather puzzling to the reader who looks to Rilke's critics for elucidation and enlightenment. For what one critic confidently asserts another as confidently rejects, and often the same critic is torn between acceptance and rejection. The reasons Rilke arouses such ambivalent emotions among his critics are not hard to find. For one thing, he was a very ambiguous man, a modern Hamlet, who refused to enter into distinct commitments. He wanted to remain open and receptive to all experiences. Like Keats he believed that the "only means of strengthening one's intellect is to make up one's mind about nothing." [26] Hence the essence of his poetry is ambiguity: it defies definition. This means that a critic is defeated before he has started. If he defines Rilke as a mystic, he is wrong; if he defines him as an esthete, he is wrong; if he defines him as a symbolist, he is wrong: Rilke was all these—had a relation to all these *and* to others besides.

For another thing Rilke was a great believer in change and was constantly changing. Thus a critic who had just praised the *Book of Hours* might be unable to do justice to the *New Poems* or vice versa. But above all Rilke's poetry represents a kind of Copernican reversal of the traditional poetic processes. This is what Auden means when he says that "Rilke's method is the direct opposite to that of the Elizabethans" or, as Professor Heller puts it: "In the great poetry of the European tradition the emotions do not interpret; they respond to the interpreted world. In Rilke's mature poetry the emotions do the interpreting and then respond to their own interpretation." [27] Unless the critic accepts Rilke's way of looking at the world, unless he is able to view it through the undivided consciousness of a child, he cannot evaluate Rilke's poetry because he does not understand it.

The more intellectual a critic is the less likely is he therefore to understand Rilke. This explains the seeming paradox that many first-rate minds are baffled by Rilke's poetry while quite unlearned people have no difficulty with it at all. It also explains Rilke's popularity and what has been called the "Rilke cult."

Now it would of course be absurd to say that you have to be simple-minded to understand Rilke. The complexity and subtlety of his work is too well known for that, but it is of a kind that demands intuitive rather than intellectual understanding because its "true foundation lies beyond the reach of limiting intellect." [28] The fact that it does appeal to the world's leading minds is a sign of the great transformation through which we are passing, a sign of what Jaspers has called "the radical disappointment of an arrogant faith in reason." [29]

Rilke's reception in France, the country where the goddess of reason was first enthroned, shows how far that disappointment has gone. Note what the French Rilke scholar, Edmond Jaloux, has to say about him:

When I began talking with Rilke it seemed to me that it was the first
time that I talked with a poet. I mean to say that all the other
poets I have known, however great they were, were poets only in their
minds; outside their work they lived in the same world as I, with the
same creatures . . . but when Rilke began to talk he introduced me to
a world that was his own and into which I could enter only by some
sort of miracle. The marvellous, the fantastic grew with his words and
through him I escaped at last from the hell of logic.[30]

For a man steeped in the tradition of Descartes this is a remarkable confession. But Rilke seems to appeal to the French
precisely because he transcends logic and opens a door into the
vast realm of the unconscious. No modern German poet has had
an equal impact on French thought. "Our country," writes Marcel
Brion,

. . . more than any other, more even than Germany herself, has accepted in its totality Rilke's message which demands sympathy and com-
munion. No French writer has judged his work from the outside, with
a cold and detached objectivity; to penetrate into one of his books
means to become a citizen of that enchanted universe which is his,
to take one's place in it. I would go further and say that you cannot
judge Rilke without loving him.[31]

Rilke was first noticed in France in 1911. In July of that year the
Nouvelle Revue Française published an article by Madame Aline
Mayrisch, under the pen name of Saint Hubert, on the *Notebooks
of Malte Laurids Brigge*. The same issue contained André Gide's
translation of excerpts from *Malte*.

Malte had appeared in June, 1910, and in September Rilke had
sent a copy to Gide. Gide's acknowledgment shows how much he
liked the book: "I have been living with you for two weeks, deeply
engrossed in your book. How grateful I am that it teaches me to
get to know you better, for that means to love you more." [32] He
says he copied a sentence from *Malte* because it went straight to
his heart. The idea of translating parts of *Malte* must have occurred to him then. We find him writing to Madame Mayrisch in
January, 1911, encouraging her to finish her study to which he and
his colleagues of the *Nouvelle Revue* are looking forward with
"cordiale impatience." It is this letter which contains the sig-

nificant sentence: "N'est-ce pas que par ce dernier livre Rilke prend place près de nous?" [33]

Madame Mayrisch's essay, praised by both Gide and Rilke, touches on most points that make up the French Rilke picture. She emphasizes the poet's "subtle and attentive sensuality from which, by some sort of immediate intuition, there emerges an extended image of life." [34] Rilke thinks with his heart, which is tormented by a Pascalian thirst for the absolute. This, she notes, is not without danger. *Malte* contains "a rather embarrassing pathological element that is not always transformed into art." [35] She mentions the role of childhood in Rilke's work: "C'est là ce qui donne au lyrisme de Rilke son accent unique, sa force, son importance." [36] She talks about Rilke's "dynamic adjectives" and the close correspondence between his thought and his style which suggests to her the idea of a skin rather than a garment. She is impressed by his verbal inventiveness, which is unlimited, but points out that at times it goes beyond the limits of the possible and that his refined taste can commit "unfortunate errors." She says that Rilke, being concerned with inner events, reveals remarkably subtle and piercing psychological insights. And yet she does not consider *Malte* a "well-made" book: it is too fervid, too uncontrolled for her taste. Still, it is so "heavy with the mystery of a living work that the commentator of this book risks above all that, for having understood it too well, he has ill divined it." [37] Many years later Paul Valéry used an almost identical phrase when he said that, although he could not understand the language of Rilke's poetry, he "divined" its meaning.

The First World War impeded but did not stop Rilke's influence in France. His French friends, notably André Gide, Romain Rolland, and Jacques Copeau, remained loyal to the German poet despite the bitter national hatred that poisoned the spirit of the two peoples. The affection they felt for him is well illustrated by the unfortunate circumstances that surround the forced sale of Rilke's personal possessions left in Paris at the outbreak of the war. For no sooner had Stefan Zweig advised Rolland in Switzerland that Rilke was about to lose his property, including letters and manuscripts, than the latter wrote to Copeau that it would be "an irreparable loss for art and an act of unreasonable cruelty to the gentle thinker and poet" [38] if this were to happen. Copeau and Gide acted at once, only to find that they were a year too late. Rilke's books and furniture, except for two boxes with personal papers, had been auctioned off in 1915. In cooperation with other writers, among them Edith Wharton, Gide did succeed in salvaging some of Rilke's papers. He returned them to the poet at the end of the war "in the name of his French friends." This episode shows that even before he had done his major work Rilke was well liked and respected in France.

The rapid increase of his popularity there in the twenties is mainly due to two factors: to the dedicated efforts of his French translator, Maurice Betz, and to his French poems published in Valéry's review *Commerce.*

Not the least interesting aspect of the Rilke phenomenon are the men and women in all countries who have devoted their talents to his service. It is a long list and includes such names as Stephen Spender, J. B. Leishman, V. M. and Edward Sackville-West, B. J. Morse, and R. C. Hull in England; Jessie Lemont, Herter Norton, Babette Deutsch, Ludwig Lewisohn, and C. F. MacIntyre in America; Leo Negrelli, Leone Traverso, Raffaello Prati, and Vincenzo Errante in Italy; Torrente Ballester in Spain; Inga Junghanns in Denmark; Stefan Napierskiego and Witold Hulewicz in Poland; L. Gorbunovoj, B. Pasternak, and Juliana Anisimova in Russia; Hsung-hua Wu in China. Although far from complete and constantly increasing—during 1951–52 no fewer than eleven Rilke translations into Japanese were brought to my notice—this list shows how universal the appeal of Rilke's poetry is.

Among the first and greatest of Rilke's translators ranks Maurice Betz. From 1923 when, as a young man, he started translating *Malte,* to his death in 1948, he was Rilke's dedicated advocate in France. A poet in his own right and a personal friend of Rilke, he succeeded in transmitting not only the thought but often the tone and music of Rilke's poetry. His eight-volume translation of Rilke's works represents a major literary achievement. With it Rilke took his place in French literature.

But Rilke has a more direct claim to French literary citizenship: the French poems he wrote at the end of his life. They are not merely translations of his German poems, although they treat similar themes. Miss Butler has called them "transubstantiations." Written in a minor key, they do not have the depth or the range of his German poems but they are not unworthy of Rilke and have genuine poetic value. That is why Valéry urged him to publish them, and Valéry's judgment has been upheld by numerous French critics. "Rilke's French poems," writes Marcel Brion, "fill a very beautiful page of French poetry which, without them—this we know today—would have remained empty." [39]

In the systole and diastole of these limpid poems Rilke's great themes lose weight and seem to float gently toward some Ultima Thule. Fate is in balance, opposites are reconciled and, as in the *Sonnets to Orpheus*, being and nonbeing know of each other. Everything is subject to "the sacred law of contrast"; even the angels have lost their terror and have become "discreet":

> How beautiful I was! That which I see
> makes me think, master, of my beauty!
> This sky, your angels,—but it was I,
> the wonder above all of not to be.

> Que j'étais belle! Ce que je vois
> me fait penser à ma beauté, o maître!
> Ce ciel, tes anges,—mais c'était moi,
> l'étonnement en plus de ne pas l'être.[40]

French critics were quick to notice that a distinct quality was introduced into French poetry by Rilke's poems, "the quality of chiaroscuro which it lacked." [41] To show their admiration they devoted an entire issue of *Les Cahiers du Mois* to him. It appeared in September, 1926, three months before Rilke's death. Among the contributors were such illustrious writers and scholars as Paul Valéry, Maurice Betz, Jean Cassou, Marcel Brion, Geneviève Bianquis, André Germain, André Berge, Edmond Jaloux, Felix Bertaux, Daniel Rops, and Francis de Miomandre. What they thought of Rilke can best be seen from the following quotations:

We can only dimly perceive this second life, this magnetic interpenetration of the self and the non-self. But Rainer Maria Rilke is at home in it. . . .[42]

We give ourselves to Rilke unreservedly, as he demands it, joyfully and with great relief because he has in abundance so many things we lack. . . .[43]

Thanks to Proust and Rilke we feel today closer to ourselves. . . .[44]

Goethe was a minister, Mallarmé a professor and even Verlaine. . . . Of Rilke one cannot imagine that he could have been anything but a poet.[45]

The existence of Rilke is identical with the existence of poetry itself; it demands from us an act of faith.[46]

The testimony of these witnesses leaves no doubt that Rilke enjoyed a considerable reputation in France in the mid-twenties. The French were charmed by the mystery that surrounded the man and by the magic of his work. Like Rilke admirers elsewhere they found it difficult to keep the two separate. They too were struck by the close interdependence between Rilke's poetry and his life, so much so that Felix Bertaux compared Rilke's life to a sonnet. Those who knew him well never stopped wondering about his "magical" presence. "Of all the unusual men that I have known," said Valéry, "one of the most fascinating and by far the most mysterious was Rilke. If the word 'magic' has any meaning at all, I would say that his person, his voice, his glance, his manners, everything about him gave the impression of a magical presence." [47] They felt that the poet was imbued with the same ineffable spiritual quality that distinguishes his work. There was no way of describing him. The man Rilke defied definition just as much as his poetry. Gide

> . . . knew of no portrait that does him justice. The features of his face, his whole physical being, seemed to be imbued with a spirituality that no brush could render. One might almost say that he was never really present in his body. One felt that he was elsewhere, in a mysterious region that was more real to him than what we call reality.[48]

These descriptions appeared in a book entitled *Rilke et la France,* which was published in Paris in 1942. Thus even the Second World War could not dim Rilke's reputation in France. On the contrary, in a world threatened by material collapse and spiritual bankruptcy Rilke's example was seen as proof that the human spirit can rise above despair. It is for this reason that some of Rilke's French friends secretly published excerpts from the poet's thoughts on war and distributed them under the nose of the Gestapo. This rare volume: *Rilke—Fragments sur la Guerre, édition clandestine imprimée par quelques amis français de Rilke,* appeared in January, 1944. Just as Auden, confronted by the desolation of the Chinese war—"when we regret that we were ever born"—had found solace in thinking of Rilke, his French friends thought of him when "their bastion was pierced, their army in retreat and violence successful like a new disease."

The rise of existentialism in the postwar period further enhanced Rilke's fame in France. For although it would be as incorrect to label him an existentialist as it is to label him a mystic, his poetry does lend support to the existentialist interpretation of the condition of man. In his book on Rilke J. F. Angelloz quotes Heidegger as saying that Rilke had expressed poetically what the existentialist expresses philosophically, i.e., the pure perilousness of human existence, man's forlornness amidst indifferent stars, his being thrust into the world where he has to exist alone, where nobody can help him: "not angels, not men." Like Kierkegaard with whose writings he was well acquainted, Rilke was imbued with anxiety, with a deeply felt awareness of the precariousness of existence. *Weltangst* was his "shadow wife"; he lived with it. He expressed it in his poetry. But he did not incorporate it in a philosophic system and the conclusion he draws from it is paradoxical. For, on the one hand, he says: "hostility is our first response"; [49] and, on the other: "to be here is magnificent." [50]

The intensity of feeling for these contradictory emotions causes great inner tensions in Rilke's work. It oscillates between total rejection and total acceptance of life, between negation and affirmation, lament and praise. It tries to reach the farthest point of despair, the point where despair risks plunging into chaos, but when it has reached it, it turns: deepest woe becomes beatitude. Rilke's belief in such a "turning point"—*Umschlag* he calls it—

forms a basic element in his *Weltanschauung*. It corresponds to
the idea of transcendence in Heidegger's philosophy: transcendence not toward God but toward the world and toward the self.
This amounts to the paradoxical belief of transcendence in immanence. It occurs very frequently in Rilke's poetry, for example
in the requiem for Count von Kalkreuth, whose suicide he
laments:

> Why could you not have waited till the point
> where heaviness grows unbearable: where it turns,
> being now so heavy because so real? [51]

> Was hast du nicht gewartet, daß die Schwere
> ganz unerträglich wird: da schlägt sie um
> und ist so schwer, weil sie so echt ist.[52]

And it occurs in his letters as a guide to life for those who ask his
advice. "If only we arrange our life according to that principle
which counsels us that we must always hold to what is difficult,
then that which now still seems to us the most hostile, will become
what we most trust and find most faithful." [53]

Like all of Rilke's ideas his *Umschlag* hypothesis is based on
lived insights, not on abstract reasoning. His own life, he felt, was
a series of "turning points" climaxing in that sudden and wholly
miraculous creative outburst at Muzot in February, 1922, which
brought forth the *Elegies* and *Sonnets*. Was it not an *Umschlag*
from the long period of sterility that had preceded it? "And everything was given once for all."

To a generation in search of new values the idea that a turning
point will come, provided we have patience to wait for it and do
not let ourselves be overwhelmed by despair, is perhaps the most
appealing of Rilke's ideas. That it should appeal to the French in
particular is not surprising, seeing that the decline of their traditional faith in reason has left a more serious void in France than
elsewhere. Having been attracted to him originally because of the
Proust-like psychological insights they gained from him, they have
come to appreciate the ethical content of his poetry: "Who speaks
of victory? To endure—that's it." [54]

In Germany Rilke's influence has been profound, as one would expect, but it has not been undisputed. Rilke himself grew alarmed when he noticed how his style began to dominate German poetry and severely rebuked those who wanted to impress him by sending him poems written in his manner. Regina Ullmann tells how sad he became when she showed him one of her poems that, she thought, he might have written. He read it and tore it up, warning her not to imitate him or anyone else but to be herself and to write as she must. For if there was one law which the artist must not violate it was that of expressing himself in his own individual, even idiopathic, style. But his warnings went unheeded. The spell he had cast over German poetry, the power of his imagery, his poetic diction, even his peculiar rhymes, proved too strong for most of his contemporaries. They imitated him eagerly; and if all the German poems written in the Rilkean manner during the last three or four decades could be collected (fortunately an impossible task), they would far outnumber Rilke's works. Herder's rebuke to the young Goethe "Shakespeare has spoilt you" could be applied to most of Rilke's imitators. It should be noted in passing that a reaction against this trend has set in, a critical re-evaluation of Rilke's place in German poetry, and that many of the younger German poets now look to Gottfried Benn rather than to Rilke for inspiration.

Another group of German Rilke admirers whose blind worship has tended to obscure his image are his numerous feminine friends and hagiographers. Most of them, with the exception of Lou Andreas-Salomé, who played a unique role in his life, were so enthralled by his magic personality that they could not describe him objectively. As a result Rilke appears in their books and memorials as a strangely incorporeal seer-saint, half hidden behind a cloud of incense that is kept burning before his altar. Miss Butler is quite right when she protests against this kind of mystification, although she is guilty of the opposite offense for "the mistake would be gross indeed if, in exploding a mere legend, one should overlook a miracle." [55] It is admittedly not easy to distinguish between the legendary and the miraculous aspects of Rilke's life, for what may be demonstrably untrue, or legendary by logical arguments may still represent a psychological truth. The

martyrdom of Rilke's childhood, for example, has been called a
legend. In his book on the young Rilke, Carl Sieber says that the
facts do not bear it out. Rilke did not have a "hard" childhood;
he was a "pampered child and a sentimental youth." [56] And more
recently Peter Demetz has reached the same conclusion. He too
finds no substance in fact for Rilke's complaint that he was a
misunderstood genius. On the contrary, he received unusual encouragement at a time when he did not deserve it at all. Dr.
Simenauer, on the other hand, points out that there are sound
psychological reasons for both these legends, that Rilke did suffer
in his childhood and felt misunderstood in Prague. The psychoanalytical approach reveals the extremely complex personality of
the poet and sheds light on the real tragedy of Rilke's life.

Resistance to Rilke in Germany has come from yet two other
unexpected quarters. Stefan George and Hugo von Hofmannsthal,
Rilke's greatest German contemporaries, were indifferent or even
hostile to his poetry. Mutual antipathy prevented George and
Rilke from doing justice to each other's work. George was rightly
critical of Rilke's youthful productions and Rilke sensed a good
deal of pretense in the works of the George circle. Its leading
critic, Friedrich Gundolf, comparing the two poets, said that
while Rilke possessed "medial" powers he lacked "human dignity."
On the other hand: "Stefan George, my own master, has glorified
in his poetry as no other the dignity of man in the universe and
thus defended the Hellenic heritage against India, the East and
even Christianity." [57] One can agree with this characterization of
the two poets and reach opposite conclusions. Instead of criticizing
Rilke's lack of dignity one can praise him for his humility and as
regards George's defense of the Hellenic heritage (a grandiloquent
statement if ever there was one) it is quite possible to assert that
Rilke's mediating position between Hellas and India, the West
and the East, anticipates the art of the future. Gundolf's con-
descending estimate of Rilke's place in German poetry, made in
1931, at a time when Rilke had already won universal recognition,
shows how far literary partisanship can mislead an otherwise
perceptive mind. "In German poetry," he said, "Rilke may last—
if not because of this message (about which I cannot prophesy)—

Rainer Maria Rilke
Head by Fritz Huf. Kunstverein Winterthur

as one of its most uncontrolled masters. By uncontrolled I mean the arbitrariness of his grasp and the absoluteness of his emotions." [58]

On the surface, at least, the relationship between Rilke and Hofmannsthal was much more cordial. The two poets met often and exchanged compliments on each other's work. Rilke presented Hofmannsthal with a number of his poems, notably with the excellent *Cornucopia*, and Hofmannsthal sent inscribed copies of his works to Rilke. But there was no real sympathy between them. In the end even Princess Taxis, a close friend of both, realized that her efforts to reconcile them had failed. She thought it was because Hofmannsthal was "a poet of life" and Rilke "a poet of death." But Rudolf Kassner, who also knew them both, comes probably closer to the truth when he says that Rilke felt Hofmannsthal was conceited, while Hofmannsthal denied that Rilke was a poet at all. Kassner calls this "a most amazing judgment from such a distinguished man" [59] but adds that the well-known essayist and poet, Rudolf Borchardt, likewise banished Rilke from the German Parnassus by not including a single Rilke poem in his anthology of German poetry. Such opinions are literary curiosities and need not detain us. They are at par with such gems of critical insight as Voltaire's opinion of Shakespeare, Goethe's opinion of Kleist and, in our time, Eliot's erstwhile opinion of Goethe. Nor do we need to concern ourselves with those German critics who resented Rilke's writing French poems or exchanging letters of courtesy with President Masaryk. Their names have long been forgotten while Rilke's poetry continues to attract readers. Indeed, an age accustomed to quantitative measurements cannot fail to be impressed by the sheer volume of Rilke literature, which "towers over Rilke's Orphic work like a mountain range." [60]

Rilke himself would probably be alarmed if he knew what an avalanche of academic response his work has released, for he had a determined aversion to the critical approach to literature. "Read as little as possible of aesthetic criticism," he admonished a young poet:

> . . . such things are either partisan views, petrified and grown senseless in their lifeless induration, or they are clever quibblings in which today

one view wins and tomorrow the opposite. Works of art are of an infinite loneliness and with nothing so little to be reached as with criticism. Only love can grasp and hold and fairly judge them.[61]

In the first of his Charles Eliot Norton lectures, delivered at Harvard in the winter of 1952–53, E. E. Cummings quoted from this passage and added: "In my proud and humble opinion, those two sentences are worth all the soi-disant criticism of the arts which has ever existed or ever will exist." [62]

More significant than the critics' response to Rilke is that of the reader. Here, too, Rilke occupies a unique position for, judging by the steadily growing publication figures of his books, the "happy few" in his case number in the hundreds of thousands.

The mass appeal of his little romantic *Tale of Love and Death of Cornet Christoph Rilke,* which is approaching the million mark, is easy to understand. The book charms the eternally romantic adolescent imagination. For the rest it is unimportant; Rilke himself thought it was overrated. More impressive is the career of the *Book of Hours.* When it was originally published in 1905 only 500 copies were printed and it took two years to sell them. A second edition of 1,000 copies appeared in 1907, a third in 1909. By 1916 the *Book of Hours* had passed through nine editions and sold 16,000 copies. Since then its popularity has grown steadily, making a new edition necessary almost every two years. By 1936, 100,000 copies had been printed; by 1946, 175,000; by 1952, well over 200,000. This is a formidable record for a book of poems, but it is in line with Rilke's other books. *Duino Elegies,* for example, one of the most esoteric and difficult poems of the age, originally printed as a special edition of 300 copies, has reached a total of well over 50,000; *Sonnets to Orpheus* 75,000; *Notebooks of Malte Laurids Brigge* 50,000; *New Poems* 40,000. If one adds to these figures reprints in anthologies, special editions and translations—and Rilke's works have been translated into all the major languages as well as into such minor ones as Lettish, Croat, Czech, Bulgarian, Hungarian, Polish, Dutch, and Finnish —Rilke's commanding position in modern poetry becomes apparent.

His name is mentioned whenever people talk about poetry. "I

shall never forget," writes Randall Jarrell in his *Poetry and the Age*, "hearing a German say, in an objective, considering tone, as if I were an illustration in a book called *Silver Poets of the Americas:* 'You know, he looks a little like Rilke.' " [63] One finds it in Hemingway's *Green Hills of Africa*; Brooks Atkinson, reviewing *Tea and Sympathy*, quotes Tennessee Williams' *Summer and Smoke* which on the title page has the anguished line from Rilke: "who if I cried . . ."; and one finds it in the mouth of people who have never read a line of Rilke or who, like Ogden Nash, make a promise each June that "they'll be literate by October":

> Lose d'Artagnan and Sherlock Holmes
> In worthier and weightier tomes,
> In Nietzsche and even preachier Germans,
> And Donne's more esoteric sermons,
> The lofty thoughts of Abelard,
> And Rilke, Kafka, Kierkegaard; [64]

Thus it was probably inevitable that Rilke's name should eventually appear in the context of our present political dilemma. This happened when the *Saturday Review* headlined an American journalist's report on Germany: "Iron Curtain Rilke." [65]

More need not be said about the extent of Rilke's impact on his age. How intensive it is, is hard to say. The notoriety of fame has undoubtedly attracted readers to him upon whom the effect of his poetry has been slight. He himself was aware of that and what he said about fame in his book on Rodin is worth repeating: "Rodin was lonely before his fame. And fame, when it came, has perhaps made him lonelier still. For, in the end, fame is nothing but the sum of all misunderstandings that gather around a new name." [66]

And yet, when all these deductions and reservations have been made, the growth of the "Rilke cult" still remains an extraordinary phenomenon which can be explained only as a sign that the Age of Anxiety feels a need for the kind of spiritual probings and intensities that Rilke's poetry contains. This is what Jean Cassou meant when he said that "we give ourselves to Rilke unconditionally, as he expects it, joyfully and with an immense sense of relief because he has in abundance so many things we lack." [67]

2   Masks and the Man

Every profound spirit needs
a mask.

Nietzsche

The process of artistic creation, deeply rooted as it is in unconscious drives, can be understood as a sublimation of the artist's inner conflicts. Rilke knew that "every work of art is the result of having-been-in-danger, of having-gone-to-the-very-end of an experience." [1] "The artistic impulse," he told Countess Sizzo, "is nothing but the constant inclination to sublimate the conflicts that endanger and strain our 'ego' which is continuously being formed anew out of such diverse and mutually contradictory elements." [2] By transforming his conflicts into works of art the artist resolves them and undergoes a catharsis. From the manner of this transformation significant insights can be gained into the nature of the conflicts which beset the man and which the artist tries to resolve. The work of art is thus the artist's most valid biography, the mirror of his inner life, and the prerequisite for an understanding of the man is an understanding of the artist: his work, his style. *Le style est l'homme même.*

Rilke's style has often been analyzed. Even those who are irritated by some of his mannerisms—a tendency toward preciosity, particularly in his early verse—agree that it is unique. "Any reader," says Holthusen,

> who, familiar with other kinds of poetry, comes across a line or stanza of Rilke's for the first time, cannot fail to be fascinated by the purely and unmistakably individual character of his language, by its partiality, self-containedness and self-sufficiency, by the intensely per-

sonal and idiomatic, even, in a sense, idiopathic quality of his lyricism.[3]

And H. W. Belmore states categorically: "Rilke's mature style is so imbued with his personality that it calls no other poetry to mind: it makes us think of Rilke only." [4]

"Exposed on the hills of his heart," Rilke struggled to reach "the last hamlet of words" only to find that higher there was "yet one remaining farmstead of feeling." Again and again he tried to reach it, forcing himself up on the "bare rock under his hands" and again and again he reached the realm of the "unsayable," encountered the resistance of language. He strained at these limitations and tried to overcome them by ingenious verbal and syntactical innovations that frequently startle the reader and seem incoherent. But as one gets used to Rilke's style these incoherences fall into a pattern until, at last, the reader shares the poet's

> swift suspicions that later,
> always, only a part will be comprehensible, always
> some single piece of existence, five pieces, perhaps, but never
> combinable all together, and all of them fragile.[5]

> die raschen Verdachte, es würde
> immer ein Teil nur, später, ergreiflich sein, immer
> irgend ein Stück, fünf Stücke, nicht einmal
> alle verbindbar, des Daseins, und alle zerbrechlich.[6]

Like erratic blocks in a familiar landscape Rilke's images stand out in German poetry. Every sensation, every impression, even the most subtle shift in feeling, he turned into a visual image. At times of great poetic tension a veritable tumult of images poured out of him. When he first encountered his angels, "those almost deadly birds of the soul," he was blinded by their terrifying presence. "Who are you?" he asked and plunged at once into a sea of metaphors:

> Early successes, Creation's pampered darlings,
> ranges, summits, dawn-red ridges
> of all beginning,—pollen of blossoming godhead,
> hinges of light, corridors, stairways, thrones,
> spaces of being, shields of felicity, tumults
> of stormily-rapturous feeling, and suddenly, separate,

mirrors, drawing up their own
outstreamed beauty into their faces again.[7]

Frühe Geglückte, ihr Verwöhnten der Schöpfung,
Höhenzüge, morgenrötliche Grate
aller Erschaffung,—Pollen der blühenden Gottheit,
Gelenke des Lichtes, Gänge, Treppen, Throne,
Räume aus Wesen, Schilde aus Wonne, Tumulte
stürmisch entzückten Gefühls und plötzlich, einzeln,
Spiegel: die die entströmte eigene Schönheit
wiederschöpfen zurück in das eigene Antlitz.[8]

No other poet, says Gundolf, not Shakespeare and no Oriental,
has transformed his feeling so fervently into metaphors; "no word
occurs more frequently with him than the word 'as.' " [9] Rilke's
flight into the image betrays a fundamental aspect of his mind:
his deep awareness of the interrelatedness of life, his tendency to
be lost in a kaleidoscopic universe of constantly changing patterns,
colors, sensations, impressions. "Staying is nowhere" in Rilke's
world. Everything is flow and counterflow of great cosmic forces
that are utterly indifferent to man. The most he can do is to accept
them, let himself be carried by them, enter into a rhythmic relation to them. This is the message Rilke tries to convey in image
after image: reject nothing—not even death.

Tears, oh tears which break forth from me
my death, blackamoor, heartkeeper,
Hold me steeper,
let them run off. I want to speak.

Giant black heart-holder.
And if I spoke
do you think silence would break?
Rock me, old friend.[10]

Tränen, Tränen, die aus mir brechen.
Mein Tod, Mohr, Träger
meines Herzens, halte mich schräger,
daß sie abfließen. Ich will sprechen.
Schwarzer, riesiger Herzhalter.
Wenn ich auch spräche,
glaubst du denn, daß das Schweigen bräche?

Wiege mich, Alter.[11]

The imagery of this little poem "of indescribable sweetness and beauty" is typically Rilkean. It is a poem about death. Now death is never "a wholly welcome guest," hence the twice repeated "tears" in the opening line. But no sooner has the sadness of death been affirmed when it is transformed into a colorful image. Death is likened to a blackamoor, a giant black heartholder. These are somber images; they evoke a child's dread of the black man, of the dark and the unknown. At this point another poet might have cried out in despair or, as Donne does, shouted defiantly, "Death thou shalt die." Not so Rilke. Choked with tears for fear of death he faces his adversary and begs him to "hold him steeper" so that his tears, his fear, may run off. He wants to speak, although he knows that there will be no answer, that there is no escape from this black giant. So he submits to him like a child crying in the dark and lets himself be rocked to sleep. Thus the balance is kept between lament and praise and the poem to death ends on a note of reconciliation: "Rock me, old friend." It becomes a blackamoor's lullaby.

Related to the visual nature of Rilke's imagery is the predominance of the noun in his style. The noun dominates everything: it is color and contour in the ebb and flow of his thought; even the verb frequently appears in substantivized form. This tendency has gone so far that some critics have objected to it; Börries von Münchhausen has accused Rilke of "substantivitis." However, this combination of the static and dynamic elements of language, which produces an effect of balance between movement and rest, is very well suited to Rilke's thought. Hence even such unusual noun forms as "the not-knowing-whither" or "this no-longer-grasping," or "this never-being-able-to-give" must be considered legitimate means of his style. But many of the nouns Rilke prefers—and, according to Baudelaire, such key words show the direction of a poet's inner compulsion—are not unusual at all. The way in which he uses them is unusual and often gives them a striking novelty and freshness.

Among such typically Rilkean nouns are "thing," "space," "inwardness," "contradiction," "relation," "center," "circle," "island," "mask," "mirror," "praise," "lament," "being," and "death." For

an understanding of Rilke's existential dilemma his use of the
words "mask," "island," and "mirror" is particularly significant.

Take the word "mask." A good example of it occurs in the last
stanza of the poem *The Death of the Poet:*

> O yes, his face was this remotest distance,
> that seeks him still and woos him in despair;
> and his mere mask, timidly dying there,
> is tender and open now like the consistence
> of an empty fruit corrupting in the air.[12]

> O sein Gesicht war diese ganze Weite,
> die jetzt noch zu ihm will und um ihn wirbt;
> und seine Maske, die nun bang verstirbt,
> ist zart und offen wie die Innenseite
> von einer Frucht, die an der Luft verdirbt.[13]

Death has torn off the poet's face (*Antlitz*) and all that now
remains is a decaying mask. But even when he was alive people
did not know his true face (*Gesicht*)—they knew his countenance
(*Antlitz*), i.e., his "life mask," which now "lies propped-up, pale
and denying above the silent cover." As to his face (*Gesicht*):

> Those who had seen him living saw no trace
> of his deep unity with all that passes,
> for these: these shadowy hills and waving grasses
> and streams of running water were his face.[14]

> Die, so ihn leben sahen, wußten nicht,
> wie sehr er Eines war mit allem diesen;
> denn Dieses: diese Tiefen, diese Wiesen
> und diese Wasser *waren* sein Gesicht.[15]

Behind these two masks—his life mask and his death mask—the
poet had remained hidden, anonymous like running water. What
death had torn off was but the outer life, the day-by-day events,
the movement on the surface—not the real face. For the real face
is indestructible.

In a much earlier prose passage Rilke had described the death of
a young girl in the same way:

> She had died. Death had not torn this life out of her. He had been
> deceived by the everydayness in her open face; *that* he had torn
> away together with the gentle contours of her profile. But the other

life was still in her, a little while ago it had rushed up to the edge
of her distorted mouth, and now it slowly ebbed away, flowed noise-
lessly within and gathered somewhere above her broken heart.[16]

Thus all we see are masks. Life, the real life, the life that matters, is invisible, "unmastered and unknown." If, in moments of
exaltation, we catch a glimpse of it, it threatens to overwhelm us
with its radiance. Hence we need masks:

> Masks! Masks! O let us blind Eros
> For who could bear his radiant face? [17]

> Masken! Masken! Daß man Eros blende.
> Wer erträgt sein strahlendes Gesicht,[18]

The mask serves a dual purpose: it conceals and it reveals.
Language, like all symbolic forms, is a mask. "It harbors the curse
of mediacy and is bound to obscure what it seeks to reveal." [19] The
artist, with whom this insight becomes an obsession, despairs of
being able to communicate at all and in the end writes mainly for
himself. This is particularly true in times when everything has
become relative, uncertain and ambiguous. Rilke, says Mason,
lived the theory of relativity that Einstein *thought* and, as a result,
his "language becomes a mask behind which the most subtle individual experiences are hidden." [20] The problem is to find the
man behind the mask.

Before this is attempted another attribute of the mask must be
mentioned: its transforming power. Every actor knows how much
he is affected by the part he is playing. Made up as a king, he *is* a
king; he lives his part. Rilke also knew "the immense influence of
a disguise." [21] In *Malte Laurids Brigge* he describes how he first
came across masks "large, threatening or astonished faces adorned
with real beards and thick or up-raised eyebrows." [22] He had never
seen masks before but he understood at once why they existed.
He tried one on and, stepping before a mirror, was overwhelmed
by what he saw. For he was no longer there, instead there stood
a great, terrifying, unknown personage before him, "an alien, unbelievable, monstrous reality." It seemed appalling to him that he
should be alone with it. "But at the very moment I thought thus,
the worst befell: I lost all knowledge of myself, I simply ceased

to exist. For one second I had an unutterable, sad, and futile long-ing for myself, then there was only he—there was nothing but he." [23]

From the frequent mention he makes of it, it is evident that the mask theme held a particular fascination for Rilke. He seems to have both invited and dreaded the loss of identity which every masquerade entails. There is the pathetic story of his childhood in which he tells how, to please his mother, he would act the part of a little girl. He would knock at his mother's door, disguise his voice and answer "Sophie" when she asked who was there. "And when I entered then (in the small girlish house-dress which I always wore with its sleeves rolled all the way up), I was simply Sophie, Mother's little Sophie, busy about her household duties." [24]

Was it the loss of identity he suffered in these childish masquer-ades that started him on his lifelong quest for his real self? Who was he? What was reality? What was behind the boy René or the girl Sophie?

At the same time all his life he delighted in acting a part: When he was with his mother in his summer vacations, proudly wearing the "Emperor's coat," the uniform of the hated military school of St. Pölten; or when he strolled along the Graben with his father on a Sunday afternoon, dressed as a dandy; or when he lived the life of a Prague littérateur, a Russian peasant, a struggling writer in Paris—did he not somehow act all these parts? And even later, when he had completely grown into the part which he had taken up so eagerly as a youth, when he had become a genuine poet—was there not a good deal of acting in Rilke's life? The elegant recluse who would stay only in the most fashionable hotels and resorts of Europe, the immaculately dressed gentleman of leisure who depended on the hospitality of his aristocratic friends, the witty raconteur, the bourgeois nobleman: where, among all these disguises is the *real* Rilke?

"Every profound spirit needs a mask," says Nietzsche, "indeed, a mask grows continuously around every profound spirit, because of the false, i.e., shallow, interpretation of every word, every step, every sign of life he gives." [25] Rilke also knew that. When he was asked about himself, he referred people to "that figure which I am

building beyond myself, outside, more valid and more permanent
. . . For: Who knows who I am? I am constantly changing." [26]
He resented all attempts to penetrate his privacy; he longed for
anonymity. He wanted to lose his self in his work. His friends
noted something strangely masklike about his face. It did not
seem to belong to him. And they agree that none of the many
pictures of him does him justice.

The key to an understanding of the tragic dichotomy in Rilke's
life is that he was an artist who knew the "ancient enmity" that
exists between art and life and wanted to transcend it. He knew it
was his fate to lose his identity, to spend himself, "pour himself
out," but he also knew that this outpouring was an act of purifica-
tion which prepared the way for the inrush of inspiration, the
Dionysiac frenzy which possessed him when he wrote his greatest
poetry. In such moments he felt he was but a mouthpiece of
Dionysus, for "Dionysus is the name for the transforming power
which forces men to become masks, masks of a suprapersonal
divine being." [27]

Seen in this light the problem of Rilke's identical nature, which
has troubled many scholars, becomes irrelevant. "A poet," Keats
told his friend Woodhouse, "has no identity, he is continuously
in for and filling some other body. . . . It is a wretched thing to
confess, but it is a very fact, that no word I utter can be taken for
granted as an opinion growing out of my identical nature—how
can it, when I have no nature?" [28]

With Rilke this dissolution of the ego went to dangerous extremes because he bestowed the energy belonging to positive
thinking upon feeling-sensation, which amounts to a reversal of
the introverted type. When this happens "the qualities of the un-
differentiated, archaic 'feeling-sensation' become paramount; i.e.
the individual relapses into extreme relatedness, or identification
with the sensed object." [29] Jung calls this state an *inferior extra-
version,*

> . . . an extraversion which, as it were, detaches the individual entirely
> from his ego and dissolves him into archaic, collective ties and identifi-
> cations. He is then no longer "himself", but a mere relatedness; he is
> identical with his object and consequently without a standpoint.

Against this condition the introvert instinctively feels the greatest resistance, which, however, is no sort of guarantee against his repeated and unwilling lapse into it.[30]

This tendency, always present in Rilke, increased in the course of his life and, while it gave incomparable insights to the poet, it caused the suffering of the man. In *An Experience* he tells how, walking in the castle garden of Duino one day at the time when the first *Elegies* began stirring in him, he leaned against the fork of a low tree and felt immediately so pleasantly supported that he gave up reading and surrendered completely to the sensation of being absorbed by nature. He felt as if from the interior of the tree "almost unnoticeable vibrations passed over to him." [31] Gentle movements penetrated his body, which seemed to lose all sense of heaviness, and he felt like a revenant who returns once more to the world that formerly had been indispensable to him. Looking back over his shoulders to the objects around him he experienced the sweet taste of their complete existence.

In a subsequent passage he confesses that he remembers other occasions when he had entered into such a state of "pure being." He mentions Capri, where the song of a bird went right through him, his body not being a barrier but part of an uninterrupted space in which "mysteriously protected there remained but one place of the purest, deepest consciousness." [32] He closed his eyes in order not to disturb this cosmic equilibrium, and presently "the infinite passed into him from all sides so gently that he thought he could feel the slight repose of the rising stars within his heart." [33] He recalls that even in his "murky" childhood he had such experiences, that he loved to expose himself to storms and to the open sensation of the plains, and that he had been deeply moved by the elemental rush of air and water and the heroic movements of the clouds. Later in his life he surrendered more and more to such experiences until in the end

. . . something gently separative kept a pure, almost transparent interspace between him and other human beings, across which it was indeed possible to exchange isolated communications but which absorbed every relationship and, becoming saturated in the process, deceived all participants like a smoky mist.[34]

Rilke realized that by entering such states of "pure being" which gave him a deep awareness of the unity of existence, he risked becoming entirely alienated from his self and not being able to communicate at all. Hence his constant desire—even while he longed to enter such states—to be "himself" again, to live a normal life with normal human relationships. Besides, there was always the danger of self-deception, the possibility that he mistook for genuine transformation what, in reality, was nothing but play acting, that he pretended to be inspired when he was only disguising his inner emptiness. The episode at Castle Berg illustrates this danger.

It will be recalled that Rilke had written a cycle of poems there which, he insisted, had been dictated to him by a mysterious Count C. W. Leishman considers them "among the most beautiful, and also, in spite of the occasional semi-dramatic element, among the most characteristic, that he ever wrote." [35] But Rilke disowned them and failed to include them in his collected works, although they are clearly superior to many he did include. What was the reason for his "strangely ambiguous attitude to these poems"? That they were "dictated" should have made him all the more ready to acknowledge them for he insisted that he had written all his major poetry under dictation. The answer to this question throws much light on his character: he disowned them because he considered them frauds. They were, he felt, the result of a make-believe identification, not a genuine transformation. He had gone to Castle Berg with the hope of rediscovering the source of that powerful poetic current which had given rise to the first *Elegies*. Duino had been destroyed in the war. He was looking for a place where his mind could once more become in tune with his angels. Castle Berg seemed promising. He went there and waited —but nothing happened, except that the eighteenth-century atmosphere that prevailed there induced him to act a scene with an imaginary count whose poems he copied. "I was not yet in the mood and able to write my own poetry and therefore, it seems, I had to 'invent,' as it were, a figure who could take upon himself that which might yet be written with that entirely inadequate degree of concentration: that was Count C. W." [36] It is true that his powers of autosuggestion were so strong that this half-serious, half-playful game threatened to get out of hand. The Count became more and more demanding and finally started dictating Italian poems. When this happened Rilke dismissed him; he did not want to be somebody else's mouthpiece. He preferred to wait for his angel.

This incident shows the danger the exalted poet has to guard against: he runs the risk of becoming an actor, of going through the motions of creative ecstasy without really experiencing anything. A work of art created under such circumstances may be formally perfect: it lacks the breath of inspiration. Rilke felt that this is what had happened in the case of the poems *From the Remains of Count C. W.*; that is why he excluded them from his works. We may regret this decision, for they are still Rilkean poems and comparable in craftsmanship to the best he wrote, but we must surely honor the integrity of an artist who refused to deceive or be deceived. However many disguises the man Rilke may have worn, the poet was sincere. He did not want those "half-filled masks." He was horrified when he discovered that the dancer of the *Fourth Elegy*—symbol of the pseudo-artist he himself might easily have become—was nothing but a disguised bourgeois; therefore he vowed:

> to wait before the puppet stage,—no, rather
> to gaze so intensely on it that at last,
> to upweigh my gaze, an angel has to come
> and play a part there, snatching up the husks [37] . . .

> zu warten vor der Puppenbühne, nein,
> so völlig hinzuschau, daß, um mein Schauen
> am Ende aufzuwiegen, dort als Spieler
> ein Engel hinmuß, der die Bälge hochreißt.[38]

The mask theme symbolizes the will to transformation which Rilke considered to be the basic principle of existence. Hence his demand: "Will transformation, o for the flame be enraptured," [39] because "that which would stay what it is renounces existence." Like all his symbols it is ambiguous and can be interpreted on various levels. It can imply a temporary disguise, a masquerade, a playful change to a different personality; it can mean a protective coloring, a necessary form of escape from the dangers and distractions of the world. Rilke's life mask was of this kind; he wore it to protect his solitude. Finally, it can mean that powerful process of inner transformation which forces men to become masks and which distinguishes the genuine artist from the virtuoso, "the clever ape of the law." [40]

The true poet is both a man transformed and a transformer. He has no other function. Outside his work he may be a philistine, a fool, or a criminal. What he is does not matter provided he turns it into poetry. The crux of the Rilke problem is that he turned his whole life into poetry. That is why it is so difficult to isolate the man. Kassner says "he was a poet even when he washed his hands." [41] And most people who met him were struck by the unmistakably poetic quality of every gesture, every sign of life he gave. In his presence they felt mysteriously remote from the world of reality and yet, they insisted, Rilke's world was as real as that which they had left behind.

It is an altogether puzzling phenomenon, this Rilkean withdrawal from the world of man into the world of poetry. He himself did not understand it, and it alarmed his friends. They noticed that it affected every aspect of his personality, even his appearance. Lou Salomé noted that "his face almost lacked the signs of age . . . his features ceased to be quite his own. His eyes stood large and anxious above his face, as if they knew that something had happened to it, as if they wanted to ask if someone, and who, had illegally appropriated it." [42]

Rilke realized he was undergoing a transformation that carried him farther and farther into the realm of incommunicable experience. It was as if the Orphic god, to whose service he had dedicated his life, had taken him by the hand and was leading him gently away from humankind. At first he struggled against what was happening to him, wanted to tear off the poetic mask and be himself again. He longed for companionship and there were times, particularly after the completion of *Malte*, when he wanted to give up writing and enter a profession. He discussed his case with psychiatrists and even considered subjecting himself to an analysis. But in the end he accepted his fate: he was a poet. For the sake of his angels he would bear his devils; on the brink of despair he would praise life:

> Oh, tell us, poet, what you do?
> > —I praise.
>
> But those dark, deadly, devastating ways,
> how do you bear them, suffer them?
> > —I praise.
>
> And then the Nameless, beyond guess or gaze,
> how can you call it, conjure it?
> > —I praise.
>
> And whence your right, in every kind of maze,
> in every mask, to remain true?
> > —I praise.
>
> And that the mildest and the wildest ways
> know you like star and storm?
> > —Because I praise.[43]

> Oh sage, Dichter, was du tust?
> > —Ich rühme.
>
> Aber das Tödliche und Ungetüme,
> Wie hältst du's aus, wie nimmst du's hin?
> > —Ich rühme.
>
> Aber das Namenlose, Anonyme,
> Wie rufst du's, Dichter, dennoch an?
> > —Ich rühme.
>
> Woher dein Recht, in jeglichem Kostüme,
> in jeder Maske wahr zu sein?
> > —Ich rühme.
>
> Und daß das Stille und das Ungestüme
> wie Stern und Sturm dich kennen?
> > :—Weil ich rühme.[44]

If, on its highest level of interpretation, the mask symbolizes the Dionysiac power of transformation which dissolves the self and forces men to become mouthpieces of a suprapersonal power: *vates*—the mirror symbol has a converse meaning: that of narcissistic self-love. The frequency with which both symbols occur in Rilke points once more to the tragic split in his personality: his longing for self-surrender and his opposite longing for self-absorption. Torn between Dionysus and Narcissus, his life was one of constant conflict.

He refers to it when, in a revealing passage in *Malte*, he complains that he is neither—neither really transformed nor really himself:

> We discover, indeed, that we do not know our part; we look for a mirror; we want to rub off the paint, to remove all that is artificial and become real. But somewhere a bit of mummery that we forget still sticks to us. A trace of exaggeration remains in our eyebrows; we do not notice that the corners of our lips are twisted. And thus we go about, a laughing-stock, a mere half-thing: neither real beings nor actors.[45]

Again he revolts against those "half-filled masks" and longs either for complete transformation, wants to be "a stirring in the god," or for complete self-absorption, for "Narcissus released and clarified."

This latter tendency which, as Simenauer has shown, constitutes a fundamental trait in Rilke's personality, is expressed in the mirror symbolism. Mirrors fascinated him as much as masks. He stood in awe of them like a child that wants to know what happens inside a mirror. Was it his double who stared at him from its impenetrable depth? Was it another? And what happened to all those faces that had once been reflected in mirrors? Whither had they gone?

> You in advance
> lost, Beloved, you whom I never met . . .
>   streets I discovered,—
> you had just walked in them,
> and sometimes in dealers' shops the mirrors
> were still dizzy with you and, startled, returned
> my too sudden image . . .[46]

> Du im Voraus
> verlorne Geliebte, Nimmergekommene . . .
>   Gassen fand ich,—
> du warst sie gerade gegangen
> und die Spiegel manchmal der Läden der Händler
> waren noch schwindlich von dir und gaben erschrocken
> mein zu plötzliches Bild—. . . .[47]

The idea that a mirror retains every image that has been reflected on its surface arouses archaic, subconscious memories. It
can be found in the folklore of most primitive societies, and traces
of it are still present in the death and marriage rites of many
peoples. According to ancient mirror magic the image in the mirror
is the soul of man, hence the superstitious belief that you can kill
your enemy if you catch his reflection in a mirror and break it:
the dead do not appear in mirrors.

This belief lies behind the mysterious midnight encounter between Malte and Erik in the picture gallery at Urnekloster, a
scene in which Rilke with the utmost economy of words succeeds
in arousing a profound sense of awe in the reader. It will be recalled that Malte was looking for the portrait of Christine Brahe,
whose ghost was a familiar sight at Urnekloster. He could not find
it; instead his cousin Erik appeared suddenly and said to him: " 'I
have brought her a mirror.' . . . 'A mirror?' . . . 'Yes, because
her portrait is not there.' . . . 'No, no,' I said. . . . Suddenly
he drew me nearer the window and pinched my forearm so sharply
that I screamed. 'She is not in there,' he breathed into my ear." [48]
All of a sudden Malte understood: Christine Brahe was not in the
mirror because she was dead. But presently Erik startled him again
with the mystifying words: "You are either in it, then you are not
here—or if you are here, you cannot be in it." [49]

In his attempt to interpret this obscure passage Bollnow concludes:

> Through the mirror man is thus transformed into a picture, so that the
> mirror can take the place of the picture. Although it can only be a
> transitory, momentary picture, nevertheless the decisive change has
> occurred through which man is transformed into a higher, meta-
> phorical being; according to the ambiguous meaning of these obscure
> and uncanny words, the relationship seems to be that you can only be
> in one or the other realm and that becoming-a-picture necessarily
> means the loss of reality.[50]

But no interpretation can account for the sense of dread Malte
experienced in this scene, or why it should affect the reader so
powerfully, unless we assume that Rilke's mirror magic evokes ancient memories in our subconscious mind. Perhaps we remember

the moment in our earliest childhood when we first saw ourselves reflected in a mirror, suddenly becoming aware of our own existence. According to the myth this was the moment when Narcissus fell in love with himself, when his libido became fixed to his own person and his ability to love anyone or anything else was destroyed. Death was the punishment the gods inflicted upon Narcissus, and modern psychiatrists agree that an extreme case of narcissism is incurable. Every child, however, passes through a narcissistic phase that marks the birth of self-consciousness or, according to Rudolf Kassner, the birth of imagination and poetry: "For the sake of his power of imagination Narcissus has to die or go through death in order to return to himself, to unity with himself, to primordial being." [51] In the life of the artist this moment is of supreme importance for, as E. E. Cummings says, artists are those "who have discovered (in a mirror surrounded with mirrors) something harder than silence but softer than falling; the third voice of 'life' which believes itself and which cannot mean because it is." [52] A narcissistic trait is therefore present in most artists. It can be quite pronounced, as it was with Kierkegaard, Tolstoy, Wilde, and Nietzsche; it can even, as it did with Rilke, go to almost pathological extremes—for that the secret wound in Rilke's life was his narcissism has long been suspected and has been confirmed by Dr. Simenauer's detailed diagnosis.

Rilke's fixation to an infantile narcissism accounts for his hopeless attempts to find an adequate love partner, for his preference for his own company, for his gospel of nonpossessive love, for his tragically lonely and restless life. It does not account for his poetry. For, as Simenauer wisely says:

> Rilke might very well have become a neurotic, as his double Malte proves. But by fashioning a work of art out of his own fate, he escaped the neurosis. We can only establish this result. What power it is, this gift of poetry, the genius of the artist, that remains the "insoluble secret" which is inaccessible to any analysis.[53]

To a mind withdrawn into itself and trying to find verbal equivalents for the flood of images that rise up in the soul, the problem of communication becomes of paramount importance. The poet realizes that language is a very blunt instrument, that it is quite unfit to render the subtle vibrations, tremors and raptures within; therefore he tries to fashion it anew, to break through the established forms of grammar and syntax, only to find that the closer he gets to his goal the more obscure he becomes. In the end he despairs of being understood at all and writes mainly for himself. Rilke's indifference to the reader stems from this insight. He knew that he could not explain how he arrived at his "lyrical sums" and that nothing would be gained by subjecting them to a critical analysis. Whenever he tried to do so, as in his letters to his Polish translator, he felt at once that it was futile: "Am I the one who is entitled to give proper explanations to the *Elegies?*" [54] All he can suggest is for the reader to get "similarly focused"; i.e., to search his soul for meaning—not his intellect. If the reader will but try to catch the images reflected in his soul, he may become aware that they are signals, indicating presences in space which to the mind seems empty. What these signals "mean" Rilke does not, indeed cannot, say; he simply notes their presence:

> And so we stand with mirrors:
> One here . . . and catch,
> Another there, reaching no real accord;
> but catching and the image from afar
> acknowledging, this pure image
> passing it to the other from the gleaming mirror.
> Ballgame for gods. A play of mirrors, in which
> three balls perhaps, or perhaps nine will cross,
> and none of which, since the world knew itself,
> even fell wide. Catchers, that's what we are!
> It comes invisibly through the air, and yet
> how wholly the mirror meets it, this
> (only in it completely present) this image,
> which only stays until we estimate
> with how much force it will go on, whither.

> Just this. And our long childhood was for this,
> distress and tenderness and long farewells,
> only for this. But this rewards.[55]

> Da stehen wir mit Spiegeln:
> einer dort . . . . . . , und fangen auf,
> und einer da, am Ende nicht verständigt;

auffangend aber und das Bild weither
uns zuerkennend, dieses reine Bild
dem andern reichend aus dem Glanz des Spiegels.
Ballspiel für Götter. Spiegelspiel, in dem
vielleicht drei Bälle, vielleicht neun sich kreuzen,
und keiner jemals, seit sich Welt besann,
fiel je daneben. Fänger, die wir sind.
Unsichtbar kommt es durch die Luft, und dennoch,
wie ganz der Spiegel ihm begegnet, diesem
(in ihm nur völlig Ankunft) diesem Bild,
das nur so lang verweilt, bis wir ermessen,
mit wieviel Kraft es weiter will, wohin.

Nur dies. Und dafür war die lange Kindheit,
Und Not und Neigung und der tiefe Abschied
war nur für dieses. Aber dieses lohnt.[56]

Another aspect of Rilke's existential dilemma, though complementary to that expressed by the mask and mirror theme, is shown by his preference for the "island" situation. We know from the drawings he made between his fourth and eighth years that islands fascinated him and that he loved drawing them. In *Malte* he refers to this love: "Mother, it is true, always insists that they were islands I was painting—islands with large trees, and a château, and a stairway, and flowers on the bank that were supposed to be reflected in the water." [57] Primarily, the island is a symbol of isolation; a piece of land cut off from the main, it reflects the situation of the isolated individual. But, since the water that surrounds an island acts like a mirror, it is a narcissistic symbol as well. Rilke often uses it in this dual meaning. In the last poem of the cycle *The Island* the lines occur:

The innermost only is near; the rest is far.
And this innermost pressed and daily
crowded with things and quite unsayable.
The island is like a too-little star
which space knows not and silently destroys
in its unconscious terribleness . . .[58]

Nah ist nur Inneres; alles andre fern.
Und dieses Innere gedrängt und täglich
mit allem überfüllt und ganz unsäglich.

Die Insel ist wie ein zu kleiner Stern
welchen der Raum nicht merkt und stumm zerstört
in seinem unbewußten Furchtbarsein, . . .[59]

Rilke's predilection for islands and mirrors accounts for the unusual attraction he felt for Venice: "It was an incredibly Venetian day, floating silver, reflected, an existence under mirrored images." [60] In *Malte* the island theme appears in wall tapestries with very little variety in them except "that there is always that oval, blue island, floating on a background of modest red. . . . Only yonder, in the last hanging, the island rises a little, as if it had grown lighter." [61] In the *Book of Hours* he describes God as beginning hesitantly "as with many islands" at the edge of his senses. In his letters he mentions "hours that are like a blossoming island. . . . It cannot hurt these island hours that there is a return to every day life. . . . Such a higher island-existence seems to me to be the future of the very few." [62] He talks of "islands in space," "islands of the heart," the "isle of work." It gave him great satisfaction that his books bore the imprint of the Insel-Verlag. In his first letter to his publisher, Kippenberg, he wrote that it was essential for his work that his connection with that firm, which had started "so sympathetically," be continued.

The island is thus also a place of refuge, a shelter in a hostile world. Indeed, Dr. Simenauer suggests that Rilke's youthful island drawings and the poet's concern with the island situation constitute "womb fantasies" emanating from Rilke's unconscious love-hate for his mother. This may sound farfetched, but Phia Rilke's influence on her son's life can hardly be exaggerated. She is the major cause of those serious psychological disturbances under which he suffered and which, had he not succeeded in sublimating them in his poetry, might easily have led to his disintegration.

By all accounts Rilke's mother was an extraordinary woman. Endowed with a fervid imagination and inordinately preoccupied with dreams of social grandeur—a strange mixture of piety and frivolity—she was ill cast in her role as the wife of a petty Austrian railroad official. That she left her husband when the boy was nine years old merely marked the end of a meaningless episode, as far as Phia was concerned, and permitted her to live the life of her girlish dreams: the life of a pious and elegant lady of leisure. Her departure from Prague came as a great shock to the sensitive child; at the same time it increased the aura of mystery that had always surrounded his beautiful mother. He thought of her with love and sorrow and confided to her his first poor verses. For her sake he rebelled against the military career his father had mapped out for him; because she had wanted a daughter he tried to conceal the fact that he was a boy. For five years he acted the part of a little girl, and Phia played with him as if he were a doll, dressing him up, showing him to her friends, making him perform little drawing-room tricks and then, suddenly, discarding him, hiding him behind a screen. He could hear his mother's laughter as she entertained her guests, his beautiful mother who would not come near him then.

All his life Rilke tried to free himself from his mother's image. He professed to hate her. "I cannot love," he said bitterly, "perhaps because I do not love my mother." [63] His intense, almost pathological hatred of dolls, which provoked his "greatest and strangest piece of prose" [64] and gave rise to the doll symbol in the *Elegies*, shows how much he suffered from his mother's thoughtless love. There is something greatly moving in the spectacle of his transmuting into poetry one of the most painful experiences of his life. And yet it is probably true that, because he loved his mother, he could not love anyone else. The ambivalence of his feeling for his mother is the root of Rilke's personal tragedy; it colored his whole attitude toward love and occasioned some of his most memorable poetry:

Mother, *you* made him small, it was you that began him;
he was new to you, you arched over those new eyes
the friendly world, averting the one that was strange.
Where, oh where, are the years when you simply displaced
for him, with your slender figure, the surging abyss?
You hid so much from him then; made the nightly-suspected room
harmless, and out of your heart full of refuge
mingled more human space with that of his nights.
Not in the darkness, no, but within your far nearer presence
you placed the light, and it shone as though out of friendship.
Nowhere a creak you could not explain with a smile,

as though you had long known *when* the floor would behave itself thus . .
And he listened to you and was soothed. So much it availed,
gently, your coming; his tall cloaked destiny stepped
behind the chest of drawers, and his restless future,
that easily got out of place, confromed to the folds of the curtain.[65]

Mutter, *du* machtest ihn klein, du warsts, die ihn anfing;
dir ware er neu, du beugtest über die neuen
Augen die freundliche Welt und wehrtest der fremden.
Wo, ach, hin sind die Jahre, da du ihm einfach
mit der schlanken Gestalt wallendes Chaos vertratst?
Vieles verbargst du ihm so; das nächtlich-verdächtige Zimmer
machtest du harmlos, aus deinem Herzen voll Zuflucht
mischtest du menschlichern Raum seinem Nacht-Raum hinzu.
Nicht in die Finsternis, nein, in dein näheres Dasein
hast du das Nachtlicht gestellt, und es schien wie aus Freundschaft.
Nirgends ein Knistern, das du nicht lächelnd erklärtest,
so als wüßtest du längst, *wann* sich die Diele benimmt . . .
Und er horchte und linderte sich. So vieles vermochte
zärtlich dein Aufstehn; hinter den Schrank trat
hoch in Mantel sein Schicksal, und in die Falten des Vorhangs
paßte, die leicht sich verschob, seine unruhige Zukunft.[66]

The refuge that he sought, but did not find, in his mother he
failed to find in any other woman. His marriage was no more successful than his mother's had been, and, although all his life he
was surrounded by women, he shrunk from entering into permanent relationships, for

> "Man must die, because he has known them." Die
> of their smile's ineffable blossom. Die
> of their light hands. Die
> of women . . .[67]

> "Man muß sterben weil man sie kennt." Sterben
> an der unsäglichen Blüte des Lächelns. Sterben
> an ihren leichten Händen. Sterben
> an Frauen.[68]

Whenever the question of marriage arose, he discreetly with-
drew into his work. And in the only instance known, apart from
Clara Westhoff, his wife and the mother of his daughter, when he
asked a woman to marry him she declined, because for her he was
"the voice of God, the immortal soul, Fra Angelico, all that is

superhumanly good, lofty, and sacred, but not a human person!" [69]
Not a human person: these words express the tragedy that was
Rilke's life. When Magda von Hattingberg wrote them she failed
to see that the cause of this tragedy was Rilke's mother, although
she mentions two incidents that clearly point to Phia's fateful hold
on her son. One refers to the shock Magda suffered when Rilke
read her his essay on dolls. She could not understand his intense
hatred of a simple plaything, did not relate it to Rilke's childhood.
The other refers to a letter from his mother that Rilke received
the last day before their departure from Duino:

> Rilke, the Princess and I spent the whole morning in the white room. I
> played for about an hour, but Rilke was silent and depressed. The
> reason for this I discovered later, for when we were alone he showed
> me a letter from his mother which had come by the early post. She
> addressed him as "Du Prachtmensch," told him of some devotional
> exercises in which she had taken part at the nunnery, and wrote of
> the saint to whom she had particularly entrusted his spiritual wel-
> fare; she begged him "not to be lukewarm in the true piety of a
> zealous Catholic," and reminded him to send her a parcel of gloves
> to clean, which he had evidently forgotten. He was to remember that
> it was her exclusive privilege to wash his gloves! I gave him back the
> letter without a word. What could I say? As he folded it up and put
> it in his note-case, he said, scarcely audibly and as though asking a
> question, ". . . Mother?" [70]

All his life Rilke tried to find the woman who would be both a
mother and a wife to him. The one who came closest to fulfilling
this dual role was Lou Andreas-Salomé. But this remarkable
woman was not willing to sacrifice her life for him. In the end he
resigned himself to his fate and, realizing that no woman could
give him the love he was seeking, he took refuge on the "island of
work."

His concern with the isolated individual, which had been stimulated by his ambivalent feeling for his mother, was strengthened by
yet another experience to which he was exposed during the formative years of his life: his childhood in Prague. Peter Demetz has
pointed out how significant it is that Rilke—like Kafka and Werfel
—was born and brought up in Prague, a town that lies outside the
German language and cultural area properly speaking, and at a

time when the awakening of Czech nationalism caused an increased sense of isolation among the German element. How
could a sensitive child help feeling that he was an outsider, that
he was different from other children; spoke a different language,
went to a different school. Surrounded by an alien people who resented his presence, he was forced to reflect upon the meaning of
life at an age when children normally accept it without question.
The anomaly of his situation must have weighed on his mind.
Here he was, a little island in a strange and menacing sea, and
condemned to an oppressive solitude.

Linguistically and socially isolated, without contact with a larger
public and thus forced in upon themselves, the German writers in
Prague were reduced to "ponder their own strange fate in the
narrow streets of the old town." [71] Their anxious quest for man's
place in society and hence in the universe, a theme that occupies
such a prominent place in the work of Rilke and Kafka, represents
an emphatic response to common childhood experiences. "Many
people," says Edwin Muir in his introduction to Kafka, "slip into
their place without being aware of it; others are painfully conscious
of the difficulty, the evident impossibility of finding any place at
all." [72] Muir suggests that this sense of isolation may have been
exacerbated in Kafka's case by the fact that he was Jewish, and
this applies to Werfel also; but even non-Jewish writers found it
hard to "slip into their place" in Prague because they belonged to
a cultural elite that was cut off from the people among whom they
lived, as well as from the mainstream of German culture.

Rilke often complained about the "homelessness of the Austrian" and about his own lack of *Heimatgefühl.*

> The town in which I grew up did not offer any real soil for it, its air
> was neither that of my breath nor of my plough. So it happened in-
> evitably that I acquired adopted homes, according to my needs, i.e.,
> I imagined involuntarily that my home was *there*, where the visible
> in its pictorial concreteness corresponded somehow more precisely to
> my instinctive needs of expression.[73]

Thus, gradually, he replaced his native town with a "composite
home" that was situated, as it were, "*above* all countries."

Nevertheless, his early verse and stories are impregnated with the baroque atmosphere of Prague: its richly ornate churches, its spires and bridges, its ancient palaces, its squares and fountains and parks. And even when he had left Prague, these were the sights he looked for in other towns and the recurrent themes of his poetry. Some of his stylistic peculiarities, his Austrian mannerisms, and in particular, the baroque elements in his style which the Dutch critic Vestdijk has noted, show that Rilke never completely escaped the formative influence of his native town. The traits of many of his characters, notably those in *Malte*, seem like variations on the theme "people of Prague" about which he wrote in his *Tuscan Diary*. They are people

> . . . who live their whole life in their own past. They are like corpses who cannot find peace and therefore live again and again in the stealth of the night their hour dying . . . they have nothing more; their smiles have withered upon their lips. . . . And progress to them is nothing but the decaying of their coffins . . . and their getting more and more brittle and tired, losing their fingers like old memories. And of these things they tell each other with voices that have died long since: thus are the people in Prague.[74]

Rilke's fondness for the grotesque and morbid aspects of life, his religious fervor, his interest in the occult, which figure so prominently in his early writings, are reflections of the Prague atmosphere, for "the real historic heritage which this town bestowed upon its poets was mystic ecstasy." [75] It ranged all the way from genuine religious experience to cheap mystagogy, from the "humanitarian rapture of Werfel to the occult horror tales of Gustav Meyrink." [76] It was a dangerous town for a boy to grow up in whose psychic equilibrium was as precariously balanced as Rilke's.

From every point of view Prague was a challenge to the German writer who spent his childhood there at the close of the nineteenth century. It kept him isolated, encouraged introspection, and— because the German spoken in Prague was an impoverished and provincial tongue—it forced him to work on his language. By dint of sheer hard work Rilke and Kafka overcame these obstacles and achieved mastery over their medium. But the fact remains that "from deficiency and not out of abundance works resulted which belong to the permanent events of contemporary literature." [77]

The power that transformed a dangerously neurotic, provincial esthete, endowed with a minor lyrical talent and driven by an excessive narcissism (Simenauer calls the latter the "motor of all artistic activity") into a world poet was Rilke's obstinate will to art. He willed to be an artist, even if it meant the death of the man: that is the real meaning of the Rilke myth. Thomas Mann's *Tonio Kröger* offers some insight into the kind of artist Rilke was:

> He did not work like someone who works in order to live, but like one who wants nothing but work because he has no regard for himself as a living person, wants to be considered only as an artist and for the rest walks about gray and inconspicuous like an actor who has taken off his makeup and is nothing as long as he represents nothing. He worked in isolation, silently, invisibly, and full of contempt for those puny artists who considered their talent a social asset and who, whether they were poor or rich, went around in fanciful or ragged clothes or wore luxurious ties, chiefly concerned to live happily, pleasantly and artistically, not knowing that good works arise only through the pressure of a bad life, that he who lives does not work and that one must have died to be a true artist.[78]

3 The Road to Damascus

Nature came over me with her breadth, with her great
exaggerated existence, as prophecy came over Saul.
Rilke, *Briefe aus den Jahren 1904–1907*

The *Duino Elegies* have been called "the most dramatic, albeit
personally dramatic, work of this century," [1] and dramatic they
certainly are, even if we disregard the drama of their composition:
Rilke's struggle with his angel. But dramatic is a term that can
justly be applied to all of Rilke's works after the powerful poetic-
visionary experience that inspired the writing of the *Book of
Hours*.

He had written and published much poetry before that time—far
too much, he thought later, and felt ashamed of it. It was melodious poetry, sweet and sad, reminiscent of Heine but without
Heine's irony; poetry that is immediately popular and finds favor
with the publishers of daily papers and women's journals. Who
would have suspected that one of the 412 contestants for a poetry
prize of one ducat, offered by the Viennese paper *Das inter-
essante Blatt* in 1891 for the best poem on the theme: "Should
ladies' dresses have trains or not?" would eventually write *Duino
Elegies*? But that is what happened. Young René Rilke's entry
did not win a prize; it was, however, considered worthy of being
printed. Thus inconspicuously started the career of one of the
greatest poets of our age.

Rilke was only sixteen at the time and probably thought very
little of the incident, except that it would show his family that he
was a poet at heart and not an officer. He often said later that the
main reason he published so much and so early was that he knew
of no other way to convince his relatives that writing poetry was

an honorable occupation. Judging by the volume of his *juvenilia* his relatives were hard to convince.

He was not yet nineteen when the Strasbourg publisher Kattentidt brought out his first volume of poems *Life and Songs*; only six copies of this little book are still known to be in existence. Their only value lies in Rilke's name on the title page. But having tasted the heady wine of authorship he could not stop, and volume after volume appeared in quick succession—in 1896 *Wild Chicory* and *An Offering to the Lares*; in 1897 *Crowned with Dreams*; in 1898 *Advent*; in 1899 *In My Honor.*

It is difficult to do justice to these poems. Rilke revised many of them and included them in his collected works under the titles *First Poems* and *Early Poems.* He did so because he felt they represented a phase of his development—and as a measure of his poetic growth they are extremely interesting—but even in their revised form he did not think much of them. Most Rilke scholars agree with him, except Heerikhuizen, who says that "the collections ADVENT and IN MY HONOUR (*Mir zur Feier*) (now entitled EARLY POEMS), contain some of the finest youth poetry that I know. Here is wonder, at least in so far as we are receptive to the sensorially intuitive beauty sought by the neo-romantics." [2]

The question is: what significance does such beauty have? That many of these poems are beautiful, some even beguilingly so, is true enough. Their melodious rhythms, evocative alliterations, and gently murmuring metaphors are very pleasing to the ear, but if one tries to grasp them they dissolve; they are like dreams one cannot quite recall.

> Can someone tell me whither
> I reach with my life?
> Do I roar with the storm,
> do I dwell a wave in the pond,
> or am I the pale, shivering
> birch in spring? [3]

> Kann mir einer sagen, wohin
> ich mit meinem Leben reiche?
> Ob ich nicht auch noch in Sturme streiche
> und als Welle wohne im Teiche,

> und ob ich nicht selbst noch die blasse, bleiche
> frühlingfrierende Birke bin? [4]

The strangeness and mystery of life are the recurrent theme of these poems; life not lived or observed but felt—intuitively felt— as oneness, and treated according to the mood of the moment as something incomprehensible:

> And when you enter you are a guest: with whom?
> You shudder as you gaze into the wilderness.[5]

> Und wenn du eintrittst, bist du Gast.—Bei wem?
> Und schauernd schaust du in das wilde Land.[6]

or as something intimate:

> In my arms forests fall asleep
> I am the ringing over them.[7]

> in meinen Armen schlafen Wälder ein,—
> und ich bin selbst das Klingen über ihnen,[8]

It is poetry that is "at home between day and dream" in the ageless, boundless land of childhood. Maidens walk in it, pale and shivering, waiting for the storm that will bend them:

> Girls you are like gardens
> on an evening in April;
> Spring on many pathways,
> but nowhere a goal.[9]

> Ihr Mädchen seid wie die Gärten
> am Abend im April:
> Frühling auf vielen Fährten,
> aber noch nirgends ein Ziel.[10]

It is pure poetry of mood, vaguely yearning for something to come, vaguely nostalgic of something that has been, perfect of its kind: sentimental, sensitive, and simple. Sometimes, it is true, the beauty of a line is marred by an excessive use of alliteration and assonance, but then again there are perfect lines with metaphor, meter and rhyme blending naturally and easily. Beauty of this kind Rilke's *Early Poems* have in abundance, and the themes they treat are typically Rilkean. But it is not great poetry. Not because it is so obviously the poetry of an adolescent—Rimbaud wrote great poetry when he was no older than Rilke at this time—but because it lacks the chief element of great poetry: it lacks a sense of engagement or, to borrow a term from Heidegger, it lacks the "resolute decision" to accept life as it is without any romantic gloss; to affirm the reality of human existence, including that of suffering, sickness, and death.

If Rilke had not made that decision he might have continued writing "beautiful poetry" for he had proved himself to be a lyrical virtuoso. But he was made of sterner stuff. He recognized the danger of "virtuosity": "the empty too-much" that comes from "the pure too-little."

That he made that decision and adhered to it is the miracle in Rilke's life, "his immensely moving achievement." [11] He conveys to the reader a sense of urgency, a deep concern with the human situation that transcends the esthetic enjoyment commonly associated with the reading of poetry. That is what Spender meant when he said that while the work of poets like Yeats and George is a dead end "Rilke opens out a new vein which the poets of the future will explore." [12] To read a Rilkean poem is an unforgettable experience for "at his bidding the soul travels as though through familiar land, but on arrival finds itself in a place where it never meant to be." [13]

The Book of Hours marks the effective beginning of Rilke's poetry. What he had written before—his prose tales, his plays, and much of his lyrics—is today mainly of historic interest. *The Book of Hours* contains the real Rilke. Symbolically enough, it is a book of prayers, a passionate hymn addressed to the Unknown God. Conceived and partly written during the closing months of the nineteenth century, it stands on the threshold of a new era.

> One feels the gleam of a new page rise
> upon which everything is still to be.
>
> The silent forces test its size
> looking at each other somberly.[14]

>   Man fühlt den Glanz von einer neuen Seite,
> auf der noch Alles werden kann.
>
> Die stillen Kräfte prüfen ihre Breite
> und sehn einander dunkel an.[15]

It is customary to cite Rilke's journey to Russia in the spring of 1899 as the outer event which occasioned the inner tensions that gave rise to the first prayers of the *Book of Hours,* entitled the *Book of Monkish Life.* And it is certainly true that Russia made a profound impression on the German poet. For the first time he experienced space, vast uninterrupted space, and its concomitant: loneliness. The Russians were lonely people "full of distance, uncertainty and hope: a people of the future." [16] He felt an immediate kinship with their piety and patience. Almost twenty years later he wrote: "Russia made me what I am, from there my inner life proceeded, the home of my instinct, all my deepest origins are there." [17] Even the revolution could not shake his faith in the Russian people. "Bolshevism," he told Princess Taxis, "is only a scarecrow to keep away the West and its self-righteous and disturbing interference." [18]

The question how closely Rilke's picture of Russia resembled the realities of Russian life does not concern us. What would be gained if it could be shown that he was wrong here or there? The point is that the impact of Russia caused those vibrations of his soul which led to the prayers of the *Book of Hours.* Why it did, he did not know himself. In a revealing letter to one of his former teachers at St. Pölten, written two decades after his Russian journey, he says that he had gained an "insight" by reading Dostoevski that had been confirmed by his visit. He found it hard to formulate precisely what this insight was. Perhaps, he says, it was something like this:

> The Russian has shown me in example after example how even an enslavement and oppression that permanently overwhelms all powers of resistance need not necessarily lead to the degeneration of the soul. There is, at least for the Slavic soul, a degree of submission which deserves the epithet perfect, because even under the most massive and oppressive pressures, it creates for the soul something like a secret space, a fourth dimension of its existence in which, however grievous conditions become, it finds a new, endless, and genuinely independent freedom.[19]

In short: what Rilke experienced in Russia, what moved him so deeply, was the visible proof of the Russian people's absolute surrender to their fate, that is, to God. For, as Lou Salomé says, the Russians do not conceive of God "as a mightily enthroned power who lifts up man's burden, but rather as a protecting nearness which does not permit final destruction: Ljeskow's Russian God who dwells in the left armpit." [20]

It is no accident that the name of Lou Andreas-Salomé occurs in connection with Rilke's journey to Russia, for it was Lou who induced him to go, who prepared him for it, and who went with him. In evaluating the impact of Russia on Rilke's poetry we must not overlook the influence of that extraordinary woman on Rilke's life. He dedicated the *Book of Hours* to her when the manuscript, which he had entrusted to her care with no idea of publication, finally appeared in print. He "returned it to her," as he said.

Rilke had met Lou in Munich in May, 1897, under not very auspicious circumstances. In one of his expansive moods the young poet had made an anonymous present of some of his lyrics to the "famous and gracious" Lou Salomé. And she was indeed famous. Although only thirty-six years old she had already published five books, among them one on Nietzsche, which had created considerable controversy. It was known that she had been a close friend and perhaps a disciple of the philosopher. Since she was a young, brilliant, and exotic girl (she was born in Russia where her father, a descendant of a Baltic-German but originally French family, had been a general) there were inevitable rumors of a romantic attachment between her and Nietzsche. These rumors, her literary accomplishments, and her unorthodox relationship to her husband, the orientalist Andreas, surrounded her with the aura of mystery of the *femme fatale*. Whether she deserved this reputation or not she certainly was the center of attraction of a large group of admirers. Among her friends and acquaintances were such famous people as Georg Brandes, Hugo von Hofmannsthal, Arthur Schnitzler, Gerhart Hauptmann, Jakob Wassermann, Frieda von Bülow, Malwida von Meysenburg, Dr. Paul Rée, Ferdinand Tönnies, Richard Wagner, Tolstoy, Turgenev, Nietzsche, Rilke, Freud. Europe's cultural elite paid homage to Lou Salomé.

This was the woman with whom Rilke, fourteen years her

junior, a young, totally unknown poet only recently arrived from the provinces, entered into a correspondence that quickly turned into love. On many occasions Rilke expressed how much this love meant to him, but perhaps never more movingly than in the letter he wrote her from Rome in November, 1903, when, after a break of more than two years, they had started to correspond again:

> I felt it then and I know it today that the infinite reality that surrounded you was the most important event of that extremely good, great and productive time. The transforming experience which then seized me at a hundred places at once, emanated from the great reality of your being. I had never before, in my groping hesitancy, felt life so much, believed in the present, and recognized the future so much. You were the opposite of all doubt and witness to the fact that everything you touch, reach, and see *exists*. The world lost its clouded aspect, the flowing together and dissolving, so typical of my first poor verses; things arose, I learned to distinguish animals and flowers; slowly and with difficulty I learned how simple everything is, and I matured and learned to say simple things. All this happened because I was fortunate enough to meet you at a time when I was in danger of losing myself in formlessness.[21]

Even if one makes allowances for the fact that Rilke was still in love when he wrote this letter, this tribute to Lou Salomé's formative influence on him shows that his journey to Russia was not the only event that "made him what he was." Lou's part was at least as great.

The period of their closest intimacy lasted almost four years, from 1897 to 1901, but they remained close friends all their lives. Such was the affinity they felt for each other that, even when they had long been separated, they reached an immediate understanding when they met again. The letters they exchanged in three decades are moving human documents; together with Lou's memoirs they permit a more penetrating understanding of Rilke's poetry, particularly of that part upon which she exerted a great personal influence: *The Book of Monkish Life.*

Its central theme is God, or more precisely a fervent searching and groping for God who is to be, the God of the future, the Unknown God who anxiously waits to be born. Rilke heralds His coming with a torrent of metaphors. God is our neighbor, separated from us only by a thin wall; He is a little bird fallen out of his nest, a cathedral, a bearded peasant, the great morning red over the plains of eternity, the forest of contradictions:

> You are the deepest one who towered,
> the diver and the spires' grudge.[22]

> Du bist der Tiefste, welcher ragte,
> der Taucher und der Türme Neid.[23]

Image after image crowds these pages. A wealth of metric patterns and rhyme schemes keeps them in constant motion. Enjambement, alliteration, and assonance, used with great effect, show what a skillful performer Rilke was on the instrument of the German language. Consider the line, "You are the forest of contradiction" ("Du bist der Wald der Widersprüche").[24] Note how the alliteration intensifies the metaphor; how suggestive the juxtaposition of forest, i.e., darkness, profusion, and contradiction. The abstract term "contradiction" is raised to a level of concreteness. God is no longer an abstraction but a coming reality; a reality full of contradictions, pregnant with growth.

The theme of the whole book is stated in the second poem:

> I am living my life in cycles that grow
> in everything growing still.
> Will the last one succeed? I do not know:
> Attempt it I will.

> I am circling round God, the tower of yore
> my cycles are centuries long;
> And I know not: Am I a falcon, a roar
> or a great song.[25]

> Ich lebe mein Leben in wachsenden Ringen,
> die sich über die Dinge ziehn.
> Ich werde den letzten vielleicht nicht vollbringen,
> aber versuchen will ich ihn.

> Ich kreise um Gott, um den uralten Turm,
> und ich kreise jahrtausendelang;
> und ich weiß noch nicht: bin ich ein Falke, ein Sturm
> oder ein großer Gesang.[26]

It contains terms that are characterisitc of Rilke's diction: God, the ancient tower around which the poet circles ceaselessly like a

falcon, things that grow like trees. The German *Ringen* at the end
of the first line, "Ich lebe mein Leben in wachsenden Ringen,"
contains a number of very Rilkean ambiguities. It suggests cycles
of growth: tree rings; the circular movement of a bird in flight,
thus anticipating the falcon image; and even the idea of effort:
ringen i.e., wrestling, struggling—the poet's determination to go
on struggling with God, even if he should never reach his goal. The
final question: "Am I a great song?" foreshadows the Orphic
answer: "Song is existence."

The insistency of Rilke's search for God is a sign that he had
undergone a powerful experience. The prayers of the *Book of
Hours* are expressions of anxiety, born of the sudden insight into
the precariousness of the human situation. Anxiety is the source
of Rilke's poetry from now on. What had been melancholy, sadness, or even a kind of romantic *Weltschmerz* before, became
Weltangst. The dread of a hostile, godless universe suddenly overwhelmed him and forced him to his knees. Anxiously he asks:
"What will you do God, if I die?" and replies: "I am afraid." For
God is man's creation just as much as man is a creature of God.

This metaphysical fear is very different from the petty personal
fears of his earlier verse. Here a soul is crying in the wilderness, a
voice trying to force an echo from the "empty nothing." From
now on for the rest of his life Rilke would work and wait for that
echo which, in moments of great, creative exaltation, he was to
hear. But for most of the time he lived at the brink of despair,
feeling that nobody, "not angels—not men," could help him.
This feeling and its sudden reversal in moments of vision—"Life
here is magnificent"—cause the dramatic tension in Rilke's work
and force the reader to face up to his fate. In this respect Rilke's
major poetry is akin to that of the Attic tragedy: it shocks the
reader and can cause a catharsis.

In her memoirs Lou Salomé describes how she had lost faith in
God early in life. The episode itself is unimportant, but it is not
hard to imagine what effect it had on Rilke's mind when the
woman he loved and admired talked to him of the "unalterable
fact of the godlessness of the universe." [27] She must have acquainted him also with Nietzsche's concept of the "Unknown

God," for Nietzschean ideas entered Rilke's mind; and when he went to Florence in March, 1898, a year before his journey to Russia, he was already convinced that God was unknown and the only way to approach Him was through art. The *Tuscan Diary* he kept for Lou, who had prepared him as thoroughly for his Italian journey as she did for their common pilgrimage to Russia, is an apotheosis of art and the artist: "How other, future worlds will ripen to Gods I do not know, but for us art is the way." [28] God is the work of a few solitary and creative minds. The mass of the people are born in chains.

> There are always three generations. One finds God; the second builds narrow temples over him and thus chains him, and the impoverished third carries away stone upon stone from the House of God in order to build their own poor huts. And then comes one which must seek God anew: Dante, Botticelli, and Fra Bartolome belonged to such a generation.[29]

During the last decade of the nineteenth century such ideas were current among artists and scholars. They represent a revolt of the creative individual against the process of leveling and the rapidly increasing ugliness of industrial civilization. In addition to the works of the recognized leaders of that revolt, Nietzsche and Carlyle, the writings of Ruskin, Pater, and Jacob Burckhardt were influential. Under Lou's guidance Rilke read most of them. He learned that the art of the quattro- and cinquecento not only gave intense esthetic satisfaction but contained spiritual values of a quasi-religious nature. Thus prepared, he arrived in Florence. What he saw there far exceeded his expectations. Confronted by the pictures and statues of the masters of the Italian Renaissance, he felt the presence of God: "The branch of the tree of God which stretches over Italy has been in bloom." The insight that

> art was a prayer, that it was piety and devotion born of the "quiet gratitude" and "deep earnestness" of a solitary individual; that poetry, originating from such "deep dimensions of the heart" was related to God and must in some way lead back to God, *that* insight—which was new around 1900—Rilke gained during the months of his stay in Florence.[30]

It is important to make this point, for otherwise the real nature of the Rilke problem is misunderstood. It is then easy to conclude, as Miss Butler does, that he suffered from "distorted and magnified ideas about the cosmic functions of art." [31] If we grant that he underwent a genuine conversion or *metanoia*, that God whom he had lost was revealed to him in the art of Botticelli or Michelangelo and in the vastness of Russia, then his problem as a poet was essentially this: could he write poetry that possessed this quality; poetry that would lead the way back to God? Was he an artist, or merely one of those "who come and go," who have "left God behind like a memory"? For "to the artist God is the last and deepest fulfillment; and when the pious say: 'He is.' and the sad feel: 'He was,' the artist smiles: 'He will be.' " [32]

All his life Rilke suffered from a profound sense of inadequacy, almost amounting to a sense of guilt, because he felt he was not equal to this task. The other, the man, constantly got in the way of the artist; the "ancient enmity" between art and life, between the artist and the virtuoso, led him at times to the brink of despair. And still he persevered. With a tenacity that stands in strange contrast to one so gentle, he carried on his quest. Rather than betray it he would be silent. The long silence that followed upon the period when he had achieved complete technical mastery is proof that he was in bitter earnest when he said: "A work of art is good [only] if it has sprung from necessity. In this nature of its origin lies its judgment. There is no other." [33]

The poems he wrote in the late autumn of 1899, a few months after his return from Russia, sprang from a twofold necessity: to give voice to his Florentine experience of art and to his experience of Russia or, more accurately, to their common source: his experience of God. In the figure of the monk he found the symbol for the poetic fusion of these two currents of experience.

It was a very fortunate find, for symbol and reality, the monk and Rilke, are in complete correspondence. At the same time the monk symbol is sufficiently ambiguous to permit subtle shifts of emphasis: it can stand for the praying Russian monk, or for the writing medieval monk—for the saint or for the artist. The saint's prayers are humble and submissive. He prostrates himself before God who can but "dimly distinguish him from things that kneel"; God, the creator of the universe who "felt the void was like a wound/ and cooled it with the world"; God "who is and is and is/ amidst the trembling time." The artist, on the other hand, feels that God is still to come: "we are building Him with trembling hands"; God is the future but "His coming contours dawn." Sometimes the two mingle and a third voice arises: the voice of the mystic. It is this voice that asks anxiously:

> What will you do, God, when I die?
> When I, your pitcher, shattered lie?
> When I, your drink, go stale or dry?
> I am your garb, the trade you ply,
> you lose your meaning, losing me.
>
> Homeless without me, you will be
> robbed of your welcome, warm and sweet.
> I am your sandals: your tired feet
> will wander bare for want of me.
>
> Your mighty cloak will fall away.
> Your glance that on my cheek was laid
> and pillowed warm, will seek, dismayed,
> the comfort that I offered once—
> to lie, as sunset colors fade
> in the cold lap of alien stones.
> What will you do, God? I am afraid.[34]
>
> Was wirst du tun, Gott, wenn ich sterbe?
> Ich bin dein Krug (wenn ich zerscherbe?)
> Ich bin dein Trank (wenn ich verderbe?)
> Bin dein Gewand und dein Gewerbe,
> mit mir verlierst du deinen Sinn.
>
> Nach mir hast du kein Haus, darin
> dich Worte, nah und warm, begrüßen
> Es fällt von deinen müden Füßen
> die Samtsandale, die ich bin.
>
> Dein großer Mantel läßt dich los.
> Dein Blick, den ich mit meiner Wange
> warm, wie mit einem Pfühl, empfange,
> wird kommen, wird mich suchen, lange—
> und legt beim Sonnenuntergange

sich fremden Steinen in den Schoß.
Was wirst du tun, Gott? Ich bin bange.[35]

In poems such as this Rilke carries on the tradition of German mysticism that started in the thirteenth century with Master Eckhart, and whose central faith is the pantheistic conception of God's oneness with the world. Angelus Silesius expresses the same thought when he says:

> I know that without me God cannot live at all.
> If I'm undone and lost, He in despair must fall.[36]

And yet Rilke was no mystic in the true sense of the word. For the true mystic negates the world: Rilke affirmed it. The true mystic distrusts his senses and mortifies the flesh: Rilke's poetry is a triumph of sensuous perceptivity. But even this statement has to be qualified. There is undoubtedly a mystic strain in Rilke, a deep longing for nonbeing and for the three modes of existence that lead to it, i.e., *via purgativa* or asceticism, *via illuminativa* or meditation, and *via unitiva* or ecstasy. This strain conflicts with the artist in him and his will to create, and thus to add to the multiplicity of the world from which the mystic wants to be freed. Fundamentally, the artist and the mystic stand on opposite poles, and the further apart they are within one individual the greater the tension under which he lives. Rilke knew the two-souls problem of Faust:

> For my voice has grown in two dimensions
> and has become a clamor and a scent:
> one wants to build God's distant mansions,
> the other, to my inner tensions,
> be angel, vision and event.[37]

> Denn meine Stimme wuchs nach zweien Seiten
> und ist ein Duften worden und ein Schrein:
> die eine will den Fernen vorbereiten,
> die andere muß meiner Einsamkeiten
> Gesicht und Seligkeit und Engel sein.[38]

The unresolved struggle between the mystic and the artist accounts for the particular tension in Rilke's life and work; unresolved, that is, until in the figure of Orpheus the mediator appears, and "for a while fate is in balance." But the Orphic resolution came to Rilke only late in life. For the most part he was torn between the two extremes. There were times when the mystic was so much in the ascendency that the artist was in danger of being silenced. This happened during the second journey to Russia.

Lou Salomé, who again went with him, remarks that she noted during the first journey how Rilke's intense devotion occasionally could not find adequate expression. The prayer did not crystallize into a poem. For there is something deeply paradoxical in the act of transforming a prayer into a work of art; it means "a reversal of cause and effect in that the secondary mode, the expression, no longer coincides with the experience itself." [39] During their second journey Rilke's inability to express what he felt became even more apparent. "Looking back upon this journey he often complained that the depth of his impressions remained without 'prayers,' but the reason for this is precisely that he 'prayed them.' " [40] She reports the extraordinary sight of Rilke "torn between the longing to kneel before each of his impressions and the opposite urge not to miss what went on creatively within him. Thus he often found himself as if transfixed at the appropriate place of listening silence and, at the same time, as if restless at the windows of an express train." [41] Is this not a perfect description of Rilke's existential dilemma: to be both the listening solitary *and* the restless voyager?

Had he lived in a more religious age, his fervor might have found release in universally accepted symbols. The Madonna cult of the late Middle Ages provided the artists of the Renaissance with an inexhaustible theme of immense spiritual potentiality. But Rilke was born at a time when "more than ever/ the things we can live with are falling away/ for what replaces them is an imageless act." For a mind like Rilke's the Empire State Building, for example, was an "imageless act" and, compared with the Cathedral of Chartres, devoid of spiritual content. There are, indeed, hardly any outer equivalents left for the activities of the soul, and the spiritually focused artist is forced either to try to reactivate the traditional images of the church, as Eliot does, or "to pour himself out into a God-creation which has lost its object." [42] Lou Salomé believed that Rilke attempted the latter and saw in this attempt the main reason both for his greatness as a poet and for the tragedy of his life: "For his task as an artist and a creator forced him to use up his human substance: where his work threatened to fail his very life was in danger." [43] Artistic failure thus became human failure, and since in Rilke's case the artistic stake was so high, was God himself, the human failure was commensurate with it, was absolute. This was the reason for Rilke's *Angst:* "the dread of being swallowed up into nothingness" [44] unless he succeeded in creating God. It was also the reason for his feeling, at times, that his art was a temptation of the devil, a form of idolatry, "a sin" in the sense in which Kierkegaard considered all poetry sinful. Lou mentions a "terrifying letter" he wrote her during the second Russian journey in which he called himself "utterly depraved" because of the presumption of his prayers. She was shocked by his psychic instability, by those sudden changes from exaltation to despair over which he seemed to have no control and which to her were symptomatic of a serious mental disturbance. She knew that, as long as he could work, there was nothing to fear. His creative spirit carried him easily over his depression. Dangerous, however, were those barren periods during which he felt a failure, both as artist and man.

He passed through such a period after he had written the first part of the *Book of Hours*, his "monk's songs" as he called them. It took him two years before he found himself once again in a state of creative exaltation, but then he wrote in eleven days all the poems of the *Book of Pilgrimage*. He felt them to be a continuation of the first prayers: "I am the same still who knelt/ before you in a monk's cowl." But there are differences. For one thing they number only thirty-four compared with the sixty-seven of the first part. Evidently the poetic current that inspired them was less strong. Russian influence is not as pronounced. Doubt has increased. The monk's confident feeling that only a "thin wall" separated him from God has given way to the pilgrim's sad insight: "the way to you is terribly far." There is a distinct increase in anti-Christian sentiment. "You do not care for Christians," he says, and wants "no waiting for the beyond, no gazing towards it/ but longing to degrade not even death." Thus the death theme, which is to figure prominently in the third part, is introduced here. The book marks the beginning of Rilke's long pilgrimage. He has left the monk's cell and God's sheltering presence and has gone out into the world: part Parzival in search of the Holy Grail, part Hamlet accompanied by ghosts.

The Book of Pilgrimage was written about six months after Rilke's marriage to Clara Westhoff during the time of his temporary estrangement from Lou Salomé. But one of the finest poems in it was a love poem, originally addressed to Lou. It has not been detected as such because it fits in perfectly with the other prayers. Lou mentions it both in her memoirs and in her correspondence with Rilke. She says he gave it to her in 1897, i.e., four years before he wrote the other poems of the *Book of Pilgrimage*—but she must be mistaken in dating it that early—and that it was the first of his poems that really moved her. Perhaps that is the reason why he included it. He wanted to show her that even though they were no longer intimate she was still his "bridge to the future." In its final, slightly revised form the poem reads:

> Put out my eyes, and I can see you still;
> Slam my ears to, and I can hear you yet;
> and without any feet can go to you;
> and tongueless, I can conjure you at will.
> Break off my arms, I shall take hold of you
> and grasp you with my heart as with a hand;
> arrest my heart, my brain will beat as true;
> and if you set this brain of mine afire,
> then on my blood I yet will carry you.[45]

> Lösch mir die Augen aus: ich kann dich sehn,
> wirf mir die Ohren zu: ich kann dich hören,
> und ohne Füße kann ich zu dir gehn,
> und ohne Mund noch kann ich dich beschwören.
> Brich mir die Arme ab, ich fasse dich
> mit meinem Herzen wie mit einer Hand,
> Halt mir das Herz zu, und mein Hirn wird schlagen,
> und wirfst du in mein Hirn den Brand,
> so werd ich dich auf meinem Blute tragen.[46]

It is a good illustration of how Rilke's poetic imagination worked. There was always the concrete person or event: Lou

Salomé, or Russia, or the Italian painters; later it would be Rodin, Baudelaire, Cézanne, Paris, and the letters of Marianna Alcoforado; later yet, Valéry and the memory of a young dancer. These and countless other persons, books, paintings, statues, churches, landscapes, historical events, and mythological, classical, and Biblical themes form the raw material out of which he distilled his poetic essences. The end product is a distillate from which all impurities have been eliminated. Not only that. Rilke's fervent soul, the catalyst in this process of transformation, adds its own intensities to the material. The result is that vibrant reality: the Rilke poem. Rich in texture and often striking in visual imagery, its most distinguishing feature is the dramatic tension that emanates from it. Even the poem given above shows it, although it was written at a time when Rilke was still learning his craft. Note how the tension grows from line to line until it reaches both its climax and dénouement at the very end. There are triumph and surrender in the climactic words: "then on my blood I yet will carry you." No ordinary lover speaks like this. The love expressed in this poem transcends its object, plunges straight into God. Here the human love partner has indeed become invisible. Only God remains.

The secret of the dramatic tension in Rilke's work, which the reader senses even if it does not make sense to him, lies in such an intensification of the feeling-emotion that a reconciliation of opposites take place: extreme joy or extreme sorrow evokes both tears and laughter. Rilke was of course not the first to make use of this paradox. The insight that life and death, love and loneliness, beauty and terror are inextricably linked stands at the core of all tragedy. But who among moderns has affirmed it more movingly? In the final chords of the *Tenth Elegy* the tragic spirit itself seems to speak:

> And we, who have always thought
> of happiness *rising*, would feel
> the emotion that almost startles
> when happiness *falls*.[47]

> Und wir, die an *steigendes* Glück
> denken, empfänden die Rührung,

die uns beinah bestürzt,
wenn ein Glückliches *fällt*.[48]

The *Book of Hours* marks the beginning of Rilke's insight into the tragic paradoxes of existence. God is such a paradox; hence the paradoxical nature of the images that try to express Him. He is the neighbor and the stranger, the past and the future, the cockcrow after the night of time: He is life, and He is death:

> You are the deep epitome of things
> that keep its being's secret with locked lip,
> and shows itself to others otherwise:
> to the ship, a haven—to the land, a ship.[49]

> Du bist der Dinge tiefer Inbegriff,
> der seines Wesens letztes Wort verschweigt
> und sich den Andern immer anders zeigt:
> dem Schiff als Küste und dem Land als Schiff.[50]

The final chapter in the *Book of Hours* bears the somber title: *The Book of Poverty and Death*. Rilke wrote it during the week he spent in Viareggio in April, 1903. It contains the same number of poems as the second book, but they are somewhat shorter— twenty pages as compared with thirty. The poetic-visionary current that had set in after his journey to Russia, giving rise to the first prayers of the *Book of Hours,* was definitely on the wane. The planned fourth book remained unwritten.

Anxiety is the keynote of these poems: deep and unrelieved anxiety. The pilgrim feels buried under mountains of fear—the fear of being lost in big cities, the fear of dying a small and petty death, the fear of becoming one of those shabby poor who drift about cheap night lodgings "without will and without world."

The poems reflect the terrors that beset Rilke in Paris and foreshadow the anguished prose of *Malte Laurids Brigge.* Appalled by the massive fraud that life in the big cities has become, he cries out for death: "the great death which we all bear within/ it is the ultimate and final fruit." He is horrified to see that even death has been cheapened. People in big cities die in hospitals, die little deaths, while "their own death hangs green and without sweetness/ a fruit within them that does not mature." Is it not time, he asks, to learn the true meaning of death and to accept it for what it is: part of life? And calling upon God, the great Lord of Death, he cries out:

> Oh do not grant the wish of the God Mother
> send us the great one who will bring forth death . . .
> Make me the mouth, Lord, of the new Messiah
> his John the Baptist and his song.[51]

> Erfülle, du gewaltiger Gewährer,
> nicht jenen Traum der Gottgebärerin,—
> richt auf den Wichtigen: den Tod-Gebärer, . . .

> Laß mich den Mund der neuen Messiade,
> den Tönenden, den Täufer sein.[52]

Thus, in a spirit of defiance, the death theme enters into Rilke's poetry. From now on it will form, together with two others, the great trinity of themes with which he is concerned almost exclusively: God, love, and death. He is deeply convinced that they have been misunderstood and neglected: that we are inadequate in love, impotent in the face of death, and ignorant of God. He tells a young poet:

> We must assume our existence as *broadly* as we in any way can; everything, even the unheard-of, must be possible in it. That is at bottom the only courage that is demanded of us: to have courage for the most extraordinary, the most singular and the most inexplicable that we may encounter. That mankind has in this sense been cowardly has done life endless harm; the experiences that are called "appearances," the so-called "spirit-world," death, all those things that are so closely akin to us, have by daily parrying been so driven out of life that the senses with which we could have grasped them are crippled. To say nothing of God.[53]

Years later he put it this way to another correspondent:

> Death . . . who is probably so close to us that the distance between him and the inner center of our hearts cannot be registered . . . was made into something external, something to be held daily at a greater distance, something that lurks in the outer voids ready to pounce on this man or the next with his baneful choice. More and more the suspicion grew up against him that he was the antithesis, the opponent, the invisible opposite in the air; the end of all our joys, the perilous glass of our happiness from which we may be spilled at any moment. . . . Nature, however, knew nothing of this banishment

which we have somehow managed to accomplish—when a tree blossoms, death blooms in it as well as life; every field is full of Death . . . [and of lovers] one can say that God is nourishing to them and that death does not harm them: *for they are full of death because they are full of life.*[54]

Rilke's "death cult" has met with serious objections even from critics who admire his poetry. Kassner says it is based on a "fallacy." The idea of a "personal death" in particular he calls a false idea. Holthusen goes even farther. According to him all of Rilke's ideas are false—i.e., the idea of nonpossessive love, the idea of an immanent God, the idea of a personal death—if they are considered outside their medium, as philosophical theses; provided, he adds, that "we assume it as proved that there are genuine criteria to distinguish between 'true' and 'false' ideas, and that a sort of intuitive logic . . . tells us whether an idea is true or false." [55]

The weakness of such reasoning is apparent. For if we have to rely on "intuitive logic" to discover the truth or falsehood of an idea we are no better off than the poet, who would be quite justified in asking why our intuition should be truer than his. There are of course ideas, once held to be true, which are demonstrably wrong, e.g., the idea that the earth is flat or that it is the center of the universe. When they appear in great classical or medieval poetry we discount them without necessarily suffering an impairment of our esthetic enjoyment. When they appear in prose or in mediocre poetry they grate on our minds. We enjoy Homer and Dante, despite the fact that they express ideas we know to be false, because we enjoy their poetry. Rilke's ideas are of a kind that cannot be proved right or wrong; all we can say is that in any given poem or prose passage we *feel* they are right or wrong. If we feel they are wrong, the reason is that he failed to express them convincingly. In that case failure means poetic failure, for "there is no poetry left, if we *feel* that the ideas are false." [56]

We shall have occasion to point out that Rilke sometimes failed as a poet and more often as a prose writer. Compared with the poetry of the *Book of Hours*, the prose of the *Stories of God*, written at the same time and treating the same theme, seems contrived. Even *Malte Laurids Brigge*—a much greater achievement than the *Stories of God*—is not as convincing as its poetic counterpart, *New Poems*. This holds true as well for the prose commentaries that Rilke wrote on *Duino Elegies*. The poetry of the *Elegies* is convincing, the prose not always. In short, Rilke's ideas are poetic ideas; they are the stuff poetry has been made of from time immemorial; they cannot be divorced from the poem: "The poetry of the *Duino Elegies* is indivisible." [57]

Returning now to Rilke's concept of a "personal death," it is well known that he found it in the writings of Jens Peter Jacobsen, whose books he was reading when he wrote the *Book of Poverty and Death*. And what has been called Rilke's "death cult"—a misleading term, for it is really a "death-life cult"—goes back to primitive vegetation myths which are basic to all religions. He found examples of it in the Egyptian and Etruscan death rites. Nor is Rilke the only modern writer who has voiced such ideas. D. H. Lawrence, a great affirmer of life, writes about death in very much the same vein:

> Unless we see the dark splendour of death ahead, and travel to be lords of darkness at last, peers in the realms of death, life is nothing but a petulant, pitiful backing, like a frightened horse, back, back, back to the stable, the manger, the cradle. But onward ahead is the great porch of the entry into death, with its columns of bone-ivory. And beyond the porch is the heart of darkness, where the lords of death arrive home out of the vulgarity of life, into their own dark and silent domains, lordly, ruling the incipience of life.[58]

Rilke was obviously not an original thinker, although his poetry provokes thought. It arouses questions that lie dormant in all of us, but it does not provide answers, except in so far as it challenges the reader to look into his own heart. What he finds there is all that matters: "Nowhere, beloved, is world but within." As a result every reader responds differently. One can reject what Rilke says or accept it, but, if one has ever read him seriously, one cannot remain indifferent. All attempts to refute Rilke's reasoning or to prove him right by logical arguments are beside the point. His poetry is based on intuitive insights, on reasons the heart understands.

Rilke used to call the *Book of Hours, Duino Elegies,* and *Sonnets to Orpheus* his undatable books. There is more truth in this than he may have realized himself, for the dates of their composition are relatively unimportant; they are undatable in the sense that they treat timeless topics. We can be moved by the anguished prose of *Malte* and get much enjoyment from many of the *New Poems* or from the *Book of Pictures*; but for the full impact of Rilke's spiritual force we must read his undatable books.

The *Book of Hours* is the earliest of these and less accomplished than the other two. Rilke himself felt that when he wrote it he did not yet have real mastery of his medium. He was overwhelmed by nature and the visions it aroused in him. He lacked the rigorous artistic discipline to mold what he felt and had to pass through a long and painful apprenticeship before he was able to express his feelings, raptures, and visions in the immaculate poetry of the *Elegies* and *Sonnets*.

The three parts of the *Book of Hours* show the direction Rilke's artistic development was to take. In the first book the monk's rapturous soul flies heavenward. God is so close that He can appear at any moment; one feels "His ascension out of the breathing heart, from which heaven is covered, and His precipitation as rain." One feels that the monk, smiling but with his face bathed in tears, has experienced God's vastness. Time has collapsed: all that remains is space vibrating with His presence. In the second book there is no such certainty. God is infinitely far. The pilgrim's fate is doubt and anxiety. The third book finally leads to the depth of despair. Life is an illusion. God is darkness, is the great Lord of Death.

In a descending curve the *Book of Hours* takes the reader from the ringing vastness of Russia to the stony silence of Paris. To endure this silence, to make beauty out of the terrors that beset him there—this was Rilke's task in the years that followed.

4 Hamlet in Paris

It is not madness
that I've uttered: bring me to the test
And I the matter will reword.
Shakespeare, *Hamlet* III. iv

In a letter to Rodin written in December, 1908, at a time when he was hard at work on the *Notebooks of Malte Laurids Brigge,* that "high watershed of his life" as he used to call it, Rilke comments on the difference between poetry and prose:

> In writing poetry one is always aided and even carried by the rhythm of exterior things; for the cadence of lyricism is that of nature: water, wind, night. But in order to write prose one must delve deeply into oneself and find the anonymous and multiple rhythm of one's blood. Prose has to be built like a cathedral; there one is truly without name, without ambition, without help: on the scaffolding and alone with one's conscience.[1]

This passage, reminiscent of Hemingway's "fourth-dimensional prose," seems an appropriate starting point for a discussion of Rilke's prose, in particular of that "prolonged monologue with his own reflection": *Malte Laurids Brigge.*

The genesis of this book can be traced back to an interesting exchange of letters with Lou Salomé that started in the summer of 1903, more than two years after their estrangement. In her last letter to the poet in February, 1901, in which she told him why she decided to leave him—a letter ominously called *Letzter Zuruf* (last appeal)—Lou had warned Rilke that she feared for his mind. She told him she had discussed his "case" with a psychiatrist friend who was quite familiar with "what you and I used to call 'the other' in you: this now depressed, now excited, all-too-timid or all-too-exalted fellow" [2] whose constant danger is a fate like Garschin's (a young Russian writer who had killed himself in a fit of melancholy) or, as Lou may well have thought, a fate like Nietzsche's. But she added "this need not be" and reminded him of the times when he had stood "whole" before her, while he was writing his monk's songs. That was where his hope lay: in his work. Although she could not help him any more she exhorted him to continue searching for his "dark God." Only in his "worst hour" was he to call her.

This he did in June, 1903. He was in Paris and had been wanting to write her for weeks but was afraid it might be too early. But finally he could not restrain himself; he had to write her for "who knows if I can come in my worst hour!" [3] He must see her, talk with her, stay in her house for one day—"one day only." Will she let him?

In her brief answer Lou assured him that he could always come to her but proposed an exchange of letters before trying a personal meeting. He was to write her all he had on his mind; she would take it straight to her heart. This promise released a flood of pent-up emotion.

Rilke first told her that he had been forced to give up his "lonely house on the moor," where he had hoped to live with his wife and child, because he could not support them. He had gone to Paris to do a book on Rodin for a German publisher and to work: "I have tried to work quietly and earnestly and am greatly disturbed to feel that I did not succeed. The town was against me; it rejected my life. It was like a test I failed." [4] Disheartened and sick with influenza, he had fled to Viareggio. There, as once before, he had found peace of mind: "The girls of my maidens' songs walked in the streets and sang." [5] In a flash the despair of Paris was transmuted into the poetry of the *Book of Poverty and Death*. But it was only a brief interval, barely a month of creative well-being. Back in Paris fear and frustration had overtaken him once more. He had used all his will power to fight it—in vain: "Far back in my childhood, in the great fevers of its sicknesses, great indescribable fears arose, fears of something too great, too hard, too near, deep unutterable fears." These same fears had suddenly returned and

> . . . did not even need the pretense of night and fever, they seized me in the middle of day when I thought I was healthy and brave, and took my heart and held it over the void. Can you understand how this is; everything changes, drops away from my senses and I feel forced out of the world where everything is close and clear into another uncertain, unspeakably sad environment. Whither? Then I felt I would not recognize anyone who might come to me and that I too would be a stranger to all, like one who has died in a strange land, alone, supernumerary, a fragment of other relationships. Then my sadness was very great and the fear arose that my worst hour could perhaps lie there in that other world from which I can return to no one.[6]

Whatever shock this letter must have caused Lou she did not say. In an obvious effort to sound casual she told him that influenza is frequently accompanied by strange mental depressions. There was no need to worry. Perhaps the fact that he wrote about his fears would help him exorcize them; and perhaps, too, that his letters came to her who was "at home in joy" and who had never had any other power except that which is innate in joy.

This answer reassured him, and he now told her more about Paris, giving form, color and contour to the unutterable fears that had overwhelmed him there. Visions of Dante and Brueghel come to mind as one reads these nightmarish pages. This is not Paris the beautiful, not the gay and light-hearted symbol of love. It is the city of the damned, the market place of hell. Corruption and decay fill every particle of its air. Behind harmless looking façades sinister acts occur. Disease, poverty, and death lurk at every corner. Hospitals:

> I have walked past large hospitals, their wide open gates making gestures of impatient and eager charity. When I passed by the *Hôtel Dieu* (mark the irony of the name) for the first time an open cab drove up with a man hanging in it; he swayed at every motion, limp like a marionette, with a heavy tumor on his long, gray, sagging neck.[7]

He tried to watch the forsaken creatures who passed him in the street with "calm and objective curiosity, like a new species of animal," [8] but was unable to maintain his detached attitude. An

irresistible pull dragged him into their miserable lives. He felt that
the fangs of the same fate that had caught them held him too.

> One evening late in autumn a little old woman stood next to me in
> the light of a shop window. She stood very quietly and I thought her
> occupied, as I was, with the display in the window and hardly paid
> any attention to her. But finally her proximity made me feel uneasy
> and, I don't know why, I suddenly looked at her strangely clasped,
> worn-out hands. There, out of these hands, slowly, quite slowly, rose
> an old, long, thin pencil; it grew and grew, taking a long time before
> it was completely visible, visible in its entire wretchedness. I cannot tell
> what horrified me in this scene, but it seemed to me that a whole
> destiny unrolled before me, a long destiny, a catastrophe that reached
> its horrible climax at the moment when the pencil stopped growing
> and, trembling gently, towered out of the loneliness of these empty
> hands. I understood finally that I was to buy it.[9]

Where do these people live, he wants to know, where do they
sleep and of what do they think when they sit for days in the
public gardens? When they talk to themselves what words are they
using? "Do they still speak in sentences or does everything rush out
of them, madly, as from a burning theater, everything that was in
them: spectator and actor, listener and hero?" [10]

Then he told her the story of the man suffering from St. Vitus
dance, told it almost exactly as he would tell it in *Malte*. A few
pages only, but what condensation of evocative power! Not a word
is out of place, none is superfluous. The outer event: a young man
walking along Boulevard St. Michel, just that: walking. He is
wearing a black overcoat and is using both his hands to turn down
his coat collar. That is all that happens outwardly. But then something starts. The young man has trouble with his collar. It seems
to have a life of its own, refuses to stay down. All of a sudden the
simple act of turning down a coat collar becomes ambiguous,
sinister. The outer event encounters an inner compulsion. Something, we do not know just what, is about to happen. A force from
within is struggling to break out. But the man fights it—fights the
onrushing sickness in his body—and continues his walk, desper-
ately trying to look unconcerned, ordinary. Rilke watches the un-
equal struggle with horrified fascination. He surrenders his own
will, offers it to the stranger "whose fear could no longer be dis-

tinguished from mine." [11] But to no avail. The man's sickness breaks out finally, "like a fire, out of all windows at once," and he surrenders to the mad convulsions of his twisting body. Rilke walks away, worn-out, defeated.

All this and much more he told Lou, imploring her to help him.

> If only I could have formed these fears, if I could have made things out of them, real, quiet things the making of which is joy and freedom and from which, once they exist, emanates calmness, nothing would have happened to me. But these fears, which fell upon me every day, aroused hundreds of other fears, and they rose up in me and against me and I did not get beyond them.[12]

To his surprise Lou did not think he needed her help now.

> In the middle of reading your last letter it happened that I forgot you completely at times: thus powerfully all you described pressed upon me. . . . I entered into a strange calm that can result even from impressions of misery if they are not created by life only but recreated after life by the artist. For you are mistaken in thinking that you suffered these things helplessly and without transforming them in a higher process. They are all here, no longer only in you but now in me also and outside us as living and self-assured things—no different from any of your poems. You are the poet of the poor and the oppressed.[13]

Rilke was elated. He read and reread her letter; for if there was one person in the world whose approval he needed it was Lou Salomé. She had rejected him in the past; she had exposed his tendency to grandiloquent words and exaggerated sentiments. She had ridiculed what she called his "pre-Wolfratshausen" moods: those abrupt changes from abject humility and self-pitying sentimentality to bold gestures of defiance. He had resented her lack of faith in him; at times he had hated her; but his hatred was born of love, and his resentment sprang from the realization that she was probably right. For he was severely honest with himself and fought against the "loud accents" of the other in him. So he had at last convinced Lou that he was a genuine artist and not just a hysterical weakling. She had seen in his confession of failure a sign of strength; it was much more than he had hoped. If Lou believed in him, could he not believe in himself? Her "great consent" to his description of his Parisian nightmares had rescued him from the desert of despair into which he had strayed . . . Or had it? After all, what had he done? He had written a letter—"only a letter!" There was no other record of the horrors he had experienced, nothing that would bear witness for him. He had lacked strength to write poetry. Perhaps it was unjust to expect that he should have been able to record those terrifying visions. Perhaps he must have patience and wait for them to be transformed in his heart. But life was passing. Might it not pass him by, leaving him empty-handed like that old woman in Paris?

However, now that Lou had encouraged him he made a new resolve to go on. He wanted to work, for he felt he had no real life outside his work. Day after day he had watched Rodin working with the calm assurance of an artist who does not have to wait for moments of inspiration. Why could he not work like that? Did he lack discipline? or strength of character? Was his will sick? Or was it perhaps "the dream in me that frustrates action?" [14] This question touches the core of his personality.

To act or not to act: *that* is Hamlet's problem. It is also the problem of that type of artist to which Rilke belonged. For the act of creating, when it springs from a strong inner compulsion, from an excess of visionary power as it were, inevitably encounters resistance. Outwardly, because there are no adequate equivalents in the visible world for the fierce activities of the soul, no "objective correlatives" for the kind of emotion experienced; and inwardly, because the will to create runs counter to a deep sense of the futility of all creation. The artist encounters the mystic in him; the longing for being, that for nonbeing. Every creative act thus becomes an act of violence.

In the *Notebooks of Malte Laurids Brigge* Rilke records his desperate resolve to "take arms against a sea of troubles." His mouthpiece *Malte* attempts to express what Eliot—writing on Hamlet—has called the "inexpressibly horrible." Both Hamlet and Malte are haunted men, both live under the compulsion that they must exorcize their ghosts, both suffer from a "mother fixation." Hamlet's sword is Malte's pen, but there is no victory for either; to lay their ghosts means death for both Danes. This they both

know and, knowing, fear it. Hamlet's "but that the dread of something after death" is echoed by Malte: "Why should I pretend that
those nights had never been, when in fear of death I sat up, cling-
ing to the fact that the mere act of sitting was at any rate a part
of life: that the dead did not sit." [15]

Rilke started working on *Malte* in February, 1904, while he was
living in Rome where his wife Clara was studying. He had no
plan, no plot, no clear idea of precisely what he wanted to do. He
simply had the urge to prove to himself that he could master his
fears. The act of writing became an act of liberation. For a few
weeks he wrote steadily, casting his thoughts into a powerful, impressionistic prose. He wrote about Paris as he had experienced it,
Paris of the Rue Toullier where he had lived when he had first
arrived: "So that is where people come to live? I should rather
have thought they came here to die." [16] He wrote of the smells,
sounds, and colors of the city, for "every city has its summer
smell." Paris smelled of iodoform, *pommes frites*, and fear. And he
wrote about death.

Death is one of the major themes in *Malte* as in the entire body
of Rilke's work. He celebrates the power and glory of death as well
as man's fear of it. "We know nothing of this going hence," and
yet it is the ultimate reality. "While the world is full of parts that
we are playing"—when you died—"a streak of something real
broke upon this scene/ green of real green, some real sunshine
and some real wood." He is horrified to see that death, like life, has
become cheap and vulgar, has lost its ancient terrible grandeur.
People no longer die their own individual deaths, just as they no
longer live their own lives. They conform. They die in hospitals, a
ready-made, mass-produced death, or in sanatoria "where people
die so willingly and with so much gratitude to doctors and nurses,
they die from one of the deaths assigned to the institution; that is
regarded very favorably." [17]

These thoughts lead him to question his own existence. What
is he doing in Paris? What sort of life is he leading—a stranger
among strangers "without a home, without inherited things, without dogs"? If only he had memories. If only his childhood were
not buried so deeply. He is learning to see: that is the only cer-

tainty he has. He is twenty-eight years old and almost nothing has happened to him. He has written a few insignificant books, a bad play, and verses: "Ah! but verses amount to so little when one begins to write them young." [18]

Then he starts thinking:

> It is laughable. Here I sit . . . I Brigge, who have grown to be eight-and-twenty years old and of whom no one knows. I sit here and am nothing. And nevertheless this nothing begins to think and, five flights up, on a grey Parisian afternoon, thinks these thoughts:
>
> "Is it possible, it thinks, that nothing real or important has yet been seen or known or said? Is it possible that mankind has had thousands of years in which to observe, reflect and record, and has allowed these millennia to slip past, like a recess interval at school in which one eats one's sandwich and an apple?
>
> Yes, it is possible.
>
> Is it possible that despite our discoveries and progress, despite our culture, religion and world-wisdom, we still remain on the surface of life? Is it possible that we have even covered this surface, which might still have been something, with an incredibly uninteresting stuff which makes it look like drawing-room furniture during summer holidays?
>
> Yes, it is possible." [19]

On and on he asks. A dynasty of questions rises in his troubled mind:

> "[Has] the whole history of the world . . . been misunderstood? . . . Is it possible that we say 'women,' 'children,' 'boys,' not guessing (despite all our culture, not guessing) that these words have long since had no plural, but only countless singulars? . . . Is it possible that there are people who speak of 'God' and mean something they have in common?" And always the terrible monotone of the answer: "Yes, it is possible." [20]

.   .   .   .

> But if all this is possible—has even no more than a semblance of possibility—then surely, for all the world's sake, something must be done. The first comer, he who has had these disturbing thoughts, must begin to do some of the neglected things; even if he be just anybody, by no means the most suitable person: there is no one else at hand. This young, insignificant foreigner, Brigge, will have to sit down in his room five flights up and write, day and night. Yes, he will have to write; that will be the end of it.[21]

It is perhaps unnecessary to say that *Malte's Notebook* does not provide answers to these immense questions, because they are unanswerable. The parable of the Prodigal Son at the end of the book, in Rilke's interpretation, says as much, for it means that they will remain unanswered until He is willing to answer them.

The fact, however, that they are unanswerable is no reason not to try to answer them. On the contrary, Rilke would say, it is one more reason why they deserve our patient and persistent attention. He does not minimize the dangers inherent in such a quest. Does not Malte's fate almost lead to the conclusion that life is "bottomless," that there are no certainties anywhere, nothing, not even that "little strip of orchard between river and rock" which he celebrates in the *Elegies?* To the untroubled mind a quest like Malte's must seem singularly futile. Does he not seem to hold "discourse with the incorporeal air?" The untroubled mind tends to dismiss the *Notebook* as a form of scapegoatism. Rilke, it says, put all his fears upon poor Malte and sent him into a land not inhabited. Such an interpretation does scant justice to the poet who accompanied his alter ego a good deal of the way and did not know in the end whether Malte had to perish so that he could live or whether the writing of the book had taken him, Rilke, "into a current which would carry him away and beyond." [22]

In any event, it proved to be a hard book to write. Soon after he had started it Rilke discovered, as he would again with *Duino Elegies*, that it was quite beyond his power to finish the task. Try as he might he could not bring himself to gaze steadily into the dreadful depths that had opened up in Paris.

In plaintive letters to Lou he tried to give reasons for his renewed failure: "When I started my new book on the eighth of February," he wrote her in April, "it became evident that my manner of working (just as my much more attentive manner of observing) has changed so that I shall probably never again be able to write a book in ten days (or nights)." [23] He took this to be a sign of progress. Would it not permit him to work steadily? Was that not what he needed for his peace of mind? At the same time he noted a new danger. What is he to do to keep outer distractions away while he is working on a long-term project? Intense concentration is possible for a week or ten days; can he keep it up for months? He did not know. All his previous experience pointed the other way. His prosebook, *Stories of God*, written in dialogue —a form he briefly considered for Malte also—was completed in seven successive nights; *Cornet* was all but finished in one sitting; and all his monk's songs, i.e., the entire first part of the *Book of Hours*, sixty-seven poems, he wrote in less than a month. Many years later, in an unparalleled outburst of creative energy, he would write the entire cycle of *Sonnets to Orpheus*, fifty-five sonnets, as well as twenty-one additional poems within a week. Hence his fear was quite justified. Could he extend the span of concentration that had produced his best work? He was afraid he could not: "This fear followed me and perhaps it is chiefly responsible for why my work faltered and broke off at the beginning of March." [24]

But this explanation did not satisfy him. In his next letter to Lou he once more took up the problem of his inability to work steadily. He gave three reasons for it: first, that he had overexerted himself in February—"I tried then to fashion and record many of my most painful Parisian impressions and felt at times, while I did it, a sharp psychic pain similar to the physical pain one feels if one lifts something too heavy"; [25] second, that the Roman climate did not agree with him; and, third, that he was troubled by the arrival of his mother.

Phia Rilke had come to Rome that spring, not because she wanted to be near her son, but because it was fashionable to spend a season in Rome. All the best people went there, and for an avid reader of the *Almanach de Gotha* and a devout Catholic, as Phia prided herself on being, a journey to Rome was clearly *de rigueur*.

Rilke dreaded her arrival. Every meeting with his mother, he felt, was a sort of relapse.

> When I must see this lost, unreal, entirely unrelated woman, who cannot grow old, then I feel that I tried to get away from her even as a child and am deeply afraid that after years and years of running and walking I am still not far enough from her, that I still have somewhere in me inner movements which are the other half of her withered gestures, broken pieces of memory which she carries in her; I am horrified then at her distracted piety, her obstinate faith, all the disfigured and distorted things she clings to, herself empty as a dress,

ghostlike and terrible. And that I am yet her child; that some hardly recognizable wallpaper door in this faded wall, which belongs nowhere, was my entrance into the world (if indeed such an entrance can lead into the world).[26]

What an echo to Hamlet's words to the queen: "Would it were not so!—You are my mother." Rilke was appalled by his mother's sham life. That she believed in it, that she was the dupe of her own lies made it all the more terrible. How hard she tried to act the *grande dame* with shawls and perfumes and elegant black gowns—she, the divorced wife of a petty Austrian railroad official. It was disgusting and ridiculous; it made him feel ashamed. And yet she was his mother. Was he not somehow involved in her fate and falsehood? Must he not redouble his efforts to be true to his own self? Had he not also deluded himself at times with grand gestures and inflated sentiments? The more he saw of his mother the more obsessed did he become of the need for truthfulness. The possibility that he too might be merely a disguised bourgeois, pretending to be an artist, worried him all his life. It occasioned the memorable lines in the *Fourth Elegy*:

> Then appeared the dancer.
> Not *he*! Enough! However light he foots it,
> he's just disguised, and turns into a bourgeois,
> and passes through the kitchen to his dwelling.
> I will not have those half-filled masks . . .[27]

> Dann erst kam der Tänzer.
> Nicht *der*. Genug! Und wenn er auch so leicht tut,
> er ist verkleidet und er wird ein Bürger
> und geht durch seine Küche in die Wohnung.
> Ich will nicht diese halbgefüllten Masken . . .[28]

If it were possible to choose one aspect of Rilke's mind and assign it a dominant role in his life and poetry, truthfulness would be the term. Kassner, who knew him well, was struck by it, and Mason writes that "Rilke's honesty, his freedom from charlatanry and pose in the great essential things of poetry and life are proved for the open-minded reader once and for all." [29] It was his mother's example that compelled Rilke to ever greater honesty.

Phia's arrival in Rome at this particular time proved to be one of those fateful interruptions in his work that Rilke had feared. She was his mother, and he could not deny her. Cézanne, it is true, refused even to attend his mother's funeral because it would distract him from his work. Such single-mindedness was Rilke's goal, too, but he had not yet reached it. He had to see his mother. For a while, at least, he had to share her unreal life, had to enter into a shallow, untrue relationship, had to pretend what he did not feel. How could he be expected to work on a book that was to be an utterly truthful record of his experiences? It would have been dishonest to try.

Once more he turned to Lou for help. He implored her to let him come and talk to her. This would be the best: if he could talk to her and watch her listen and be silent. And once more Lou told him to be patient. Truth and error, victory and defeat are mysteriously blended in everything that succeeds in life. Even bacilli are a necessary part of it: *that,* she said, is the miracle of life. She advised him to look upon his mother as a necessary irritant in his life, a source of fermentation that would yet bring out what lay dormant in him. For the rest she counseled patience. She told him that she too had been working on a book she loved doing but had fallen sick and been forced to stop; "One must have patience," everything depended on that.

It has been pointed out how much Rilke owed to Lou Salomé. This extraordinary woman whose love had transformed an immature, sentimental youth into the poet of the *Book of Hours,* who, by taking him to Russia, had initiated him into a whole new world—a world of spaciousness and picty—that became an integral part of his poetry, now guided him through another difficult period of his life. For what he was trying to do was nothing less than to reverse his natural bent. The introvert dreamer wanted to become a conscious craftsman; the exalted mystic, a recorder of reality; the lyric poet, a sculptor in words. He wanted to overcome "the ancient curse of poets, always bewailing themselves instead of saying"; wanted to transmute himself into words "doggedly, as the carver of a cathedral/ transfers himself to the stone's constancy." Orpheus wanted to become Apollo.

It was a desperate undertaking, fraught with danger, and marked one of the great turning points in Rilke's art. Lou warned him in vain that "words do not build like stones, real and concrete things, they are symbols rather for indirectly transmitted suggestions and in themselves far poorer, less substantial than a stone." [30] He persisted; he had to learn to make things out of words: realities. Had he not said in his book on Rodin that Baudelaire had made poems that seemed "formed and not written, lines that felt like reliefs, and sonnets that bore the burden of an anxious thought like pillars with confused capitals." [31] Cost what it may, he would become a sculptor in words.

The violence to which Rilke subjected himself during these years is reflected in *Malte* and, to a lesser degree, in the *New Poems*. The latter, products of the same period, treat many themes that occur in *Malte*, just as *Malte* treats many themes that Rilke had touched upon in his private correspondence. It is a fascinating experience to follow the threefold transformation of a personal event to its final poetic form. Rilke's art clearly mirrors his life, *is* his life; song is existence.

Malte's multiple fears, his account of the desolate lives of the poor of Paris, his sense of solitude, his desperate efforts to penetrate the mystery of existence, these and many other themes that occur in the later pages of *Malte*—a remarkable description of Venice in autumn for example—reappear in the *New Poems*. But in the process of being transformed from prose to poetry they have undergone subtle changes in spirit as well. While many passages in *Malte* leave the reader with a sense of agitated despair, most of the poems, even when they treat the same subjects, reach beyond despair. "Only a step," says Malte, "and my deep woe would be beatitude. But I cannot take that step." [32] In the *New Poems* that one step was often taken: therein lies the difference between Rilke the poet and Rilke the chronicler of *Malte*.

But this is anticipating. It took years before Rilke felt he had mastered his new technique sufficiently to finish his "prosebook," as he called *Malte* at this stage. After the Roman debacle he went north and spent the rest of the year in Sweden and Denmark. As always in times of crisis he needed a change of scenery. Italy no longer suited him. Its bright lights, strong colors, and sharp contours did not invite close observation. The Italian skies with their picture postcard sunsets seemed to him singularly "empty, deserted, sapped dry." There was nothing to investigate there. It was all surface "and behind the last trees which stand flat like stage props against this indifferent photographer's background— everything stops." [33] He felt the Italian past had left no room for the present, hence "the sham life of this vanished people, the empty phrases of its epigone art, the gardenflower beauty of d'Annunzio's verses." [34] Was not his first trip to Viareggio, which "for all my efforts ended in nothing," proof that Italian influences were not really helpful to him?

He decided to go north because "northern and more serious countries have inured my mind to soft and simple things." [35] To prepare himself for his journey he started learning Danish even while he was still in Rome. He wanted to read Kierkegaard and planned to write a monograph on Jacobsen, whom he had long admired, and who had become really necessary to him now that he had found that "Jacobsen's and Rodin's words often agree to the letter." [36]

When he finally reached Copenhagen in June, he was enchanted with it. It is "an incomparable town, strangely ineffable, all nuances: old and new, lighthearted and mysterious." [37] Unfortunately he could not stay there for, through the good offices of Ellen Key, he had received invitations from two Swedish families. He would spend the better part of the next six months in the pleasant country houses of Borgebygård and Furuborg. It was a welcome change from his boarding-house existence in Paris and Rome. His spirits revived quickly, and his letters from Sweden sound carefree, almost happy. "Many legends live with us," he told Lou, "perhaps also people of the past of great families, but they terrify no one." [38]

He writes of long walks in fields and parks, of lonely vigils in northern nights, of great autumnal storms and of sleigh rides "into the soft countryside where everything had become distance." [39] Better yet: he sent Lou a poem that had been "torn out" of him, the first in a "long, long time." Did it mean that he had overcome the crisis and would now be able to take up his interrupted work on *Malte* again? If Lou thought so, he soon disillusioned her. No, he was not yet well enough for that; he needed time to recuperate. Also he "lacked courage" to work on the book started in Rome.

But perhaps it was not only courage he lacked. Perhaps he realized that the almost casual manner in which he had started the book violated the rule of objectivity that he now demanded of a work of art. For all he had done so far had been to fashion his Parisian experiences. As a result the book consisted of a number of powerful but transparently autobiographical scenes. He could conceivably have continued in that style without even the attempt at objectivization. But this was precisely what he did *not* want to do. He wanted to create a work of art that could bear witness for him. He did not want to make a confession in the manner of Rousseau or even in that of Goethe's *Werther*. This must be said, because *Malte* has been described as a sort of *Werther manqué*.

That Rilke failed to get outside himself, that he did not succeed in making Malte a real protagonist, is true enough; that he was aware of his failure is evidenced by his weary admission to Lou that "the good Ellen Key, of course, has confused me with Malte and has given me up." [40] It is also true, however, that failures are sometimes more significant than successes. In T. S. Eliot's opinion *Hamlet, qua* work of art, is also a failure, and "we must simply admit that here Shakespeare tackled a problem which proved too much for him." [41] Judged by the Aristotelian rules of drama all of Shakespeare's plays are failures, and yet Herder called Shakespeare "Sophocles' brother." If we measure *Malte* by the standard of objectivity set by Flaubert for the modern novel, Rilke certainly failed. But soon after the book was published André Gide wrote that with it Rilke had taken his place beside the French writers. Perhaps the best measure of Rilke's failure or success is the fact that he struggled off and on for six years to cast *Malte* into an objective mold. Only the Duino angels proved more obdurate to his summoning will.

Significantly, his failure to write his "prosebook" in Rome was counterbalanced by the success of three remarkable poems in prose, later turned into verse: *Orpheus. Eurydice. Hermes; Tombs of the Hetaerae;* and *Birth of Venus*. Kassner says that he received the "first great and decisive impression" [42] of Rilke's genius from them; and if we compare them with the tortured prose he wrote at the same time we understand why he found *Malte* such a hard book to write. He was a poet; prose was not his proper medium. And yet, by forcing himself to write prose he learned to objectify his feelings and to control his craft. In the development of Rilke's poetry *Malte*, therefore, represents an important phase.

He left Rome in June, 1904, in the hope of finding a more congenial environment than the Italian capital for his work on *Malte*. That hope proved illusory; the book did not progress, at least not outwardly. Inwardly, however, Rilke's six-month stay in the north added an important element to *Malte*; here Rilke projected Malte's childhood. It was not his own childhood in Prague —the book in this respect deviates considerably from the autobiographical approach used in the Parisian scenes—it was a childhood spent in spacious country houses in the north among royal chamberlains, counts, and princesses. Neither the setting nor the people bear any resemblance to the bourgeois milieu in which Rilke grew up and which he described with such puckish humor in his youthful sketch *Ewald Tragy.*

The change is interesting. All his life Rilke complained about his hard and lonely childhood and felt the need to "perform it once more." Now he had a chance to do so, a chance to rid himself of the horrors he had suffered at home from a vain and empty mother who played with him like a doll, from a sorry crowd of maiden aunts and uncles who tried to bring him up in the genteel tradition of the Austrian bourgeoisie, from the drill sergeants of his military schools. Why did he not take it? Was it still too painfully close to him? Did he want to get away from the biographical approach altogether? Or did he realize, as an artist, if not otherwise, that there was no real substance to his claim to a particularly hard childhood? Carl Sieber, at any rate, is of the opinion that all the talk of the martyrdom of Rilke's childhood is a legend: "One cannot write a novel about it." [43]

It is certainly noteworthy that Rilke never wrote his "military school" novel, although he frequently planned to do so; it is also noteworthy that the mother theme is treated very differently in his poetry from the way it is in his letters and that Malte's mother bears no resemblance to Phia Rilke. She is much more like the mother celebrated in the *Third Elegy* who, with her slender figure, displaces the surging abyss that terrifies her child at night. When Malte is terror-stricken, when he is perishing with fright of the monsters that invade his dreams, his mother comes to his bed holding up a light: "O mother, O you only one . . . who took it upon yourself, saying: 'Do not be afraid; it is I.' . . . Is there any power like your power among the rulers of the earth?" [44]

Whatever the reasons for this change, it occasioned such memorable scenes in *Malte* as the death of Christoph Detlev Brigge of Ulsgaard; the events at Urnekloster centering round Count Brahe and his female relations: Mathilde, Abelone, and the revenants Christine and Ingeborg; and the story of the Schulin family "an able race of independent women" modeled after the women of Borgebygård. The weird account of the hand, "a larger, extraordinarily thin hand," that reached out of the wall to meet Malte's groping hand in the dark, and the incident with the masks are undoubtedly based on personal experiences. They reflect borderline situations between reality and the unknown, shrouded in the dim twilight of a northern sky. Chiaroscuro predominates; gone is the naked/terror of the Parisian scenes. The sense of the past is greater than the fear of the present.

In addition to Malte's childhood, conceived during Rilke's stay in the north, another element enters the story here, much more discreetly to be sure but not without importance. Rilke became acquainted with the writings of the young poet Sigbjørn Obstfelder, one of Norway's leading impressionists. Perhaps he had already heard of him in Paris, but it is almost certain that he only started reading him at this time. In a letter to a young girl he mentioned admiringly that the poet Obstfelder had once described the face of a young man, "it was (when he began to speak) as if there was a woman in him." [45] Rilke thought this description would fit every poet who begins to speak. And he sent Lou one of Obstfelder's books because "there are certain things in it which I have learned to love." [46] But he was probably more moved by Obstfelder's fate than by his poetry. For here was a gifted young poet who had gone to Paris, had struggled to survive there, and had perished, not quite thirty-four years old. Was this not Malte's fate also: a young writer in Paris, poor, lonely, a stranger among strangers, lost in a city that was against him? Could he not think of the young Norwegian while he worked on *Malte* and thus, imperceptibly, shift his ground somewhat from the all-too-personal protagonist of the earlier parts? At least he could try. While it would be going too far to say that the poet Obstfelder is the prototype for Malte, it was important that Rilke learned of him at this stage.

When he left his Swedish hosts at the end of the year, he was once again at a loss what to do and where to go. He would have liked to spend the Russian New Year with Lou in Göttingen. He wanted to talk with her, read her his new poems, and find out if he could take some courses at the university. But most of all he wanted to see her. "This time I must not miss you; seeing you again is the only bridge to the future." [47] But again she put him off. Later in the year perhaps, not now. So he continued his peripatetic course, which led him from Bremen to Lahmann's sanitarium in Dresden and back again to Worpswede and Berlin.

Gradually the pattern of his life became set: restlessly, in search of himself, he crossed and recrossed the continent. Germany, Austria, France, Italy, Scandinavia, Switzerland, Spain, briefly even North Africa, provided him with temporary shelter. He was here today, gone tomorrow, leaving a trail of luminous letters behind, reports of a soul in travail. Many people crossed his path: young people who felt that his anxiety was their anxiety, members of old families who were attracted to him because he possessed a high degree of personal charm and the manners of an eighteenth-century aristocrat—and women. Women were fascinated by him and remained faithful to his memory even when he left them— and he left them all. It was always the same: a brief encounter, a passionate embrace, and a gentle parting. There was no permanence: "for staying is nowhere." Love, too, was a process of constant transformations in the course of which the beloved became a friend and the friend a memory. Even his wife Clara, first his partner in solitude, then for a while his traveling companion,

was in the end little more than one of his numerous correspondents. Only Lou Salomé occupied a fairly constant place in
his life: she was his confidante and his mother confessor. There
were misunderstandings between them, too, but he never lost
confidence in her. Even as he lay dying in Switzerland he asked
his doctor to write to Lou, for he felt she was the only person who
knew what was wrong with him.

On two occasions Rilke confided to Lou that the "turning
point" in his life, which must come if he was to live, had not come
yet; once in 1905 and again in 1914. Between these two dates falls
the completion of *Malte.* It has already been said that objectivity
was the goal he wanted to attain when he started *Malte.* He
pursued it with a single-mindedness that left him exhausted when
the book was finally finished—"like Raskolnikov after the deed."
And the crisis that led to *Malte* was followed by the even more
prolonged crisis that led to the *Duino Elegies.*

Malte was conceived in Paris and finished there, for in Paris
Rilke learned to see objectively. His poetic-visionary powers, released in Russia, were subjected to a rigorous discipline in the
French capital. Diligently and patiently he studied the works of
the great French craftsmen: Rodin, Baudelaire, Jammes, Flaubert,
Cézanne. He spent hours in the Louvre gazing at the pictures of
the old masters and absorbing every detail. For it was not only a
new technique, it was a new way of life into which he tried to
enter.

> I tried that in the Louvre recently. I had been there a few times and it
> was like looking at great activity; thus things kept happening and hap-
> pening there before me. And then, a short time ago, there were only
> pictures and many too many pictures, and everywhere someone standing,
> and everything was disturbing. And then I asked myself why it was
> different today. Was I tired? Yes. But wherein did this tiredness consist?
> In the fact that I let everything possible come into my mind; in that
> everything possible went right through me like water through a reflec-
> tion, dissolving all my outlines into flux. And I said to myself: I will no
> longer be the reflection but that which is above. And I turned myself
> over so that I was no longer upside down, and closed my eyes for a brief
> moment and drew myself about me and stretched my contours, as one
> stretches violin strings, until one feels them taut and singing, and sud-

denly I knew I was fully outlined like a Dürer drawing, and I went thus
before Madonna Lisa: and she was incomparable.[48]

Such passages as this one written to Clara, and they occur frequently in his letters at this time, show what a conscious effort
he made to reach a state of pure receptivity. Nothing must interfere with it; even the activities of his mind must be excluded. He
must learn to penetrate the object with his steady gaze. He must
develop a sixth sense of differentiation, note the subtlest nuances
of color and contour, distinguish between almost imperceptible
shades of meaning. He must learn to see, and he must record
what he sees.

> Yesterday I spent the whole morning in the Jardin des Plantes looking
> at the gazelles. *Gazella Dorcas*, Linné. There is a pair and a single one.
> They lay in the grass a few paces from each other, chewing, resting, look-
> ing. As women look out of pictures they, too, gaze out of something with
> a soundless, final turn of the head. And when a horse whinnied one of
> them listened, and I saw the coronet of ears and horns round its slender
> head. Were the ears of the deer in Al Hayat also grey (as pewter is to
> gold, so is this grey to the colour of the other hair), and with a soft, dark,
> dendriform drawing inside? I saw one of the gazelles get up, but only for
> a second—it lay down again immediately after; yet while it was stretch-
> ing and testing itself I could see the magnificent workmanship of the
> legs (they were like barrels of rifles cocked to fire).[49]

These descriptions, poetically compressed, reappear in a sonnet
written at this time and included in *New Poems*, where the
choicest fruits of Rilke's undivided attention are gathered. They
once again show what he meant by *Umschlag*: that sudden reversal—almost like an electric discharge when the tension on the
poles has become too great—from receptivity to spontaneity.

But *Malte* remained obdurate. He could not finish the book because it still lacked a unifying theme, for

> . . . the necessary unity was no longer that of a poem, it was that of
> the personality which had to come alive from beginning to end in its
> endless complexity. An irregular, broken rhythm impressed itself upon
> me and pulled me into many unexpected directions. . . . I wrote many
> pages at random. Some were letters, others notes, pages from a diary,
> poems in prose. In spite of the structural density of this prose entirely

new to me, it felt like a constant groping about, a march into darkness which never seemed to end.[50]

He tried hard to superimpose a unity but failed on two counts: first, he failed to make Malte a saint. Sainthood would have been a unifying principle. He thought of making Malte another Saint Julian the Hospitaler who bedded himself with the leper, conquering his fear and disgust: "Dost thou perhaps intend, O God, that I should leave everything and love them?"[51] Second, he failed to give substance to his doctrine of nonpossessive love.

In an important letter to his wife, written in Paris on October 19, 1907, he explains Malte's failure on the first count:

You surely remember . . . that passage from the *Notebooks of Malte Laurids Brigge* about Baudelaire and his poem *The Carrion*. I could not help thinking that without this poem the entire development toward objective expression, which we now recognize in Cézanne, could never have begun; that poem in its inexorability had to be there first. Artistic observation had first to conquer itself so far as to be able to see, even in the horrible and apparently only repulsive, that which is, and which, together with all other being, *has value*. Aversion from any kind of existence is as little permitted to the artist as selection: a single rejection at any time thrusts him from the state of grace, makes him wholly and entirely sinful. When Flaubert retold the legend of St. Julien-L'Hospitalier with so much circumspection and care, he gave it that simple credibility amidst the miraculous, because the artist in him agreed with the decisions of the saint, consented to them happily. To bed oneself with the leper, to share with him one's own warmth, even the heart warmth of nights of love, this experience must, at some time or other, have been in the life of an artist as a compulsion to his new happiness. You can imagine how moved I was when I read that Cézanne even in his last years knew this poem—Baudelaire's *Carrion*—by heart and could recite it word for word. Behind this devotion, in a small way at first, begins holiness: the simple life of a love that has endured, that without ever praising itself on that account advances to everything, unaccompanied, inconspicuous, wordless. . . .

And all at once (and for the first time) I understand the fate of Malte. Is it not this: that this test was too much for him, that he did not pass it in reality, although in his mind he was convinced of its necessity, so much so that he sought it out so long instinctively that it finally clung to him and never left him? The book of Malte, when at last it shall be

written, will be nothing but the book of this insight exemplified in one
for whom it was too great.[52]

Rilke realized that Malte's failure to measure up to the task he
assigned him conveys to the reader a sense of hopelessness. He
therefore warned people

> . . . whose spiritual development is tender and questing, against find-
> ing analogies in the "Notes" for what they are suffering; whoever gives
> way to temptation and goes parallel with this book must of necessity
> sink down . . . it will be pleasurable only to those who undertake to
> read it *against the current*, as it were. Strictly speaking, however, I would
> not place it in anybody's hands, I would *let it simply be there*, seeing that
> it has the good conscience not to have fashioned itself irresponsibly.
> Certainly there is nothing to *learn* from it, as we ordinarily understand
> this word; for that you must keep to the *Neue Gedichte* [*New Poems*],
> where you can at least feel how every object may turn into work and,
> once resolutely and honestly mastered, reveal itself in absolute grandeur.[53]

The counterpart to Malte's quest for love that embraces everything, even the most repulsive, is the quest of the Prodigal Son
for nonpossessive, intransitive love, i.e., love in which the object
has completely disappeared. In the unrequited love of the great
lovers who succeeded in freeing themselves from the loved one
and whose pure emotion, no longer deflected by anybody or anything, could hurl itself directly at God, Rilke discerned a state
of exaltation unknown to the satiated. He mentions their names,
a whole catalogue of lover saints: Gaspara Stampa, Louise Labé,
Marianna Alcoforado, Bettina von Arnim, the Countess of Die,
Héloise, Marceline Desbordes, Rose of Lima, Theresa of Avila,
Mechthild, Eliza Mercoeur, and insists that their lives prove that
this kind of love is possible. It is time, he says, that we learn from
them, for "ought not these oldest sufferings of ours be yielding
more fruit by now?"

T. S. Eliot, in the second epigraph to *Sweeney Agonistes*, quotes
St. John of the Cross: "Hence the soul cannot be possessed of the
divine union, until it has divested itself of the love of created
beings." [54] The concept of "intransitive love" is thus not unknown
in mystical writings. But it still remains a puzzling problem, and
Rilke's examples are by no means convincing. His insistence on it,
despite the protests of his friends, shows that it was deeply rooted

in his psychology. Even Rodin's healthy skepticism could not deter him:

> I speak to him of all her [Marianna Alcoforado's] rapture transformed, and the woman's will *beyond* gratification; he does not believe it; and unfortunately he has so many female saints in support of his view who bear out the contention that they used Christ as a sort of concubine: as a sweet *ersatz* for virility, as the tenderest paramour that could be had, could still, at long last, be had. Over against that I have my Nun. And I show how, in her few letters, she has grown out beyond the lover, and I know it is true. And I vow that if ever the Count of Chamilly, surrendering to her last letter, had returned, she would have been unable to perceive him at all, just as you do not see a fly down below from the balcony of a tower. And I am inexorable and will not depart an inch from my Nun.[55]

As one ponders the meaning of the strange pages in the second half of *Malte* in which the love theme predominates, pages filled with macabre scenes from remote and unfamiliar corners of history: the unmasking of the false czar, the downfall of Charles the Bold, the madness of King Charles the Sixth—one gets intermittent insights into Rilke's vision, powerful reminders of the proximity of horror and holiness. But the picture is not a steady one. One is left agitated but not convinced, or at least not convinced in the sense that even the irrational can carry conviction when it is presented poetically.

Occasionally there is fusion of form and content. In the scene of the blind newspaper vendor in the Luxembourg Garden—with its moving epilogue: "My God, it struck me with sudden vehemence, thus then art Thou! There are proofs of Thy existence" [56] —Rilke's power of expression is commensurate with his vision. And his description of Malte's Petersburg room neighbors, particularly that strange character Nikolai Kusmitch, inventor of the time bank, has a Kafkaesque condensation of symbolic force.

But in other places the reader's interest slackens. What is he to make of that pale Ophelia, Abelone, Malte's soul mate? No matter how hard one tries to get close to her, she remains a shadowy figure. Indeed, an unkind critic might easily echo Malte's words, when he first becomes aware of Abelone's existence: "Why is Abelone here?" Beautiful, beautiful Abelone, she floats in and out

of the story like an astral body. All we know of her is that she
sings. To be sure this is intentional, for Malte says: "I shall tell
nothing about you, Abelone. Not because we deceived one another
—since even then you loved one whom you, loving one, have
never forgotten, and I loved all women—but because only harm
would come from the telling." [57] When she finally disappears, or
rather when her memory, evoked by a mysterious stranger who
sings an unknown German song in a Venetian drawing room,
fades away, that same critic might again echo Malte: "No one had
expected it."

How powerfully, by contrast, Venice is described, Venice in
autumn when all the "somnolent foreigners" have left and when,
suddenly,

> . . . one morning the other Venice is there, the real Venice, awake,
> brittle to the breaking point, and not in the least dream-like: This Venice,
> willed into being in the midst of nothing and set on sunken forests,
> created by force, and in the end so thoroughly manifest. This hardened
> body, stripped to necessities, through which the sleepless arsenal drove
> the blood of its toil, and this body's penetrating spirit, ever spreading,
> more powerful than the perfume of aromatic lands. This inventive state,
> that bartered the salt and glass of its poverty for the treasures of the
> nations. This beautiful counterpoise of the world, which even in its em-
> bellishments is full of latent energies ever more finely ramified—this
> Venice! [58]

The ambiguity that lies at the heart of Venice—the contrast
between its glittering mask and its fierce foundations, between the
make-believe and the real Venice—fascinated Rilke. Here was
a living symbol of all he wanted to express, proof of the vitality of
those invisible, subterranean forces that determine our destinies:
life behind fate. "Fate loves to invent patterns and designs. Its
difficulty lies in its complexity. But life is difficult because of its
simplicity." [59]

In the *New Poems* he treated the Venetian theme four times.
The arresting *Late Autumn in Venice* is essentially a poetic
version of the prose passage given above. But is it really a prose
passage? Would it not be more correct to call it a prose poem?
Many of *Malte's* formal problems could be solved more easily if
it were possible to distinguish clearly between prose, poetic prose,

and poems in prose. Goethe's distinction, according to which poetry may be irrational but "in prose, reason is and may and should be at home" [60] is clearly not applicable to Rilke's prose and is, in any case, of dubious validity. All we can safely say is that, although Rilke set out to write a "prosebook," *Malte* is most successful in those passages that come closest to being poetry, and least when he attempts discursive interpretations.

A case in point is his interpretation of the parable of the Prodigal Son at the end of the book. It contains passages of great poetic beauty to which the reader assents wholeheartedly and without question; only when the reasoning of the whole story is considered do doubts arise, not necessarily because the reader feels that Rilke is wrong but because he wonders whether Rilke may not be right. In either case the immediacy of the poetic impact is lost. The parable owes its prominent place in *Malte* to the fact that Rilke saw in it a possibility of giving symbolic expression to the twin themes of fear and love.

Love is the theme of the Biblical story. It celebrates God's love for man; for man who was lost and is found, for the sinner who repents and returns. Transgression, repentance, forgiveness: this is the meaning of the story Jesus told the Pharisees when he wanted to explain to them the nature of God's love of man. It states one of the basic precepts of Christianity: salvation through repentance.

The changes the parable underwent in the hands of Gide and Rilke reflect the changed position of the Christian faith. In Gide's version, with which Rilke was familiar, transgression had become revolt, and repentance renunciation. The Prodigal Son revolted in the name of individualism against being coerced into a mold alien to him. He left home in search of himself, and returned only because he could not bear the burden of this quest. Weariness of spirit and cowardice made him come back—not repentance. Henceforth he would be an obedient son, just like his older brother. He would follow the dictates of society and would not try to be different. He would conform. His return is thus an admission of defeat. But when his younger brother—a new character Gide introduced into the story—tells him that he, the

younger brother, will leave his home and his parents, the Prodigal
Son encourages him to do so: "Be strong. Forget us, forget me.
May you never return." [61] It is evident that Gide did not share
Jesus' concern with the repentant sinner. He sympathized with
the unrepentant rebel. Rilke did likewise.

In his version the departure of the Prodigal Son is motivated by
one basic fear: the fear of being loved. For "to be loved means to
be consumed." "What he desired was that inner indifference of
spirit which sometimes, of an early morning in the fields, seized
him so unalloyed that he began to run, that he might have neither
time nor breath to be more than a transient moment in which the
morning becomes conscious of itself." [62]

Like Malte, the Prodigal Son wants to experience pure consciousness, wants to live the flow and rhythm of life that pulsates
at the heart of the world, wants "to rub off the paint, to remove
all that is artificial and become real." [63] But that is precisely what
those who love him prevent him from doing because, loving him,
they try to make him over in their image. "You were the person
for whom they took you . . . the person for whom, out of his
brief past and their own desires, they had long fashioned a life
. . . which lay day and night under the influence of their love." [64]
How could he escape from their confining love? "Should he stay
and pretend to live the sort of life they ascribe to him, and grow
to resemble them in his whole appearance?" [65] He decided to go
away: "Go away forever. Not until long afterwards is he to
realize how firmly he had then resolved never to love, in order not
to put anyone in the terrible position of being loved." [66] Bravely
he bore the cross of his solitude, the terrors of poverty, the fear of
death: "That was the time which began with his feeling himself
a part of the universe and anonymous, like a lingering convales-
cent. He did not love, unless it were that he loved to live." [67] At
this time, too, he realized the "extreme remoteness of God," whom
he "almost forgot in the hard task of drawing near Him." In the
end he returned because he wanted once more to perform his
childhood, which he felt he had "simply allowed to slip past while
he waited." [68] He returned—but "we know not whether he remained." [69]

Rilke, in effect, reverses the sense of the parable. While the Bible says that man is lost until God's love finds him, Rilke implies that God is lost until man's love finds Him. This vision of a non-loving God removes Rilke from Christianity and places him near the prophets of the Old Testament. Malte relives the drama of Job: "Terrors are turned upon me: they pursue my soul as the wind. . . . The days of affliction have taken hold upon me. . . . I am become like dust and ashes. I cry unto thee and thou dost not hear me: I stand up and thou regardest me not." [70]

It is thus not surprising that Rilke's favorite reading during the time when he struggled with *Malte* was the Book of Job. Written, as it almost certainly was, before the giving of the law, this, probably the oldest book of the Bible, shows the dawn of man's consciousness of evil. With the coming of Christ the emphasis shifted from the awareness of evil to the promise of salvation. It seems that we are approaching another dawn of consciousness of the existence of evil, to judge by the concern some of our leading writers have shown for this theme. Their predecessors in the nineteenth century, Kierkegaard, Dostoevski, Melville, were concerned with essentially the some problem that Rilke treated in *Malte* and, more convincingly, in his major poetry. It is of course true that the older poets, Shakespeare and Dante above all, did not lack a sense of evil—Hamlet is as horror-struck as Malte—but with them the awareness of evil was balanced by their faith in God. When this faith is absent, evil reigns supreme and leads man to the brink of despair. This is Malte's fate as it was Rilke's. But while Rilke is carried beyond despair by his poetry we are left wondering what will happen to Malte. Will he find God? Will his suffering finally evoke a response from Him who alone knows "how to love with a penetrating, radiant love?" We do not know. All we know, when the final curtain on the *Malte* drama is rung down, is that the play will go on. The catharsis has yet to come. And perhaps the most fitting epitaph for this logbook of a tormented soul—Rilke himself knew that it lacked unity—is the conclusion Hamlet arrives at in the passage on providence: "The readiness is all."

5 The Magic Circle

Magic is here. Into the realm of charm
the common word seems lifted high above . . .
and yet it's real like the cock-bird's call
for the invisible dove.

Hier ist Magie. In das Bereich des Zaubers
scheint das gemeine Wort hinaufgestuft . . .
und ist doch wirklich wie der Ruf des Taubers,
der nach der unsichtbaren Taube ruft.

Rilke, *Sämtliche Werke*

The keynote of the response that Rilke's *New Poems* evoked among the critics when they appeared in 1907 and 1908 was struck by Felix Braun in a review in *Süddeutsche Monatshefte*: "The customary conception we have of lyric poetry is no longer adequate, for these poems represent a marvelous transposition of plastic art into poetry; indeed, as if this mystic union of two fundamentally foreign arts were not enough, a third appears—from afar, to be sure, but with decisive force: music." [1] Schellenberg in the *Xenien* also noted the "greater objectivity" of Rilke's *New Poems*, and Stefan Zweig, who reviewed them in the *Literarische Echo*, agreed that Rilke's latest book "belonged more to sculpture than to lyric poetry." [2] He noted the "unprecedented intensity of observation" with which Rilke "penetrates the object" and "makes dead things vibrate in a frightening and almost ghostly way." "A deeper penetration seems impossible; indeed, in some poems Rilke has perhaps gone beyond the limits of poetry. There is in him something of the insatiable daring of the Alpinist who is attracted only by peaks that have never been climbed." [3] In his conclusion

Zweig expressed the hope that the next phase in Rilke's development would go beyond "this unheard-of plastic art—here an end in itself" and that it would become "a means to a more intensive production." [4]

Other readers voiced this hope even more vigorously. They were shocked by the poet's indifference to their susceptibilities, by his insistence on the horrible and repulsive aspects of life. They had come to see in him a master of impressionistic verse (*Cornet*), of subtle and suggestive word-pictures (*Book of Pictures*), and of passionate prayers. In the *Book of Hours* they had heard the voice of a modern mystic whose pantheistic fervor aroused genuine religious feelings. Here at last was a poet who reaffirmed the glory of God amidst a "superficial generation."

In the *New Poems* everything was different. The sweet dreams of Rilke's earlier verse had turned into nightmares. Pale kings were no longer crowned with dreams: maggots crawled in the velvet of their thrones. The romantic knights and languid maidens, the moonlit parks, the melancholic evenings had disappeared; disappeared also the monk and the pilgrim. Instead a host of strange and frightening characters had arisen: the sick and insane, the beggars and the blind, leprous kings, diseased courtesans, tortured saints, and fierce prophets of the Old Testament. And God was nowhere in sight.

It is true: there were also strange and wonderful flowers, animals, statues, parks, and landscapes, but the first impression one gets from reading these "bewitched and bewitching poems" [5] is a sense of menace, a feeling that behind the ordered surface of life fierce forces are at work.

It was therefore not surprising that many readers felt uneasy about these poems. Some critics, like Wilhelm Michel reviewing them in *Münchener neueste Nachrichten*, considered them "poetic aberrations," an opinion that can be heard even now; Heerikhuizen, for example, seems to share it. Even Rilke's friends were obviously at a loss what to say about them. Lou Salomé wrote him that she did not find *New Poems* as "suggestive" as the *Book of Pictures* or the *Requiem* but added she was still trying to find him in them "as in a dense forest where much is hidden." [6]

As a rule Rilke did not pay much attention to what critics said about his work, but he was clearly disturbed about the reaction of his friends, for he found it necessary to write lengthy letters in defense of his books.

> Concerning these more recent books [he wrote Baron Uexküll] I can assure you of my good, clear conscience: every word, every interval between the words in those poems came into being from extreme necessity, in the consciousness of that ultimate responsibility under whose inner tribunal my work is carried out. Perhaps shortcomings in my nature or omissions to be made up in my development are the cause of that hard objectivity and unfeeling quality of what is portrayed: perhaps more pleasing ways are conceivable: I must continue on mine, difficult as it is.[7]

It must have come as a great disappointment to him that the very objectivity he had labored so hard to attain, now that he had attained it, displeased his friends. Evidently they wanted him to continue in the manner of the *Book of Hours* when "nature was still a general incitement for him, when he did not sit before her, when he went along with her and saw—saw not nature but the images she inspired in him."

They failed to see what effort it had cost him to "turn himself over" and to "stretch his contours" so that he could observe with that "hard objectivity" which he had learned to admire in the work of the great French craftsmen. They did not seem to realize that it would have been far easier for him to let himself be carried by the stream of his feelings, but that was precisely what he did not want to do, for "verses are not, as people imagine, simply feelings (we have these soon enough); they are experiences. In order to write a single verse, one must see many cities, and men and things." [8]

Things: that is what he wanted to make now, realities. Others might write verses; he would follow Rodin's example, would "transmute himself into the words," obstinately, like those master craftsmen who built the great cathedrals. He would work like a sculptor, carve his words, deliberately, patiently, and with the utmost regard for detail. For to make a thing meant to hide nothing and to overlook nothing, to know all the surfaces and all the profiles. Only thus can a thing arise, only then is it an "island" and completely lifted out of the "continent of vagueness."

"We talk as if thought was precise and emotion vague. In reality there is precise emotion and there is vague emotion. To express precise emotion requires as great intellectual powers as to express precise thought." [9] Meticulous care with the use of language is as much a prerequisite for the expression of precise emotion as it is for the expression of precise thought. This insight Rilke gained during his years in Paris. He learned his craft; he entered deeply into the spirit of language. Words, he now realized, are not merely sounds vaguely evocative of moods and feelings, they are tools that demand careful and precise handling. Formerly he had been carried away by them, had surrendered to their music, had been at the mercy of rhyme and rhythm. Now he wanted to control them.

An almost Flaubertian obsession for *le mot juste* took hold of him, and he was distressed when he discovered the many imperfections of language. There was no exact German equivalent for the word "palm," he found after consulting Grimm's dictionary. To call the multiple movements on the inside of a hand *"Handfläche"* seemed to him an unpardonable inexactitude of the German language; as for *"Handteller"*—"but that is the palm of a hand stretched out to collect alms, to beg, serving as a plate! What a confession in this insufficiency of our language!" [10] And there is the scene in *Malte* where Felix Arvers had to correct a mispronounced word before he could die because "he was a poet and hated vagueness." This, then, was Rilke's aim in the *New Poems*: he wanted to demonstrate that by accurate observation and precise expression artistic mastery could be attained over everything, even over the most repulsive subjects.

In retrospect he thought it had been his aim even in his earlier books, although he had then lacked the skill and the patience to achieve it.

> Do you not believe, dear friend, that even the *Book of Hours* was all filled with the determination in which (one-sidedly, if you will) I have been growing? To consider art not as a *selection* from the world, but rather as its total transformation into the glorious. The marveling with

which art flings itself upon things (all things, without exception) must
be so impetuous, so strong, so radiant, that the object has no time to
think of its own ugliness or depravity. In the sphere of the terrible there
can exist nothing so renunciatory and negative that the multiple action
of artistic mastery would not leave it behind with a great, positive surplus, as something that affirms existence, [something that] wants to be:
as an angel.[11]

The role of the angel in Rilke's work will be discussed in the
following chapter. Here, it will be noted, the angel stands for that
glorious affirmation of existence which a work of art leaves behind,
no matter how forbidding and terrible is the subject with which it
deals. Since all things "without exception" can be transformed
into art there is no limit to the angelic host, a vast positive surplus
remains, and, despite fate, life is magnificent.

Things: no word appears more frequently in Rilke, none is so
charged with emotional overtones. "Things. While I say this word
(can you hear?) a stillness arises; the stillness that surrounds
things. All movement ceases, becomes contour and out of the past
and the future something permanent is formed: Space, the great
peace of the unhurried things." [12]

Rilke's things are not simply objects: a piece of wood, a stone,
or a jug; they are objects seen by man, understood by man, loved
by man. Without man's transforming love they remain objects.
To see the thing in the object, to free it from the "continent of
vagueness," *that* is the task of the artist, or, as he would later say,
that is what man is here for.

> Are we, perhaps, here just for saying: House,
> Bridge, Fountain, Gate, Jug, Olive tree, Window—
> possibly: Pillar, Tower? . . . but for saying, remember,
> oh, for such saying as never the things themselves
> hoped so intensely to be.[13]

> Sind wir vielleicht *hier,* um zu sagen: Haus,
> Brücke, Brunnen, Tor, Krug, Obstbaum, Fenster,—
> höchstens: Säule, Turm. . . . aber zu *sagen,* verstehs,
> oh zu sagen *so,* wie selber die Dinge niemals
> innig meinten zu sein.[14]

Love is the prerequisite for this act of liberation. "If you wish
that a thing speak to you, you must take it for a time as the only

thing that exists, as the only reality which your active and exclusive love places in the center of the universe." [15] The artist who
fails to do that, who lacks either the patience or the devotion to
love things, will always remain on the "periphery of art." In the
example of Rodin and Cézanne Rilke saw proof that the great
artist is the dedicated man. "Since it was given to Rodin to 'see
things in everything' it became possible for him to make things,
for that is the great secret of his art." [16]

If it is possible to see things in everything, the world of things
obviously transcends the world of objects. It can include animals
and men. "Rodin is quite open when he is with things," Rilke told
Lou, "or when men and animals move him quietly like things." [17]

He himself, it is true, was ill at ease with men. They rarely
moved him as deeply as things did. "I cannot make use of human
models (proof: I do not make them yet) and shall be occupied for
years with flowers, animals, and landscapes." [18] There were times
when he worried about this shortcoming of his nature. "Perhaps
I shall now learn to become a little human," he wrote Princess
Taxis after the completion of *Malte;* "hitherto my art has really
come into being at the price of my insisting always on *things;* this
was self-willed of me and, I fear, arrogant." [19] He even wondered
whether he had not overdone the intense concentration he had
applied to the writing of *New Poems,* the close attention to detail,
the uninterrupted gazing: "For, behold, there is a limit to gazing."
To Lou he confided that he had won the long battle of looking and
that now the time had come for some "heartwork." But in the end
he understood that there was no turning back, he would have to go
on watching and waiting:

> Even if the lights go out, even if I'm told
> "There's nothing more". . . .
> I'll still remain. For one can always watch.[20]

> Wenn auch die Lampen ausgehn, wenn mir auch
> gesagt wird: Nichts mehr—, . . .
> Ich bleibe dennoch. Es giebt immer Zuschaun.[21]

Elisabeth von Schmidt-Pauli reports a moving incident that
shows how determined he was to continue in the manner of his

"plastic poetry." During a walk in Munich in 1918 she told him
that his friends were afraid his obstinate insistence on objectivity
might do permanent damage to his lyrical talent and that it was
perhaps the cause of his long sterility, but Rilke stopped her and
pointed to a tree that stood alone on the lawn:

> You see, that is what I want to do and nothing else: I would like to say
> this tree so that only the tree would speak in my words, exactly as it is,
> without any addition of my own. In my poem *The Ball* I succeeded in
> doing that; there I expressed nothing except the almost inexpressible
> phenomenon of a pure movement. That is why it is my best poem.[22]

The significance of this passage lies not in the judgment expressed (poets are not the best judges of their work), but in the
spirit it bespeaks: Rilke's determination to restrain his lyrical
fervor and to work, watch, and wait. He would be silent rather
than compromise his sense of artistic integrity. "It is moving to
realize," says Lou Salomé in her memoirs, "with what courage of
avowed objectivity Rilke worked, as if he wanted to clip his lyric
wings and stay on the ground." [23] And not the least important
factor in the growth of the Rilke myth is the dedication with which
he applied himself to his art. "A dedicated career like Rilke's becomes an heroic career" [24] writes Louise Bogan, and Heerikhuizen
says that "Rilke's silence during the last three years of the war can
be regarded as one of his greatest poems, possibly even the
greatest." [25]

The first clear manifestation of the spirit of objective expression
Rilke had found in Baudelaire's poem *The Carrion:* "It had to be
there first in its inexorability." [26]

There is nothing unusual in the theme of *The Carrion.* It treats
the relationship between love and death, a topic that has a peren-
nial appeal to the romantic imagination. Rilke's *Cornet* and
Goethe's *Werther* are illustrious examples of it. The significance
of Baudelaire's poem does not lie in the theme, it lies in the manner in which the theme is presented, in the utterly unsentimental
and unromantic treatment. Baudelaire's death is a putrefying
corpse "roasting and sweating poisons" with its "legs in the air
like a lustful woman"; "flies buzz over its putrid belly out of which

black battalions of maggots flow like a thick liquid." Two lovers out for a walk on a fine summer morning chance across it. The stench is so strong that the girl almost faints. But the poet makes her look at it, forces her to face death, describes it with inexorable truthfulness. And yet the cumulative effect of these terrifying and obscene images of decomposition is not disgust, nor is it beauty in the traditional sense of the word, no "joy forever." It is the shock of recognition that follows upon the realization that a profound, if painful, truth has been stated; a truth about death which, when it is accepted, is stronger than our fear of death, for it means that death is only a process of transformation; "And the sky saw this superb corpse/ open up like a flower." Rarely has the paradox of death—life flowering amidst corruption—been so powerfully expressed as in this poem. It is not surprising that it made a profound impression on Rilke, who wanted to "make things out of fear" and to wrest beauty out of terror. "The terrible has shocked and frightened man," he wrote to Countess Sizzo, "but where is there sweetness and beauty that has not at times worn *this* mask, the mask of the terrible? Life itself—and we know nothing outside it —is it not terrible?" [27] In *The Carrion* Baudelaire had shown that it was possible to penetrate the mask of the terrible; that is why Rilke saw in it a challenge to utter artistic honesty.

He did not measure up to this challenge in every one of the 175 poems that comprise the two parts of *New Poems*. Some, like the *King of Münster*, are merely horrible and leave no positive surplus behind; others, like *The Experience of Death* and *Song of the Sea*—excellent poems though they are—fall short of the "hard objectivity" he tried to attain; although, if that were taken as the sole yardstick, few poems would wholly qualify because Rilke rarely succeeded in excluding himself entirely and the *New Poems* breathe his spirit as unmistakably as any he wrote, but the tendency toward objective statement is present in most.

It can be seen by such purely formal devices as the frequent use of the sonnet, which now entered into Rilke's poetry and was destined to become the vehicle for some of his most significant poetic utterances. It can also be seen by the care he took in arranging these poems. He obviously tried to achieve a parallel order of thematic development for the two parts. It is not a rigid order: there are transitions and interpolations, but on the whole *New Poems I* and *II* follow parallel courses. Each part begins with a classical theme: the first part with *Early Apollo,* the second with *Archaic Torso of Apollo.* Upon the classical follows the Biblical theme with a group of poems such as *The Departure of the Prodigal Son* in the first part and *Saul among the Prophets* in the second. The Biblical theme is followed by the medieval theme, and that by the general theme: Paris. In addition both parts contain poems about flowers, notably *Blue Hydrangea* in the first and *Pink Hydrangea* in the second part (which Rilke briefly considered as title poems); animals, such as the famous *Panther* in the first part and the *Flamingos* in the second; towns and landscapes— Bruges in the first, Venice and Naples in the second; and figures. Among the latter, three poems on Buddha are noteworthy. Two appear in the first part, and the final poem in the second is addressed to *Buddha in His Glory.*

Thus like a great arc the course of action in *New Poems* leads from classical antiquity through Christianity to the modern world and comes to rest in Buddha, "the center of all centers." The inner intensity of Indian mysticism is the counterpoise to the pure form of Greek art: Buddha complements Apollo, and we experience reality as oscillations between these two poles. Many individual poems seem to be variations on this general theme: they start with plastic clarity and end on a quasi-mystic note. Take, for example, the *Panther,* one of the earliest of *New Poems,* and one of Rilke's favorites because it had shown him "the way to artistic honesty."

> His vision from the passing of the bars
> has grown so weary, it holds nothing more.
> He feels as though there were a thousand bars
> and behind a thousand bars no world.
>
> The padding of his strong and supple stride
> that in the very smallest circle turns,
> is like a dance of strength around a hub
> in which a mighty will stands stupefied.

Only from time to time the pupil's film
soundlessly parts—an image caught
goes through the tensioned stillness of the limbs—
and ceases to exist within the heart.[28]

Sein Blick ist vom Vorübergehn der Stäbe
so müd geworden, daß er nichts mehr hält.
Ihm ist, als ob es tausend Stäbe gäbe
Und hinter tausend Stäben keine Welt.

Der weiche Gang geschmeidig starker Schritte,
der sich im allerkleinsten Kreise dreht,
ist wie ein Tanz von Kraft um eine Mitte,
in der betäubt ein großer Wille steht.

Nur manchmal schiebt der Vorhang der Pupille
sich lautlos auf—Dann geht ein Bild hinein,
geht durch der Glieder angespannte Stille—
und hört im Herzen auf zu sein.[29]

The first words of this poem go straight to the heart of the matter: the most striking feature in an animal's physiognomy is its eyes. For, as Rilke would say in the *Eighth Elegy*, "With all its eyes the creature-world beholds the open . . . what *is* outside we know from the [animal's] face alone." [30] The panther here described, however, is in captivity, is behind bars. These bars stand between him and the openness beyond. He cannot avoid them; whichever way he turns there are bars, a thousand bars and behind them—nothing. The terrible monotony of his meaningless and fragmented existence is underlined by the repetition of the keyword "bars" and by the grating assonance of the broad "ä" in the German version: *Stäbe . . . Stäbe . . . gäbe . . . Stäben.* The quatrain ends with awful finality: *"keine Welt."*

But there are force and rebellion in the imprisoned animal. Although weary, it keeps on pacing. The strength and suppleness of its movements are well brought out by the alternating vowels "ei" and "a" in German:

Der weiche Gang geschmeidig starker Schritte,
der sich im allerkleinsten Kreise dreht. . . .

They reach their climax in the third line:

> ist wie ein Tanz von Kraft um eine Mitte

and come to an abrupt end in the fourth:

> in der betäubt ein grosser Wille steht.

At this point the panther's contours are tightly drawn. A stalemate has been reached between the caged animal and the outer world: the stalemate of stupefaction. Then an inner movement begins, quietly and almost imperceptibly but with an uncanny force that seems to drag the reader into the cage. Suddenly he is no longer looking at the panther from the outside, he is inside, feels the smooth nictitating membrane sliding open, shudders as the image passes through the tense stillness of the limbs and dies away in the heart. By an act of pure verbal magic the panther's fate has become the fate of the reader. He, too, is behind bars and can only catch intermittent glances of what lies beyond; their meaning he cannot grasp. Paralyzed by the sudden shock of what blinding vision, his body stiffens and becomes a transmission line that leads to the heart. For the heart alone can withstand shocks that terrify the mind and leave the body numb.

"The strange and almost frightening effect of many of [these] poems . . . [is that] they seize upon the beholder and drag him in. The poet is not outside the object described; he is not contemplating it, although he has contemplated it; he is in the object itself, and at a given moment he pulls the reader in as well." [31]

In an interpretative analysis of the poem *The Donor*, which, like *The Panther*, appears in the first part of *New Poems*, H. J. Weigand calls this phenomenon "the miracle" in Rilke's work, the sudden "break-through of grace," and says he knows of no German poet "who is more at home in the sphere of the miraculous" [32] than Rilke. In the translation of Leishman, according to whom "nothing like these poems had been written before; nothing like them has been written since," [33] *The Donor* reads:

> The painters' guild completed their commission.
> Perhaps the Saviour never blessed his zeal;
> perhaps no bishop honoured his submission

as in this picture, granted him remission,
and touched him lightly with the seal.

Perhaps that was the whole point: so to kneel
(just as it's all that we have ever known):
to kneel: and hold with choking breath one's own
contracted contours, trying to expand,
tight in one's heart like horses in one's hand.

So that, if something monstrous should appear,
something unpromised and unprophesied,
we might dare hope it would not see nor hear,
and might approach, until it came quite near,
deep in itself and self-preoccupied.[34]

Das war der Auftrag an die Malergilde.
Vielleicht daß ihm der Heiland nie erschien;
vielleicht trat auch kein heiliger Bischof milde
an seine Seite wie in diesem Bilde
und legte leise seine Hand auf ihn.

Vielleicht war dieses alles: so zu knien
(so wie es alles ist was wir erfuhren):
zu knien: daß man die eigenen Konturen,
die auswärtswollenden, ganz angespannt
im Herzen hält, wie Pferde in der Hand.

Daß, wenn ein Ungeheueres geschehe,
das nicht versprochen ist und nie verbrieft,
wir hoffen könnten, daß es uns nicht sähe
und näher käme, ganz in unsre Nähe,
mit sich beschäftigt und in sich vertieft.[35]

The poem again starts with a precise statement. In the title and
the first line the world of late medieval and Renaissance painting
comes to life; the custom of commissioning religious paintings as
personal memorials with the figure of the donor included among
the saints and prophets, often in a kneeling posture, for these
worldly Maecenases had reason to be concerned about their fate
in the hereafter. In the picture that served Rilke as a model the
donor obviously received a bishop's blessing. But it was not the
blessing that moved the poet. Rilke did not believe that grace
could be bestowed from the outside. That is why he rejected the
idea of the mediator. Indeed, perhaps the donor of this picture

was not blessed at all, and the bishop's gesture nothing but a pious sentiment on the painters' part. Perhaps he did not even know the Saviour. Perhaps the real blessing was his being on his knees. For a man who kneels submits himself directly to God.

The sense of urgency with which Rilke insists upon the act of kneeling in this poem and in many others—as in the *First Elegy* the saints "went impossibly/ on with their kneeling, in undistracted attention"—is transferred to the reader. "A pulsebeat goes through the poem," [36] forcing the reader upon his knees and initiating him in the mystery of undistracted devotion. How superbly the immense concentration of the heart is expressed in the image of tightly holding the reins of a team of horses in one's hand! The swift onrush of feeling that wants to run away from us is checked and forced to stay tense and trembling in the heart.

Having thus prepared the reader, Rilke confronts him in the final stanza with the pure perilousness of existence. Something monstrous appears, we do not know what it is, but that it exists is beyond doubt. It grows, it takes on form, it approaches. Again by an act of sheer magic the poet makes us believe in the unbelievable, causes us to feel that we are seized by it. Will it help us? Will it destroy us? We do not know. All we can hope for is that it is too much preoccupied with itself to notice us and that, being on our knees, we are invulnerable. For, as he says in a later poem:

> And if they are overpowered,
> if before life and death they kneel
> a new measure is given to the world
> with this right angle of their knees.[37]

> Und überwältigt sie's,
> und stürzen sie ins Knien vor Tod und Leben,
> so ist der Welt ein neues Maß gegeben
> mit diesem rechten Winkel ihres Knie's! [38]

The act of kneeling represents one of the most convincing outer equivalents for the activities of the soul. Basically it is a religious attitude, whether it is the lover who kneels before his beloved, the defeated who kneels before the victor, or the saint who kneels before God. Above all, Rilke thought, it was the proper posture for the artist. He must have experienced the mystery of kneeling, must know that a man upon his knees "is greater, spiritually speaking, than a man standing upright." [39] Otherwise he risks forfeiting that divine grace without which a work of art remains empty.

The difference between the monk in the *Book of Hours*, who lies prostrate before God, and the artist in *New Poems*, who kneels before his work, is that the former is carried away by his fervor and pours himself out into the world while the latter concentrates his feelings in his heart. Absolute surrender and pure concentration are the two modes of being in which man experiences the divine. St. Francis in the *Book of Hours* and Narcissus in Rilke's major poetry symbolize this polar situation.

To what extreme Rilke carried the concentration of his heart can be seen in the poem *The Solitary*, which depicts the isolation to which he subjected himself much of his life in order to reach a state of undistracted devotion:

> No; my heart shall turn into a tower,
> I to a carving from its cornice curled:
> Where nothing else exists from hour to hour
> But pain, ineffability, and world.
>
> Only a thing lost in immensity,
> Which day and night with light and darkness grace,
> Only a last lingering and longing face
> Thrust into being's unsilenceable sea,
>
> Only an uttermost stone face, not less
> Obedient to its inner gravity,
> Which the wide spaces, slaying silently,
> compel to ever greater happiness.[40]

> Nein: ein Turm soll sein aus meinem Herzen
> und ich selbst an seinen Rand gestellt:
> wo sonst nichts mehr ist, noch einmal Schmerzen
> und Unsäglichkeit, noch einmal Welt.
>
> Noch ein Ding allein im Übergroßen,
> welches dunkel wird und wieder licht,
> noch ein letztes, sehnendes Gesicht
> in das Nie-zu-Stillende verstoßen,
>
> noch ein äußerstes Gesicht aus Stein,
> willig seinen inneren Gewichten,

das die Weiten, die es still vernichten,
zwingen, immer seliger zu sein.[41]

Again the first line unlocks the rest: the poet's determination to concentrate his feelings in his heart. The startling "no" at the beginning points to the preceding struggle and sums up the poet's resolution not to be deflected from his course. He will force his heart to turn into a tower, which juts out, a self-contained rock, into the vast indeterminate space of being. Rilke was fond of the word "tower"; he used it frequently as a symbol of strength, solitude, and watchfulness. In the poem *Saint George*, for example, the maiden's prayer stood "like towers" beside him in his fight. Here it refers to the immense effort of concentration with which he applied himself to his work. In *The Donor* this effort is expressed in the image of holding the heart like horses in one's hand; now a higher degree of concentration has been reached: the heart has become a tower. It should be noted that *The Donor* appears in the first part, *The Solitary* in the second. Rilke's poetry clearly tended in the direction of ever greater concentration.

> As I arranged these poems [he wrote his publisher when he sent him *New Poems II*], I gained the impression that this new volume would form a very fitting sequel to the previous one: the course of action runs almost parallel, only somewhat higher, it seems to me, and toward greater depth and wider distance. If a third volume should be added to the other two, it would have to show a similar intensification in the more and more objective mastery of reality from which follows quite naturally the more comprehensive significance and clearer validity of all things.[42]

He did not write a third volume of *New Poems*, and it is hard to see how he could have exceeded the degree of concentration he had reached in the second. For when the heart turns into a tower it ceases to exist. Death is the limit of pure concentration, just as it is the limit of absolute surrender. This is but another way of saying that man experiences the divine in the shadow of death. "Almost deadly birds of the soul" Rilke called the angels, who represent a state of "pure being," and "almost deadly is the glow of all poems" where concentration is maximized.

The Solitary states the extreme case of the artist's will to transform the world; as in the *Picture of Dorian Gray* the artist's life becomes a work of art. At the same time the tower image— "tower": that classic symbol of male creativity—and Rilke's desire to "thrust it into being's unsilenceable sea" suggest his unconscious wish to overflow and spend himself. Consciously he longs for concentration, wants to be an "uttermost stone face," but he knows that this is impossible. Even the hardest stone is worn away. "The wide spaces" will annihilate it.

It is important to remember that in Rilke's cosmology Space, not Time, is the great transformer. Time has collapsed. "Does it really exist, Time the destroyer?" he asks, and answers: "The ghost of transitoriness/ passes through those who humbly accept it/ as though it were smoke." [43] Kassner, who first emphasized the spatial character of Rilke's poetry, says that "if there was or could be for Rilke's mind any notion of a circumference, a comprehended-comprehensiveness, an enclosure and a fence of the world: it was Space and nothing else, the Space of the visionary, the Space into which God's creative energy places things, the mythical Space of transformations." [44]

In *New Poems* Rilke tried to thrust pictures into this space, self-contained rocks of music: things. To this end he devoted an immense amount of spiritual energy. "It is this active spiritual energy . . . which differentiates [these poems] sharply from descriptions no less faithful, imaginative or beautiful. It is magic." [45] Like all magicians Rilke discovered, however, that "in the end we yet depend/ on creatures we created." The writing of these poems exhausted him. Like his *Goldsmith* who suddenly felt, while he was working on a gem, that "the savage creature thrust its rasping/ claws with metallic hatred into me," [46] Rilke felt paralyzed when he had written these poems, spellbound like his *Magician:*

> Decision falls. The spell begins anew.
> He knows, the call has countered the denial.
> His face, though, stands at midnight, like a dial
> with meeting pointers. He is spell-bound too.[47]
>
> Entscheidung fällt. Die Bindung stellt sich her.
> Er weiß, der Anruf überwog das Weigern.

Doch sein Gesicht, wie mit gedeckten Zeigern,
hat Mitternacht. Gebunden ist auch er.[48]

It has been noted that Rilke was particularly fond of casting his spell over old things: old houses and parks, family portraits, churches, sarcophagi, mirrors, and fountains. For this reason Miss Butler thinks that a fitting title for these poems would be *The Sense of the Past*. But this is misleading, for when Rilke takes us back into the past, when, as is often the case, the action occurs in a setting of faded aristocratic elegance, he does not arouse historical memories, we are not moved to reflect upon the past, we feel that we are part of it: the past is present. It is this sense of the presence of the past that makes the reading of these poems such an unforgettable and often disturbing experience. Take, for example, the poem *Before Summer Rain*:

Quite suddenly, from all the green around,
something—you hardly know just what—has gone;
you feel the park itself drawing in upon
the windows and growing silent. The last sound

is the rain-piping dotterel in the wood,
reminding you of somebody's *Jerome*—
there rises so much zeal and solitude
from that one voice the cataract to come

will listen to. The lofty walls, arrayed
with ancient portraits, as though recollecting
they should not listen to our talk, withdraw.

The faded tapestries are now reflecting
the uncertain light we in our childhood saw
those afternoons when we were so afraid.[49]

Auf einmal ist aus allem Grün im Park,
man weiß nicht was, ein Etwas, fortgenommen;
man fühlt ihn näher an die Fenster kommen
und schweigsam sein. Inständig nur und stark

ertönt aus dem Gehölz der Regenpfeifer,
man denkt an einen Hieronymus:
so sehr steigt irgend Einsamkeit und Eifer
aus dieser einen Stimme, die der Guß

erhören wird. Des Saales Wände sind
mit ihren Bildern von uns fortgetreten,
als dürften sie nicht hören, was wir sagen.

Es spiegeln die verblichenen Tapeten
das ungewisse Licht von Nachmittagen,
in denen man sich fürchtete als Kind.[50]

The setting of this poem—an old house in an old park with its nostalgic associations of a declining aristocratic culture—is typically Rilkean. His preference for this setting, reflected in the pattern of his life, his sojourns in ancient castles and manor houses, his attachment to members of some of the oldest families in Europe, has led to the charge that he was a snob at heart and that his art is "decadent." "A snob is always suspect,"[51] says Simenauer, who claims that "a high degree of snobbism can be detected in Rilke,"[52] although he adds that "Rilke's snobbism was no ordinary snobbism,"[53] that it was perhaps "only a part he played." Kassner, on the other hand, did not notice "the slightest traces of vanity"[54] in Rilke's character and calls him "a very truthful person." Stefan Zweig likewise praised Rilke's "complete modesty." Be that as it may, the charge that Rilke's poetry is decadent is certainly untenable.

Note the sense of menace that grows out of these few aristocratic props. The reader's awareness is roused to the presence of a powerful, subterranean vitality. "The park is drawing in upon the windows": there is no clear distinction left between outside and inside. The change outside causes a change within. Quite imperceptibly the conversation takes a new turn, becomes graver. Even the walls are affected. They withdraw. The uncertain light, reflected in the faded tapestries, brings up recollections. Childhood arises, and all the strange fears of childhood. "Something— you hardly know just what—has gone." The certainty of the phenomenal world has gone. A door has opened, and we are made aware that there is something else: a world we knew so well when we were children.

Thus in poem after poem Rilke penetrates the mask of things. Under his steady gaze the phenomenal world dissolves, and in its place there arises a vibrant reality, quite unsuspected, strange and frightening.

A textbook example of his technique is his treatment of the theme, Venice. This magnificent town has had few rivals as a source of artistic inspiration; there is hardly a poet who has not tried to capture its spirit. And yet how many Venetian poems go beyond stating surface clichés: gondolas, canals, St. Mark's Square, the Doge's Palace? Goethe's *Venetian Epigrams* do avoid the sentimental pitfalls into which writers on Venice are prone to fall, but they are critical and philosophic reflections on the state of Venice and the world in general. They do not try to recapture the spirit of the town. In Rilke's poem *Late Autumn in Venice* the whole town arises: its present decline and its past grandeur, the glitter of its surface splendor and the fierce will that forced its foundations down into the bottom of the sea:

> The town no longer drifts now like a bait
> that tries to catch all the emerging days.
> Harsher the glazen palaces now grate
> against your view. And from the gardens sways
>
> summer like a bunch of puppets
> heads down, tired, killed outright.
> But from the dark soil of primordial woods
> a will arises: as if over night
>
> the ruler of the sea were to increase
> twofold the galleys in the watchful port
> to tar with a new fleet tomorrow's breeze
>
> which suddenly, oars beating in accord,
> flags flying and impatient of the wait
> takes the full wind, all radiant, all fate.[55]

> Nun treibt die Stadt schon nicht mehr wie ein Köder,
> der alle aufgetauchten Tage fängt.
> Die gläsernen Paläste klingen spröder
> an deinen Blick. Und aus den Gärten hängt
> der Sommer wie ein Haufen Marionetten
> kopfüber, müde, umgebracht.
> Aber vom Grund aus alten Waldskeletten
> steigt Willen auf: als sollte über Nacht
> der General des Meeres die Galeeren

verdoppeln in dem wachen Arsenal,
um schon die nächste Morgenluft zu teeren
mit einer Flotte, welche ruderschlagend
sich drängt und jäh, mit allen Flaggen tagend,
den großen Wind hat, strahlend und fatal.[56]

The immediate occasion that gave rise to this poem was Rilke's stay in Venice in November, 1907. He had been there often before and had paid homage to this "dream of a town" in four poems written in the traditional manner, complete with marble palaces, canals, and gondolas. Now he realized that these were mere surface impressions, false and misleading. The better he got to know Venice the more he felt that it was an incomprehensible town, as though it existed in mirrors. It was the first time he saw Venice under a dull wintry sky, and he found that

> . . . this Venice seems to me almost hard to admire; it has to be learned over again from the beginning. Ashen its marble stands there, gray in the grayness, light as the ashy edge of a log that has just been aglow. And how unexplained in its selection is the red on walls, the green on window shutters; discreet and yet not to be surpassed; bygone, but with a fullness of transiency; pale, but as a person turns pale in excitement.[57]

His object in writing this poem was to present the "real" Venice, the Venice tourists do not see, which he described in that memorable prose passage in *Malte* quoted above: "awake, brittle to the breaking point, and not in the least dream-like." [58] The proper setting for this Venice was autumn, for what season could be more fitting for a town whose virile past stands in such marked contrast to its insipid present? In two striking images the tension between past and present is expressed. Venice is a "bait" luring people to come and see her just as, at the height of her power, she had lured the Levantine trade and made herself mistress of the Adriatic —and a far richer catch it was than those "somnolent foreigners" she now attracts. But all this is past. The Venetian summer is gone. All that remains of the great show are a few lifeless puppets. Here we have the second image, "puppets." This is one of Rilke's favorite symbols; he likes it because "he can use it either to express the universal human or the definitely nonhuman, or both at the same time." [59] In this poem it provides an effective bridge between the dramatic past of Venice and its listless present.

In six lines Rilke succeeds in transforming the familiar picture postcard impression we have of Venice and showing that in reality it is a ghost town. Its "glazen palaces" (note that there is no "marble" here, for marble means strength and vitality and would be quite out of place) are brittle and can break at any moment.

But then the inner movement starts: the fierce will that founded Venice asserts itself, rising irresistibly from the submerged forest upon which the town rests. In a breath-taking succession of images this will takes on form and recreates the past: a new ruler is born, a new fleet arises, colorful, restless, and ready to challenge fate. The sonnet ends on a note of triumph. Its final two adjectives *"strahlend und fatal"* sound like a fanfare announcing the departure of this magnificent fleet. The incredible has happened: before our eyes the past has risen; we have witnessed the rebirth of Venice. By tearing off the mask of time Rilke has freed those timeless forces that lie hidden at its foundations. The reader, shocked by this sudden release of spiritual energy, wonders and asks himself: "What is time? When is Now?" [60]

The immediacy of this shock is of course lost in the translation, which at best gives but a distant echo of the original force.

> In German the very language of the poem expresses the tension of the political will . . . there is a constant tension between the nouns and the verbs, the inactive and the active elements of language. . . . Soft ä and ö sounds prevail in the first quatrain, fuller ü, o and u sounds in the second one. The first half of the sestet is distinguished by its sharp strident e's. . . . The second half abounds in bright, bellicose a's. . . . A movement of the will from tension to explosion determines the character of the sonnet ·down to the last details of verse and language.[61]

In the *New Poems* Rilke shows that, if a determined will to form is applied to a singular thing, a field of tension between reality and transparency is set up. It is this tension which shocks the reader and gives him heightened insights into the nature of existence. The effort required to set up this field of tension is well described in a later poem:

Which of the daringly-devised creations
can beat us in our fiery enterprise?
We stand and strain against our limitations
and wrest things in we cannot recognize.[62]

Von allen großgewagten Existenzen
kann eine glühender und kühner sein?
Wir stehn und stemmen uns an unsre Grenzen
und reißen ein Unkenntliches herein,[63]

It was to be expected that the immense amount of spiritual energy Rilke used up in writing *New Poems* and *Malte Laurids Brigge* would leave him exhausted; and it seems that spiritual exhaustion is in large measure responsible for the mood of despondency into which he fell after he had completed these books. It was always the same: as soon as a book was finished he lapsed into a serious crisis that affected both his mind and his body. He felt weary, despondent, and sick and looked back longingly to that period of creative well-being he had experienced during the writing of *New Poems*, "when I expected nothing and nobody and the whole world streamed towards me only as an ever greater task which I answered clearly and surely with pure achievement." [64] At the same time he knew that "the terrible thing about art is that the further you progress in it the more it demands of you the extreme, the all-but-impossible." [65]

In his *New Poems* and in *Malte* he had tried the "all-but-impossible." He had strained against his limitations, had stretched his contours and forced himself to stay on the ground. "As his nature was purely romantic-intuitive, however, was averse to being bound and was imbued with an intense fear of material reality, fierce inner conflicts arose within him . . . [which make] his work of this period . . . so lacking in harmony." [66] These words, in which Heerikhuizen tries to explain the serious crisis in Rilke's life, are a reminder of the dangerous extreme to which he carried his ideal of objective expression.

It is quite likely that he overstrained himself, that his "uninterrupted gazing" had finally numbed his spontaneity: "And now I sit here and look and look till my eyes ache, and point it out to myself and say it over and over, as though I had to learn it by heart," [67] he confessed to Lou. But there was no response. Everything left him obstinately empty. He concluded that he applied too much force to his impressions: "I stay too long in front of them, I press them into my face, and yet they *are* impressions of nature, even if you let them lie quietly for a while"; and he added sadly, "Au LIEU DE ME PÉNÉTRER LES IMPRESSIONS ME PERCENT." [68]

This state of paralysis of his creative faculties lasted for years. It was paradoxical: here he was, a master of expression who suddenly found nothing to express, an accomplished poet at the height of his powers who felt empty and superfluous. There were times when he wondered whether he should not stop trying to write altogether and, like Rimbaud, take up some useful occupation. He consulted doctors and psychiatrists. In his letters to Lou he again mentioned the need for a "turning point," just as he had done after he had written the *Book of Hours*. It will be recalled that his fervent search for God during the second Russian journey had not produced any poetry. He had prayed his prayers instead of writing them. Now he had reached the opposite extreme. His fervent search for the thing in the object had stifled his heart:

> For, behold, there is a limit to looking,
> and the intently looked-at world
> longs to bear fruit in love.
> Work of sight is achieved,
> now for some heart-work
> on all those pictures, those prisoned creatures within you
> You conquered them; but do not know them as yet.[69]

> Denn des Anschauns, siehe, ist eine Grenze.
> Und die geschautere Welt
> will in der Liebe gedeihn.

> Werk des Gesichts ist getan,
> tue nun Herz-Werk
> an den Bildern in dir, jenen gefangenen; denn du
> überwältigtest sie: aber nun kennst du sie nicht.[70]

He felt it was imperative that he change his life. But could he change it? Had his "terrible will to art" so stunted his spontaneity that now that he had achieved technical mastery of expression the source of his inspiration had dried up? It took an angel to answer this question. While he waited for that answer he may well have pondered the "imperious message . . . which radiates from the *Archaic Torso of Apollo*." [71]

Although we never knew his lyric head
from which the eyes looked out so piercing clear,
his torso glows still like a chandelier
in which his gaze, only turned down, not dead,

persists and burns. If not how could the surge
of the breast blind you, or in the gentle turning
of the thighs a smile keep passing and returning
towards that center where the seeds converge?

If not, this stone would stand all uncompact
beneath the shoulders' shining cataract
and would not glisten with that wild beast grace

and would not burst from every rift as rife
as sky with stars: for here there is no place
that does not see you. You must change your life.[72]

Wir kannten nicht sein unerhörtes Haupt,
darin die Augenäpfel reiften. Aber
sein Torso glüht noch wie ein Kandelaber,
in dem sein Schauen, nur zurückgeschraubt,

sich hält und glänzt. Sonst könnte nicht der Bug
der Brust dich blenden, und im leisen Drehen
der Lemden könnte nicht ein Lächeln gehen
zu jener Mitte, die die Zeugung trug.

Sonst stünde dieser Stein entstellt und kurz
unter der Schultern durchsichtigem Sturz
und flimmerte nicht so wie Raubtierfelle;

und bräche nicht aus allen seinen Rändern
aus wie ein Stern: denn da ist keine Stelle,
die dich nicht sieht. Du mußt dein Leben ändern.[73]

6 Dolls and Angels

Alas, as I was hoping for human help: angels
suddenly stepped silently over
my prostrate heart.

Ach, da wir Hülfe von Menschen erharrten: stiegen
Engel lautlos mit einem Schritte hinüber
über das liegende Herz.

Rilke, *Sämtliche Werke*

In the last stanza of the *Fourth Elegy* Rilke asks anxiously:
"Who'll show a child just as it is? Who'll place it within its constellation, with the measure of distance in its hand?" [1] The commentator on those two great poetic cycles, *Duino Elegies* and *Sonnets to Orpheus*, might ask with equal anxiety: Who can place
these poems within their constellations? How can they be judged,
what measure would do them justice?

It does not help us much to be told by Miss Butler that, "as a
profoundly tragic record of the isolation of genius, *Duino Elegies*
is unparalleled in the history of poetry," [2] nor by Heerikhuizen
that it is "the most dramatic, albeit personally dramatic, work of
this century." [3] Expressions like "the most monumental, most
difficult and most ambitious" poetic utterances of this or any age,
which are found frequently when the *Elegies* are discussed, simply
prove Mephistopheles' point: "When ideas are lacking words are
readily at hand." Lest this be taken as an unjust criticism of Rilke's
critics, it should be noted that one must have a good deal of
sympathy for them. It is difficult to avoid superlatives when writing
about these poems. Rilke himself called them "the most mysterious dictation of his life." [4]

In the introduction of his translation of the *Sonnets to Orpheus*

Leishman gives an excellent explanation of the nature of the difficulties that Rilke's major work offers to any interpretative criticism: "Again and again I feel, in reading him, that we have come round the spiral to another 'dawn of consciousness', where language is in the making, and where myth and symbol must often supply the place of not yet thinkable thoughts." [5] The critic's dilemma is understandable. Language and logic are the tools of his craft, but the genius of Rilke's poetry is *mythos* not *logos*, *intuitio* not *ratio*. It is well to remember, as C. G. Jung has pointed out, that "rational truths are not the last word, there are also irrational truths. In human affairs what appears impossible upon the way of the intellect, has very often become true upon the way of the irrational." [6]

Rilke often insisted that the key to an understanding of these poems is to become "like-minded." This is easier said than done, for the average reader, focused on the "real" world and equipped by experience and training to apply rational criteria to every phenomenon he encounters, is baffled by what seems to him unreal or irrational. He may be aware of the existence of irrational forces; if he is a student of psychology he may be willing to grant that "the unconscious disposes of a whole world of images whose boundless range yields in nothing to the world of 'real' things"; [7] but face to face with these images in the works of such poets as Blake, Hölderlin, or Rilke, his first response is likely to be puzzled disbelief. He cannot rid himself of the suspicion that what is not intelligible is not true and inclines to dismiss such artists as visionaries, mystics, or madmen. "Those who have been told that my works are but an unscientific and irregular Eccentricity, a Madman's Scrawls, I demand of them to do me the justice to examine before they decide." [8] The despair underlying this Blakean outburst is a sign that he lived in a society that was "differently focused" and to whom his prophetic utterances must have seemed like the outpouring of a disordered brain.

The charge that his major poetry is the expression of a "nobly vainglorious mind" has also been directed against Rilke, but on the whole he has met with a much more favorable response from his contemporaries than either Blake or Hölderlin did from theirs.

The reason for this is not necessarily that Rilke was a better poet, but that he lived at a time when the traditional values of Western man were collapsing. Rilke's *Weltangst*, his dread of a hostile universe, his very personal experience of man's forlornness amidst indifferent stars—*"le néant vaste et noir"* (Baudelaire)—his insistence upon the tragic nature of human existence: these are aspects of his poetry that contemporary experience affirms. Two world wars and the fear of worse to come have shaken the premises of an "arrogant faith in reason." We are no longer certain that man is a rational animal, or even that he could become one. We fear that Faust's insatiable thirst for knowledge will lead to the destruction of the world:

> Woe! woe!
> You have smashed it,
> the beautiful world,
> with a mighty blow;
> it tumbles, it falls!
> A demigod has destroyed it! [9]

These words of the Chorus of Spirits in Goethe's *Faust* have taken on a new meaning and urgency for us. We have seen the primordial chaos that lurks behind the ordered surface of life, and we know we need new values, a deeper and more comprehensive interpretation of reality and of man's place in it. We need a world view that does not exclude pain, suffering, sickness, or death and does not evade the issue of our being here by taking refuge in a utopian hereafter. Confronted by the disintegrating forces of the intellect, we need to return to the inner sources of our strength. For while "man's mind is discord, the heart unites"; or again, in Goethe's words:

> Oh mighty one
> of the sons of earth!
> More beautiful
> build it up,
> in your heart build it up again! [10]

to which the *Ninth Elegy* provides the echo:

> Earth, isn't this what you want: to arise
> invisibly within us? [11]

Erde, ist es nicht dies, was du willst: *unsichtbar*
in uns erstehn?—[12]

The reception accorded to Rilke and the growing interest in
Blake and Hölderlin seems indicative of a shift of emphasis in the
West from a predominantly outward to a more inward direction
of life. In any case, the prerequisite for an appreciation of Rilke's
major poetry is such a shift. The reader who wants to understand
it must get "spiritually focused," must assume that "the infinite
does not decrease when the finite grows," and that "the miracle
remains." [13]

That the *Duino Elegies* and the *Sonnets to Orpheus* are poetic
miracles is acknowledged even by critics who question the validity
of Rilke's world view and the truth of his ideas. Perhaps the chief
reason these poems have attracted so much comment is their
wholly miraculous nature, for, although miracles cannot be explained, the urge to interpret them is irresistible. Rilke himself
could not resist it. He left a considerable body of quasi-exegetic
writings on them, to which most commentators refer, and which
offer valuable insights into the processes of Rilke's mind. As commentaries to the poems themselves they have to be used cautiously.
Rilke was a far better poet than an interpreter of his own poetry.
However, what he said about the relationship between *Elegies* and
Sonnets should be borne in mind because it brings out an essential
fact: both cycles belong together, like two movements of one piece
of music. To interpret one without considering the other gives an
incomplete and therefore misleading impression of Rilke's major
poetry: "Elegies and Sonnets sustain one another at all points,—
and I deem it an infinite grace that I have been able, with the
same breath, to swell these two sails: the little rust-coloured sail of
the Sonnets and the gigantic white canvas of the Elegies." [14]

In this chapter two aspects of the *Elegies* will be considered: the
nature of their conception and genesis, and the significance of
two of their major figures: angel and doll.

The prolonged crisis in Rilke's life that followed upon the
completion of *Malte* in 1910 was briefly overcome by the creative
euphoria in 1912 when, at Duino, he encountered the angel and
conceived the cycle of the *Elegies* (completing the first two and

writing fragments of others); it reached a climax of despair in 1915 with the *Fourth Elegy* and, coinciding with the deepening universal crisis of the first World War, was not resolved until 1922, when in Muzot "all his powers spoke," not only permitting him to finish the cycle of the *Elegies*, but also presenting him with the totally unexpected gift of the *Sonnets*. After this immense achievement he experienced a brief Indian summer during which his French poems and some of his most mature *Late Poems* ripened, but which was cut short by his rapidly deteriorating state of health (he suffered from leukemia) and his agonizing death in December, 1926. Although the *Elegies* are thus not Rilke's last work and perhaps not even his greatest—there is a growing opinion that the poetry of the *Sonnets* is more perfect—they occupy a unique place in his work and in the history of poetry. Like *Malte* they document the anguish of a soul grievously sick but whose very sickness was transformed into poetry. For this was the miracle of Rilke's art: it integrated his life; without it he might have been lost, might have fallen victim to the fierce disintegrating forces within him—as Nietzsche and Hölderlin did. His art saved him. At the same time, he wanted to get beyond it: "Fundamentally, Rilke only wanted one thing of poetry: to overcome poetry, to get beyond it. . . . Whither? To the 'proof.' " [15] In these words Kassner reveals one of Rilke's basic paradoxes. He was obsessed with the desire to penetrate the mask of things and reach their essence. Being a poet, he had to use words as tools; but words are masks too, hence:

> Fortunate those who know that behind
> language the unsayable looms;
>
> Glücklich, die wissen, daß hinter allen
> Sprachen das Unsägliche steht; [16]

for this insight enables them to understand it without words. On the other hand, what proof have we that there is anything behind the mask?

> Lovers, to you, each satisfied in the other,
> I turn with my question about us. You grasp yourselves.
>   Have you proofs? [17]

Liebende, euch, ihr in einander Genügten,
frag ich nach uns. Ihr greift euch. Habt ihr Beweise? [18]

"They do not have them, neither the man nor the woman. Hence the poet." [19]

While the poet in Rilke thus saved the man—he admitted freely that his work was "really nothing but a self-treatment"— there were times when the man revolted against the poet and longed for a life of normal human relationships.

> Never have I looked more passionately than in the last year towards those who pursue some good, regular occupation which they can always do, which depends more on intellect, brain-power, understanding, skill—whatever it is—than on those mighty tensions of one's inner life over which one has no control. They are not exaltations, that much is certain, otherwise they could not induce such an indescribable reality in the spirit; but they are so immeasurable in their impetuosity and recoil that one often thinks the heart could not bear such extremes on both sides. . . . Only by . . . some great aberration, probably, can art proceed from nature.[20]

He confessed that he was "a little horrified" when he thought of all the violence he had put forth in *Malte*, "how in my consequent desperation I plunged clean through to the back of things, behind death itself, so to speak, so that nothing more was possible, not even dying." [21] He felt like a "photographic plate that had been exposed too long" and hoped to find someone who would share his solitude. At the same time he knew that "it is a bad sign . . . [this] incessant longing to lodge my aloneness with some person," and he thought with a "sort of shame" of his best time in Paris, that of *New Poems*, "when I expected nothing and nobody and the whole world streamed towards me only as an ever greater task which I answered clearly and surely with pure achievement." [22]

But Paris no longer inspired him. Mechanically he went through his daily routine, tried to work, but discovered that there was no response. Thinking that he perhaps needed a change of scenery, a completely different environment, he accepted an invitation to a journey to Africa, visited Tunis, Algiers, Egypt, gazed with awe upon the incredible "temple-world of Karnak"; but, when he returned to his room in Paris, he felt as empty as before. As often during barren periods he busied himself with translations because, as he told Princess Taxis, "writing is after all better than not writing, and perhaps it will provoke an angel and make him jealous." [23] To Lou, on the other hand, he said that he was not interested in writing merely for the sake of writing and was scornful of artists who "have got themselves in hand by outwitting and exploiting their own known inadequacies": "I stand too definitely on the side of my nature, I have never desired anything from it which it did not give forth greatly and happily from its very ownest impulses, almost as though I were not there." [24] And yet he longed for work and "sometimes, I think, it longs for me—but we do not get together." [25]

In the end he decided that he must be sick and consulted a psychiatrist. His wife, who was undergoing analysis at the time, advised him to do likewise. Lou, however, counseled against it. She told him that an analysis might indeed drive out his devils, but that it might also injure his angels. This gave him pause, for, although he knew that things were not going well with him, he was

> . . . nevertheless moved by nothing so much as by the incomprehensible, the stupendous marvel of my own being which was so impossibly biassed from the start and which yet travelled from salvation to salvation, as through ever harder stone, so that, whenever I think of not writing any more, this fact alone dismays me, the fact of not having recorded the absolutely miraculous line of this so strangely lived life.[26]

But once again, as during critical periods in the past, providence came to his rescue—this time in the person of Princess Taxis who put her beautiful property, Castle Duino on the Adriatic, at his disposal. She invited him to spend the winter there alone, except for the servants necessary for his well-being, so that he could give undivided attention to whatever angels or demons would deign to appear to him. Rilke lived at Duino from October, 1911, to May, 1912, trying to work out the equation of his life. And it was there, at the end of January, 1912, that the vision he tried to express in the *Elegies* came to him.

It would be difficult to imagine a setting more beautiful, a landscape more apt to arouse the poetic imagination than that in which he now found himself:

> This castle, immensely towering above the sea, which, like a promontory of human existence, looks out with many of its windows (one of mine included) into the most open sea-space, directly into the universe, you might say, and into its generous, all-surpassing spectacles—while inner windows on different levels open on quietly enclosed ancient court-yards, around whose old Roman walls later periods have fashioned graceful baroque balustrades and playful figures. But behind it, when you step out of its solid gates, there rises, as inhospitable as the sea, the empty Karst, and the eye, void of all small impressions, is strangely moved by the little castle garden which in places where the castle does not border on the precipice tries to stretch down like the surf; then the game park on the next projection along the shore line assumes prominence; bordering it there lies, hollowed out and in ruins, the yet older castle which preceded this very ancient one and where, according to the legend, Dante is said to have stayed.[27]

It is tempting to think that the *Divine Comedy* and the *Duino Elegies* have a common birthplace; but, whether this is true or not, it has often been noted that Rilke's poetry has Dantesque qualities, especially with regard to the visual nature of his imagery. The tone of deep, metaphysical anxiety that permeates the *Elegies* constitutes an additional element of affinity between the two poets:

> Who, if I cried, would hear me among the angelic
> orders? And even if one of them suddenly
> pressed me against his heart, I should fade in the strength of his
> stronger existence.[28]

> Wer, wenn ich schriee, hörte mich denn aus der Engel
> Ordnungen? und gesetzt selbst, es nähme
> einer mich plötzlich ans Herz: ich verginge von seinem
> stärkeren Dasein.[29]

To be sure, Rilke's angel is not the Christian angel of the New Testament. We must rid our minds of the gentle, white-robed messenger of God, as Raphael and Botticelli painted him, if we want to grasp the meaning of the angel of the *Elegies*. He is more nearly akin to the angel of the Old Testament with whom Jacob wrestled until he was blessed, although Rilke himself insisted that "the angel of the *Elegies* has nothing to do with the angel of the

Christian heaven (rather with the angelic figures of Islam . . .)." [30]
But this explanation is more ingenious than convincing for, no
matter how much his conscious mind rejected Christian concepts,
there is no doubt that these were deeply embedded in Rilke's sub-
conscious and influenced the creation of the angel symbol. The
difficulty of locating a specific angelic prototype for Rilke's angel
should not, however, cause us to assume that he is simply a
"pseudonym for God," as Dehn and Holthusen assert. Like all of
Rilke's symbols the angel has a protean nature: "Now he represents the glorious essence of pure being, now the terrifying demon
of artistic vocation, then again the ebb and flow in historic becoming and finally (as Cämmerer calls him) the messenger,
citizen and gatekeeper of the invisible. His basic meaning remains
artistic." [31]

In a letter written at Duino a few days after Rilke had completed
the *First Elegy*, when he may already have been occupied with
the *Second*, whose main theme is the nature of the angels, he
mentioned the case of the Portuguese nun, Marianna Alcoforado,
whose unrequited love seemed to him

> . . . so wonderfully pure because she refrains from projecting the
> current of her feeling further and further into the Imaginary, but with
> infinite strength leads the genius of this feeling back into herself again:
> bearing *it*, nothing else. . . . Had she, glorious beyond all measure,
> given way for an instant she would have plunged into God like a stone
> into the sea, and had it pleased God to do to her what he does to
> the angels continually—casting their radiance back into themselves again
> —I am certain she would have become an angel on the spot, just as
> she stood there in this grievous convent, an angel deep inside her, in her
> deepest nature.[32]

The angel thus symbolizes intensities of feeling that are not
directed outward but concentrated in the heart, which, under the
impact of their radiance, becomes an angel or, as one might say,
experiences pure being. Perhaps one could think of the sun's rays
caught in a concave mirror and concentrated on an object, which,
under their impact, bursts into flame. Indeed, the *Second Elegy*
uses the mirror image for the angels; they are "tumults of stormily
rapturous feeling, and suddenly, separate mirrors, drawing up their
own outstreamed beauty into their faces again."

Such an apotheosis of Narcissus is alien to the Western tradition and to its conception of love as an outgoing force. Judged by it Rilke's poetic ideas amount to a reversal of the natural order. There were times when he thought so himself, for example, when he told Princess Taxis: "I do not think anybody has ever experienced more vividly to what an extent art goes against nature; it is the most passionate inversion of the world." [33] And Hans Carossa felt that "something strange and Eastern had come with Rilke into the German dreamworld, a Yoga spirit which no longer carries singing nature innocently within, but uses will power to force his rays through the burning glass of his soul, concentrating them in one point, until it bursts into song." [34]

Bursting into song, encountering an angel, or experiencing pure being—whichever terms are used to express the inexpressible—means the dissolution of the phenomenal self and the entering into the transcendental Self, the Atman of the Upanishad. "The Old Testament puts it this way," Rilke said in another letter written at Duino at this time, "that it is impossible to see an angel without dying of him." [35] A year later he expressed the same thought in the poem addressed *To the Angel:*

> Shine, o shine and let the constellations
> look upon me. For I fade away.[36]

> Leuchte, leuchte! Mach mich angeschauter
> bei den Sternen. Denn ich schwinde hin.[37]

Two attributes are inherent in the nature of the angel. He is glorious because he is at home in that vast open world that knows neither past, present, nor future, but only pure space or pure being. He is terrible for us because we can experience pure being only at the cost of losing our identity:

> We have never, not for a single day,
> pure space before us into which flowers
> endlessly open. There is always world
> and never nowhere without no: that pure,
> unsuperintended element one breathes,
> endlessly knows, and never craves. A child
> sometimes gets quietly lost there, to be always
> jogged back again. Or someone dies and *is* it.[38]

Wir haben nie, nicht einen einzigen Tag,
den reinen Raum vor uns, in den die Blumen
unendlich aufgehn. Immer ist es Welt
und niemals Nirgends ohne Nicht: das Reine,
Unüberwachte, das man atmet und
unendlich *weiß* und nicht begehrt. Als Kind
verliert sich eins im Stilln an dies und wird
gerüttelt. Oder jener stirbt und *ists*.[39]

Death is the entrance into the angelic state of being:

Oh, to be dead at last and endlessly know them,
all the stars! For how, how, how to forget them! [40]

O einst tot sein und sie wissen unendlich,
alle die Sterne: denn wie, wie, wie sie vergessen! [41]

But we fear death:

Because being here is much, and because all
this Here and Now, so fleeting, seems to require us and
strangely concerns us.[42]

Aber weil Hiersein viel ist, und weil uns scheinbar
alles das Hiesige braucht, dieses Schwindende, das
seltsam uns angeht.[43]

If Rilke had been a true mystic the Here and Now would not
have concerned him. The fact that he was wholeheartedly on the
side of the angel, for whom the earth does not exist, and on that
of the earth, for whom the angel does not exist, caused the fierce
tensions in his life. Thus he says in the same breath: "Oh, to be
dead at last" and "Life here is glorious." That he succeeded in
reconciling these "pure contradictions" by elevating them into
the "realm of praise" is his unique achievement, albeit a trans-
logical one, for, "seen from the standpoint of logic, there exists,
as ever, no third—between the logical: 'either . . . or'. But between 'intellectus' and 'res' there still is 'anima', and this 'esse
in anima' makes the entire ontological argument superfluous." [44]

The vision Rilke had at Duino was that of the world as seen by
the angel. "This world regarded no longer from the human point
of view, but as it is within the angel, is perhaps my real task," [45]
he told a correspondent in October, 1915, at a time when he was

trying to recapture it. The "perhaps" should give us pause; it shows that he was not at all certain about his task, for "what is man that he should do this, that he should travel in the opposite direction against [everything?]" [46] What would remain of his humanity? The angels are utterly indifferent to man: "I regard them as aggressors par excellence, and here you must defer to me, I have paid the price: for when, on my return from a profound occupation with things and animals, I longed to be instructed in human kind, behold, the next but one stage, the angelic, was set before me: thus I have bypassed people and am now looking cordially back upon them." [47]

In this he was mistaken. It was not at all easy to look back upon people, and, while his soul labored to transform the world in the spirit of the angel, his whole being ached for love:

> Were you not always
> distracted by expectation, as though everything
> announced a beloved? [48]

> Warst du nicht immer
> noch von Erwartung zerstreut, als kündigte alles
> eine Geliebte dir an? [49]

His letters reveal how close to a complete breakdown he came at this time. To Lou he confessed that his body threatened to become the caricature of his soul and that he continued to wait anxiously for someone who would share his solitude. Terrified by his vision of total human isolation, he shuddered, hesitated, and let it slip by without having fully reported it. This explains the abrupt break in the composition of the *Elegies* and his frantic search for a more human solution. "Yes, the two elegies are there," he wrote Lou from Spain where he had gone after he had left Duino,

> but only by word of mouth could I tell you what a small and bitterly truncated fragment they form of what was once given into my power. With conditions and powers like those when the *Book of Hours* was begun—what could I not have achieved. If only I could see you, dear Lou, that is my great hope now. Often I tell myself that it is only through you that I am linked with humankind.[50]

For years the conflict raged between the artist in Rilke and the man: the artist wanted to recapture the vision he had had at Duino, the man dreaded it; the artist wanted to be carried into the realm of angelic exaltation, the man wanted to love and be loved. "Art or existence: this is and remains Rilke's problem." [51] It is moving to watch him struggle with it, now putting his entire hope in art, now in life, but all the time trying to reconcile them. The desperate tone of his letters to Lou shows how severe the conflict was and how little she could help him. For, although he thanked her for her sympathy and said that "the rest is now for me and for the angel, if only we cling together: he and I and you from afar," [52] he knew very well that, if an angel pressed him against his heart, he would "fade in the strength of his stronger existence."

It was obvious that he needed a counterweight to the terrifying, superhuman figure of the angel. He needed another symbol, a symbol of pure outwardness, fully visible, all matter and no spirit —hence the direct opposite to the angel—a creature, moreover, whose relationship to man was similar to man's relationship to the angel. He found it in the figure of the doll. Doll, in Rilkean terms, means *Umschlag* from the angel. The question of how he found it and how much, if anything, he owes to Kleist's essay *On the Marionette Theatre* does not concern us here. Like the angel, the doll had appeared in Rilke's poetry before it assumed its role in the *Elegies* and undoubtedly represents a "most personal" experience, intimately connected with memories of his own "doll childhood."

The German for doll is *Puppe*. But *Puppe* has two other meanings as well, marionette (puppet) and chrysalis (pupa). One reason for Rilke's fondness for the word *Puppe* is the suggestive power of this trinity of meaning and the possibility of imperceptibly shifting the emphasis from one meaning to the next—transformation within the word, the mythopoeic process par excellence. A typically Rilkean symbol, it is complex, ambiguous, and yet, at the same time, strikingly simple. It calls forth a whole range of associations, from earliest childhood memories to the most mature reflections on the metamorphic processes of life.

Rilke distinguishes three levels of *Puppe*. At its lowest level it means doll: that lifeless creature on whom we wasted our first innocent love, in whose presence, "as it stared fixedly at us, we first experienced (if I am not mistaken) that void in feeling, that stoppage of the heart, during which we would perish, did not the whole of gently moving nature lift us, like something inanimate, over abysses." [53] Having no fancy at all, a doll is less than a thing; it is a soulless usurper of a child's genuine love. On the next higher level *Puppe* refers to the marionette. A marionette is a lively doll; it is full of imagination and hence "just as much more than a thing as a doll is less." Rilke thought that "a poet could easily fall under the spell of a marionette." Indeed, is not the relationship of the poet to the marionette similar to that of God to man? Does not a poet "make puppets" according to his image? Finally, on the highest level, *Puppe* means chrysalis and heralds the birth of a winged creature. The range of meaning of *Puppe* thus extends all the way from the most lifeless to the liveliest, from doll to butterfly. During Rilke's struggle with the angel the doll symbol took on more and more prominence, until in the *Fourth Elegy* both were joined: "Angel and doll! Then there's at last a play" [54] ("Engel und Puppe: dann ist endlich Schauspiel" [55]).

It has been said that Rilke's basic problem was "art or existence," though it would be more correct to say "art *and* existence" for he really wanted both. His problem was that he wanted both absolutely, that he did not want to compromise his art for the sake of his life, nor his life for the sake of his art.

> Ultimately, each of us experiences only *one* conflict in life which constantly reappears under a different guise,—mine is to reconcile life with work, in the purest sense; and where it is a question of the infinitely incommensurable work of the artist, the two directions stand opposed. Many people have helped themselves by taking life easily, by snatching what they needed from it . . . or by turning life's values into an intoxication whose wretched enthusiasms they hurriedly flung into art; others have no alternative but to withdraw from life—asceticism—and *this* way is of course much cleaner and truer than that rapacious cheating of life for the sake of art. But for me even asceticism cannot be considered. Since in the last analysis my productivity proceeds from the plainest adoration of life, from the daily, inexhaustible wonder of it

(how could I have been productive otherwise?)—I would see it as a
lie to reject any of the currents that flow towards me; in the end every
such failure must express itself in your art—however much art may
gain potentially from it—as a certain hardness, and there take its re-
venge: for who can be open and affirmative on such sensitive ground
if he has a mistrustful, restrictive and anxious attitude towards life!
So one learns, oh how slowly, that life travels over endless starting-
points—to what end, finally, can one apply one's little abilities? [56]
I do not want to tear art from life. I know that somehow and somewhere both belong together.[57]

That art and life belong together is of course true, but it is
equally true that an "ancient enmity" exists between them. The
artist, obsessed with his work, has no time to live. Cézanne did not
even have time to attend his mother's funeral, although he loved
her. He loved his work more. During his years in Paris Rilke also
possessed this obstinate will to art; at least he thought he possessed
it, for even then there were times when he felt he could not go on.
Particularly during the completion of *Malte* he often indulged in
the strange afterthought of giving up writing. He may never have
been serious for he knew that, while it was difficult to live with
his art, life without it was inconceivable. In a letter to Dr. Gebsat-
tel, rejecting psychiatric treatment, he clearly stated his dilemma:

> After the most serious reflection I have come to the conclusion that I
> could not allow myself the loophole of psychoanalysis unless I were
> really determined to start a new (if possible, uncreative) life on the
> other side of it, a change such as I sometimes promised myself on the
> completion of *Malte Laurids Brigge* and often since then in tired moods,
> as a sort of reward for all I have gone through. Now, however, I must
> confess that these plans have really never been quite serious, that be-
> neath such evasions I still feel bound with infinitely strong ties to what
> has been begun, to all the happiness and misery it entails, so that,
> strictly speaking, I can wish for no change, no intervention from the
> outside, no relief save that which is inherent in endurance and in the
> ultimate triumph.[58]

We know now that he was right, and that with the *Elegies* and
Sonnets he did achieve ultimate triumph, but only after he had
endured what must have been surely the most agonizing vigil in
the history of poetry. He first had to deny both—life and art—
before he could burst out into jubilant affirmation:

Earth, isn't this what you want: to arise
invisibly within us? Is it not your dream
to be one day invisible? Earth! invisible!
What is your urgent command, if not transformation?
Earth, you darling, I will! O, believe me, you need
your springs no longer to win me: a single one,
just one, is already more than my blood can endure.
I have now been unspeakably yours for ages and ages.
You were always right, and your holy idea
is Death, friendly Death.

Look, I am living. On what? Neither childhood nor future
are growing less . . . Supernumerous existence
wells up in my heart.[59]

Erde, ist es nicht dies, was du willst: *unsichtbar*
in uns erstehn?—Ist es dein Traum nicht,
einmal unsichtbar zu sein?—Erde! unsichtbar!
Was, wenn Verwandlung nicht, ist dein drängender Auftrag?
Erde, du liebe, ich will. Oh glaub, es bedürfte
nicht deiner Frühlinge mehr, mich dir zu gewinnen—, *einer*,
ach, ein einziger ist schon dem Blute zu viel.
Namenlos bin ich zu dir entschlossen, von weit her.
Immer warst du im Recht, und dein heiliger Einfall
ist der vertrauliche Tod.

Siehe, ich lebe. Woraus? Weder Kindheit noch Zukunft
werden weniger . . . . . Überzähliges Dasein
entspringt mir im Herzen.[60]

These exuberant final chords of the *Ninth Elegy*, written at
Muzot in 1922, and echoing the spirit of Beethoven's *Ninth
Symphony*, show the distance Rilke had traveled from that day in
January, 1912, when he had set out on his journey. Accompanied
by doubt and despair, and weighed down by the universal tragedy
of the first World War, he had nevertheless reached his goal: he
had conquered negation. This seemed to him an event of more
than private significance: "For therewith a measure is given for
the inexhaustible stratification of our nature; and how many who,
for one reason or another, believe they have been torn asunder
might not draw from this example of continuability a peculiar
consolation?" [61] He thought that somehow this consolation had
found its way into the *Elegies*, thus becoming a source of solace

to the reader. And as he lay dying in Switzerland Lou Salomé advised him to draw comfort from the *Elegies*, as some of her patients had done.

But this is anticipating. For the triumph of the *Ninth Elegy* was preceded by the despair of the *Fourth*, written in Munich in the winter of 1915, and by years of silence during which he lost all hope that he would ever again enter into the spirit of these poems.

In many ways the *Fourth Elegy* is the most personal, hence the most difficult, of all. Miss Butler comments that it is

> . . . a hard poem . . . to like, even when the intellectual difficulties
> it presents have been partially overcome, on account of its hard tone
> of contempt for all human values and its convulsive efforts to transcend
> them. It came from an atrophied heart and an arrogant mind, rigidly
> determined to divorce life from art at any cost. . . . Yet, for all its
> grimness, it has tragic proportions. . . .[62]

E. E. Stahl says that in the *Fourth Elegy* "in language and imagery of unusual suggestiveness, but replete with esoteric meaning, Rilke passes judgment on human nature." [63] Mason, who analyzed it closely, concluded that "the entire *Fourth Elegy* can be understood correctly only from the exceptional position of the poet." [64] Bassermann, on the other hand, does not think that any adequate interpretation of the *Fourth Elegy* exists and suggests that it be left "obscure"; he quotes with approval Rilke's words that where obscurities exist "not explanation but inclination" leads to understanding. Finally, the well-known Catholic theologian Romano Guardini, who subjected the *Elegies* to a close philosophic scrutiny, concluded that Rilke's vision was defective: "Human existence is not as Rilke says it is. He has cut out from it what forms its center: the human personality, its responsibility, love and fate." [65]

Before turning to the *Fourth Elegy* let us recall that the major themes of the first two *Elegies* had been the hopelessness of the human condition:

> Alas, who is there
> we can make use of? Not angels, not men. . . .

> Ach, wen vermögen
> wir denn zu brauchen? Engel nicht, Menschen nicht. . . .[66]

Only the youthful dead, the forsaken lover, and the hero are "more than ourselves," "glow in the fullness of the heart," while the rest of us, "when we feel, we evaporate and breathe ourselves away." We pass by everything like an "airy exchange," and, even if we could hear the voice of God, we could not endure it. Hence all we can do is "listen to the suspiration, the uninterrupted message that grows out of silence."

In the *Third Elegy*, which Rilke started at Duino in 1912 and finished in Paris in 1913, this theme is taken up again, but here it is not fierce and indifferent angels against whom man's forlornness is projected, here the antagonist is the "hidden, guilty river-god of the blood":

> Oh, the Neptune within our blood, oh, his terrible trident!
> Oh, the gloomy blast of his breast from the twisted shell! [67]

> O des Blutes Neptun, o sein furchtbarer Dreizack.
> O der dunkele Wind seiner Brust aus gewundener Muschel.[68]

In pictures of compelling beauty the dark splendor of sex is revealed, the fierce powers of the id that entangle the sleeping youth. How innocent he looks in his sleep and how seemingly protected, but within: "who could avert, divert, the floods of origin flowing within him?" Alas, there is no caution within that sleeper. He gets tangled up in fierce inner events, primitive patterns overwhelm him, he is at the mercy of bestial preying forms, but, oh:

> How he gave himself up to it! Loved.
> Loved his interior world, his interior jungle,
> that primal forest within, on whose mute overthrownness,
> green-lit, his heart stood.[69]

> Wie er sich hingab—. Liebte.
> Liebte sein Inneres, seines Inneren Wildnis,
> diesen Urwald in ihm, auf dessen stummen Gestürztsein
> lichtgrün sein Herz stand.[70]

The reader is taken through the world Dostoevski and Freud explored, the underworld of the soul. He witnesses the rising of a *deus absconditus*, the return of primordial chaos, and, shuddering, he asks: Where can man find refuge? Placed between indifferent cosmic forces that combine to suppress him and fierce chthonic forces that lie dormant in his blood, his fate is indeed tragic:

and already the knowing brutes are aware
that we don't feel very securely at home
within our interpreted world.[71]

und die findigen Tiere merken es schon,
daß wir nicht sehr verläßlich zu Haus sind
in der gedeuteten Welt.[72]

In the two and a half years that lie between the composition of the *Third* and the *Fourth Elegy* two events occurred that left a deep imprint on Rilke's mind: his encounter with Benvenuta and the sudden emergence of the "remote, incredible War God."

Benvenuta was the name he gave to the gifted pianist, Magda von Hattingberg, who now entered his life. On the face of it the affair was no different from others that had preceded it or would follow: it started with exalted expectations, passed through a brief moment of passion, and ended in disillusionment. And yet, while the course it took followed a familiar pattern, it came at a time in Rilke's life when everything hung in the balance, when "between stuffed and lifeless dolls and remote and invisible angels [his position] was utterly and excruciatingly lonely." [73] Benvenuta's coming, he felt, was a sign that his long patience had finally been rewarded: here, at last, was the partner of his solitude.

The manner of their meeting undoubtedly heightened the sense of mystery the affair had for him from the beginning. It started with a letter he received from a total stranger about his *Tales of God*. Benvenuta wrote that she had just finished reading the book and wanted to thank him for it "because it had given her so much comfort." In her conclusion she referred to the fact that he had dedicated the book to Ellen Key and added: "I have never yet wished to be anyone but myself, but now nothing would please me more than to be metamorphosed into Ellen Key, so that that dedication would be mine; I am convinced that my love for the *Tales of the Almighty* [*Tales of God*] is greater than anyone else's in the world." [74]

Habent sua fata libelli. It is strange to think that of all of Rilke's books *Tales of God* was to become the indirect cause of his painful discovery that he was incapable of love, that the human solution was not his solution, and that he was fated to go on alone, wrestling with his daimon.

The episode lasted only four months, but in that time Rilke wrote some of the most passionate letters of his life, "Titans of letters that broke out of him like molten lava from Mount Stromboli." These letters, he told Benvenuta, were the testament of his whole life, "and if one day the hour you know of should come . . . then bear testimony, for you are called to be my witness, you who hold the legacy of my life in your blessed hands." [75] Even before they had met he asked:

> Is it possible?—Did God send you to me in the years of my mortal need to give me strength to survive? Can I sense the world, breathe its air, in the certitude that it contains you, my friend, as I know it contains God?—God, whom I have felt so illimitably in the joy of my work, as you have in your music.[76]

Again and again he assured her that she had just come in time to save him and that

> . . . the life of the mind for which I have been struggling all these unbearable years (the mind that is so mightily mind that it can sweep all things into itself, excluding nothing), that infinite life of the mind comes true for me in you; I glimpse, as it were, a country of all innocence. . . . I feel it—it is your nature to grasp me as a whole, you greater circle round the infinite circle of my heart.[77]

But he also warned her that hateful feelings went through his soul at the sight of the human condition, that there was "much evil" in him, and that the "chill of an alien fate had fallen upon him."

The impetuosity of these letters, the fact that they were addressed to her by a famous poet, both frightened and fascinated Benvenuta. She suspected even then that "he suffered from a nameless affliction that lay exclusively in himself and in his mortal substance," [78] but she agreed to meet him. On the train to Berlin he wrote her a poem that sums up his existential dilemma and reads like a prolegomenon to the *Elegies:*

Oh, I went through thickets like a breeze,
escaped like gusty smoke from every roof;
where others found in custom joy and ease
like a strange custom I remained aloof.
My hands went forward fearfully
into the fateful clasp of other hands;
in that outpouring every heart expands,
and I could but myself outpouréd be.

You see, we need a foothold in the dust
even to gaze upon the planet's track,
for trust can only come of others' trust,
all giving is no more than giving back.
The night asked nought of me; but if I peer
up to the firmament bestarred,
the marred to the eternally unmarred,
Whereon stand I? Am I here? [79]

Ach, wie Wind durchging ich die Gesträuche,
jedem Haus entdrang ich wie ein Rauch,
wo sich andre freuten in Gebräuche
blieb ich strenge wie ein fremder Brauch.
Meine Hände gingen schreckhaft ein
in der andern schicksalsvolle Schließung;
alle, alle *mehrte* die Ergießung:
und ich konnte nur vergossen sein.

Siehst du, selbst um das Gestirn zu schauen,
brauchts ein kleines irdisches Beruhn,
denn Vertrauen kommt nur aus Vertrauen,
alles Wohltun ist ein *Wieder*tun;
ach, die Nacht verlangte nichts von mir,
doch wenn ich mich zu den Sternen kehrte,
der Versehrte an das Unversehrte:
Worauf stand ich? War ich hier? [80]

For a few weeks it seemed that Benvenuta could appease Rilke's daimon. In her presence he seemed happy and cheerful. She opened to him the world of music, which had been all but closed to him before; he in turn read her his poems and told her the story of his "so strangely lived life." Finally he took her to Paris, his Paris, the town where he had been more miserable and happier than anywhere else. Benvenuta was enchanted with it, and everything pointed to a happy conclusion of his long search for love and human companionship. But when he asked her to stay with him "always," she hesitated, for she was troubled to notice that when they were together he seemed unable to work. With the same exclusiveness with which he had formerly dedicated himself to his work, he now devoted himself to her. She mentions that once he showed her a manuscript, *The Seven Poems of the Unknown,* which he had recently finished:

> He read them aloud, but at first I thought they were by someone else; there is an alien tone in them that does not belong to him. He must have guessed my thoughts, for he suddenly said, "They are no good, are they?" I told him he had probably written them when he was not calm and ready enough. . . . [And he replied:] "Do you think that I can ever be ready again? Isn't that all over?" [81]

His face looked ashen and incredibly sad; he wanted to "creep away like a beast dully dying" to spare his friends the sight of his unworthiness.

Deeply disturbed, Benvenuta tried to comfort him, advising him to rid himself of everything and everybody that impeded his work and go back into seclusion. But it was useless. "Cannot you see," he said, "that the flaw is after all irreparable, even when your healing hand touches me?" [82]

She must have realized then that nobody could help him, but she agreed to make one more attempt. He asked her to come to Duino with him, to see the place where he had encountered the angel and to listen to the two *Elegies*. Perhaps he hoped that by bringing together the work he loved and the woman he loved he could achieve the long-desired synthesis of life and work. If so he was to be cruelly disappointed.

At first everything went well. Benvenuta was enchanted with the old castle and charmed by her hostess, Princess Taxis. There were music, poetry, and good conversation; there were walks in the castle garden, drives along the Adriatic, visits to Venice. And, most important of all, Rilke seemed relaxed and at ease.

But then the moment came when, all of a sudden, their world collapsed. According to Benvenuta:

> Rilke had received some colored pictures of dolls—I believe from the woman who had made them. They looked as though they had been

modelled on insane persons or on those sick from taking opium. He
showed them to me and I thought them frightful. I was shocked when
Rilke said he found them "moving and beautiful." I answered: "The
test of a toy is whether children like it. But any healthy and innocent
little girl would be scared by these horrors." [83]

Rilke replied that there were no children in the lives of these
dolls, that they had "outgrown children's comprehension and
begun, as it were, their own independent life." Benvenuta thought
it very odd that from a harmless plaything could arise such a
monstrous nonplaything.

But Rilke became almost vehement. "A toy gets worn out and bad,"
he cried. "Don't say that the badness of a toy is innocent. It needs
all the unbounded innocence of children to keep permanently harmless all that is dirty and depraved in a toy. Just imagine that such an
object had become deformed and depraved in the hands of adults—
it would fill you with unspeakable loathing." [84]

Benvenuta disagreed violently, and when, to convince her, he
read her his essay on dolls, she became more and more upset.
"Suddenly I had an irrepressible desire to cry. 'Rainer,' I said, 'I
cannot listen any more. Forgive me, but it hurts me. It is very
silly and childish of me, and I don't even know why your hatred
of dolls affects me so much, for after all it is your hatred, not
mine—but I cannot go on. I find it horrifying.' " [85]

Their breach became final a few evenings later when Rilke read
from the *Elegies*.

Today Rilke read aloud some fragments of the *Elegies*. They are an
image of himself as he now is—or always was? Who knows? I cannot
possibly think that he will not complete them. I can understand that
this work, born of suffering, probably demands the final renunciation
of all safe, warm, human life. I understand now what he means when
he makes the sailor's bride bid him go because it is his fate to live in
danger in strange and alien lands. The poem made a deep impression
on me, but I also felt its complete hostility to life, and my whole mind
resisted it.[86]

It must have come as a bitter disappointment to Rilke that of
all those who heard him read the first *Elegies* Benvenuta was the
only one who failed to respond to the positive surplus of their

poetry. For if she was right, if they were "hostile to life," if they left that impression, rather than that the condition of man was tragic, he would have considered them poetic failures. For even in his bitterest moods, even when he despaired of human existence, he never failed to praise life, all of life, including its most terrifying aspects, and he had little respect for artists who tried to tear it down. Hemingway's "life's a dirty trick" would have offended him deeply. And almost the last words reported of him, spoken at the height of the painful illness that led to his death, were "You must never forget, my dear, that life is magnificent." [87]

It would thus be wrong to think that the inadequacies of his own life, which the Benvenuta episode revealed so clearly, had affected his judgment about the value of life. All it had done was to make him realize that in a human sense *his* life was forfeit, that he must not look for human help, that his salvation lay in his poetry. The result of his failure to find a human solution was a renewed faith in his art.

He did not take his failure lightly. The insight that nobody could help him, that he was condemned to be alone forever, almost unhinged him. There was again a sharp physical reaction. He felt weary and despondent:

> But now my triumph-tree is breaking,
> the storm is breaking my slow
> triumph-tree.
> Loveliest in my invisible
> landscape, making me better
> known to invisible angels.[88]

> Jetzt aber bricht mir mein Jubel-Baum,
> bricht mir im Sturme mein langsamer
> Jubel-Baum.
> Schönster in meiner unsichtbaren
> Landschaft, der du mich kenntlicher
> machtest Engeln, unsichtbaren.[89]

A few weeks later the war broke out. For a brief moment his private sufferings were swept aside as he watched the great popular upsurge, the intoxication with which all peoples plunged into a roaring fate. Carried away by the universal enthusiasm, he wrote five songs in praise of the incredible War God. But even then, in the midst of the contagious frenzy that surrounded him on all sides, he confessed that:

> like a ship's syren, there howls within me at night
> the vast interrogation "Whither, whither, whither?"
> Does the god from his lofty shoulder see where we are going?
> Is he casting lighthouse-beams to a struggling future
> that has long been looking for us? Is he a knower?
>   Can he
> possibly be a knower, this ravaging god? [90]

> Dennoch, es heult bei Nacht wie die Sirenen der Schiffe
> in mir das Fragende, heult nach dem Weg, dem Weg.
> Sieht ihn oben der Gott, hoch von der Schulter? Lodert
> er als Leuchtturm hinaus einer ringenden Zukunft,
> die uns lange gesucht? Ist er ein Wissender? *Kann*
> er ein Wissender sein, dieser reißende Gott? [91]

He soon learned the answer: No, it was not a god at all who had come, it was a spirit of destruction wearing a patriotic mask and usurping genuine feelings of kin and country for its own sinister ends. The war had only lasted a few weeks when he was appalled by the lies and hypocrisy that turned this tremendous event into a disease, and now

> . . . the magnificence, the sacrifice, the resolution that are occurring continually are being imprisoned in the chaos of wretchedness and untruth, swallowed-up by the "enterprise" of this war which is to bring profit—glory? Oh no, all these conceptions have become meaningless through their employment by the newspapers—the world has fallen into the hands of men.[92]

Can nobody stop it? he cried. "Why are there not a few, three, five, ten, who stand together in the public squares and shout: enough! And are shot and at least give their lives so that it be enough, while those on the front now only perish to make this monstrous thing last and last." [93]

As the war continued month after month he asked himself more and more insistently: what good was it to be an artist now? "Can art heal wounds? Can it sweeten the bitterness of death? It does not comfort the desperate, it does not feed the hungry, it does not clothe the freezing." [94]

In this mood of despair he wrote the *Fourth Elegy*. The Benvenuta episode had shown him that he was incapable of love; the war made him doubt the value of art. Formerly he had felt that "it was awful that old men [he had Strindberg in mind] could end like twenty-year-old Dauphines whose last words were: *Fie de la vie, ne m'en parlez plus.*" [95] Now he himself despaired, if not of life, at least of man's part in it. For is it not man who constantly interrupts the great unity of life?

> Outstript and late,
> we suddenly thrust into the wind, and fall
> into unfeeling ponds.[96]

> Überholt und spät,
> so drängen wir uns plötzlich Winden auf
> und fallen ein auf teilnahmslosen Teich.[97]

Unlike the migatory birds man does not fall in with the rhythm of nature, he thrusts against it, fights it, hence: "hostility is our first response."

Having thus introduced the theme of human inadequacy, he turned to himself. What was his own position? he asked, and in what follows he passed stern judgment on his life and work:

> Who's not sat tense before his own heart's curtain?
> Up it would go: the scenery was parting.
> Easy to understand.[98]

> Wer saß nich bang vor seines Herzens Vorhang?
> Der schlug sich auf: die Szenerie war Abschied.
> Leicht zu verstehen.[99]

In the *First Elegy* he had said "for staying is nowhere," and he would end the *Eighth* with "we live our lives forever taking leave." It is therefore "easy to understand" that "the scenery was parting" as the curtain of his heart goes up. The question is: What is he parting from in the *Fourth Elegy*?

> The well-known garden,
> swaying a little . . .[100]

> Der bekannte Garten,
> und schwankte leise: [101]

Is he thinking here of his early poems? Of the nostalgic, neo-romantic garden sentiments with which his "first poor verses" abound? He had long since dismissed them as inconsequential because there was nothing behind them, they were just youthful vapors "swaying a little."

> Then appeared the dancer.
> Not *he!* Enough! However light he foots it,
> he's just disguised, and turns into a bourgeois,
> and passes through the kitchen to his dwelling.[102]

> dann erst kam der Tänzer.
> Nicht der. Genug! Und wenn er auch so leicht tut,
> er ist verkleidet und er wird ein Bürger
> und geht durch seine Küche in die Wohnung.[103]

In commenting on this passage Günther says that "now he sees himself in the figure of the dancer, God's dancer at the time of the *Book of Hours,* sees himself as the enthusiast who is enraptured by the sound of his own voice," [104] and, bitterly, he turns his glance away. "Not he!" For was he not a "disguised bourgeois" when he wrote these poems? Did he not pretend to be an artist while, in reality, he was a young father who worried where the next meal was to come from?

> I will not have those half-filled masks! No, no,
> rather the doll. That's full.[105]

> Ich will nicht diese halbgefüllten Masken,
> lieber die Puppe. Die ist voll.[106]

In *Malte* already he had deplored this being "a mere half-thing: neither real beings nor actors." Here he goes further. Rather than be half artist, half bourgeois, he will be a doll. There is nothing half and half about a doll: it is stuffed full, completely outside, mask through and through. True, it is a desperate wish, this wanting to become a doll, for it amounts to a renunciation of his humanity, but, if being human means to be a "half-filled mask," if it means to *appear* more than to *be,* he would rather be a doll. A doll is what it appears to be, a doll is genuine. Death, too, is genuine:

```
                                        I'll force myself
to bear the husk, the wire, and even the face
that's all outside. Here! I'm already waiting.
Even if the lights go out, even if I'm told
"There's nothing more,"—even if greyish draughts
of emptiness come drifting from the stage,—
even if of all my silent forebears none
sits by me any longer, not a woman,
not even the boy with the brown squinting eyes:
I'll still remain. For one can always watch.[107]
```

```
                                        Ich will
den Balg aushalten und den Draht und ihr
Gesicht aus Aussehn. Hier. Ich bin davor.
Wenn auch die Lampen ausgehn, wenn mir auch
gesagt wird: Nichts mehr—, wenn auch von der Bühne
das Leere herkommt mit dem grauen Luftzug,
wenn auch von meinen stillen Vorfahrn keiner
mehr mit mir dasitzt, keine Frau, sogar
der Knabe nicht mehr mit dem braunen Schielaug:
Ich bleibe dennoch. Es giebt immer Zuschaun.[108]
```

He will face up to death, he will not sneak away when the puppet show is over and "greyish draughts of emptiness come drifting from the stage." What a powerful image this is of death approaching—"greyish draughts of emptiness"—you can feel it on your face. But most of us cannot bear an "empty stage," just as most of us do not dare to face up to death. "What creatures are these that have to be poisoned out of life?" he asked in the poem *Death*, written concurrently with the *Fourth Elegy*. They have to be driven away:

```
Else, would they stay? Has this hard food, in fact,
such power to infatuate,
they'd eat for ever, did not some hand extract
the crusty present, like a dental-plate?

Which leaves them babbling. Bab, bab, ba. . . . .[109]
```

```
Blieben sie sonst? Sind sie denn hier vernarrt
in dieses Essen voller Hindernis?
Man muß ihnen die harte Gegenwart
ausnehmen, wie ein künstliches Gebiß.
Dann lallen sie. Gelall, Gelall! . . . . .[110]
```

Terrifying though these poems are and close to the edge where language plunges into dadaistic babbling, they show how determined Rilke was to penetrate the mask and reach reality. He would face up to death, and he would face up to the doll. Here "doll" probably refers to his *New Poems*. They were the result of such intent gazing, and they were perfect of their kind, the best he had done, but they were still only puppets. To make them he had had to renounce life, had to sit and watch: "For one can always watch."

But can one? Was he right in renouncing life for the sake of these puppets? At the end of his life Michelangelo is supposed to have said: "What is the good of having made so many puppets?" [111] When he first heard of this Rilke could not understand it. But now the question disturbed him also. He needed reassurance and called on his father as a witness, his father who was the first to "taste his life," "that turbid first infusion of my Must" [112] (*"den ersten trüben Aufguß meines Müssens"* [113])—his father who had been alarmed to see him grow into an artist and who was yet fascinated also by "the after-taste of such queer future." Was he right? Rilke asked him.

Was he right? he then asked those who loved him and whom he had forsaken:

> because the space within your faces changed,
> even while I loved it, into cosmic space
> where you no longer were . . .[114]

> weil mir der Raum in eurem Angesicht,
> da ich ihn liebte, überging in Weltraum,
> in dem ihr nicht mehr wart . . . .[115]

The ellipses at the end of this passage signify, as ellipses often do in Rilke's poetry, that he had reached the edge of the sayable. There were no further words, there was no answer to the question, Was he right? Instead he had to make a decision. It was a fateful decision for it amounted to a rejection of humanity, an attempt to transcend it and to bring about a synthesis of art and life on an extrahuman level:

when I feel like it,
to wait before the puppet stage,—no, rather
gaze so intensely on it that at last,
to upweigh my gaze, an angel has to come,
and play a part there, snatching up the husks.
Angel and doll! Then there's at last a play.
Then there unites what we continually
part by our being there.[116]

wenn mir zumut ist,
zu warten vor der Puppenbühne, nein,
so völlig hinzuschaun, daß, um mein Schauen
am Ende aufzuwiegen, dort als Spieler
ein Engel hinmuß, der die Bälge hochreißt.
Engel und Puppe: dann ist endlich Schauspiel.
Dann kommt zusammen, was wir immerfort
entzwein, indem wir da sind.[117]

Right or wrong, he is determined to go on watching and making puppets. Perhaps an angel will come after all, perhaps his gazing will provoke an angel, forcing him to breathe life into lifeless puppets. What poetry that would be! Angel and doll: the union of pure spirit and pure form enacting the pure event. It can happen only if we do not interfere, if we let ourselves be played, if the spirit enters us completely; in short, if we cease to be men and become masks of Dionysus. Guardini calls this a "gigantic, mythical but terrifying idea," [118] for it amounts to a denial of the human center and proclaims as the ideal of existence a state of ecstasy. Clearly such an ideal does not represent the human norm. Rilke is thinking here of the artist in the grip of his daimon, the artist carried beyond himself by a creative upsurge. He is thinking of that state of exaltation during which men speak with tongues; he is thinking of what happened to him at Duino and what was to happen again at Muzot, when in a few days "with trembling hands" he wrote most of his major poetry:

All in a few days, it was an unspeakable storm, a tornado of the spirit (as in Duino), the very fibres and tissues cracked in me—there was never a thought of eating, God knows what nourished me. But now it is done. Done. Amen. So here is the triumph I was holding out for,

through everything. . . . This was what I wanted. Just this and nothing more.[119]

In the words of the *Fourth Elegy* the miracle of such a creative
explosion occurs when doll (pure receptivity) and angel (pure
spontaneity) meet. "Then there's at last a play":

> Then at last
> can spring from our own turning years the cycle
> of the whole event. Over and above us
> there's then the angel playing.[120]

> Dann entsteht
> aus unsern Jahreszeiten erst der Umkreis
> des ganzen Wandelns. Über uns hinüber
> spielt dann der Engel.[121]

Undoubtedly Rilke is reporting here a very personal experience.
The angel symbolizes that state of ecstasy which possessed him
during the high tide of his poetic creativity. But it is one thing to
say that it was a personal, even idiopathic, experience and another
that it lacks general significance. A considerable body of the folklore of all peoples deals with "men possessed." The founders of all
religions, the saints and prophets bear witness to the mighty inrush of inspiration, and so do the poets: hence the term *vates*. In
modern times Hölderlin, Blake, and Nietzsche have reported
similar experiences. Nietzsche's description of what happens when
the spirit assails man closely parallels Rilke's: "You hear but do
not seek; you take but do not ask who gives; a thought flashes
through you like lightning, with necessity, without hesitation as
to form—I have never had a choice." [122]

Rilke thought that the sudden insight into the nature of existence, which the artist gains when he is in the grip of his daimon,
the dying gain, too—for "surely they must suspect how full of
pretext/ is all that we accomplish here, where nothing/ is what
it really is"—and sometimes children standing "within the gap
left between world and toy."

The child in the state of innocence, before it has been "turned
around" and made conscious of time, death, and world, when "behind figures there was more/ than the mere past, and when what

lay before us/ was not the future," occupies therefore a key position in Rilke's world. How can a child be shown just as it is? he
asks in the final stanza of the *Fourth Elegy*. That an elegy which
deals with dolls and angels should be concerned with the child
is not hard to understand; however, Rilke's concern here is not
with the child but with the child's death. Thus he touches on one
of the main themes of the *Elegies*: the duo-unity of life and death.
In three lines—surely among the strangest lines in poetry—he
poses the problem:

> Who'll make its death
> from grey bread, that grows hard,—or leave it there
> within the round mouth, like the choking core
> of a nice apple? . . . .[123]

> Wer macht den Kindertod
> aus grauem Brot, das hart wird,—oder läßt
> ihn drin im runden Mund, so wie den Gröps
> von einem schönen Apfel? . . . .[124]

It is a strange question. Who, he asks, which power could make
a child's death? Where is the artist who could portray it? If a
sculptor were to make a figure of it he would use bronze or stone.
Here the proposed material is bread. Imagine a figure kneaded of
bread dough that "grows hard." Gray bread: grayness and hardness
are attributes of death. Bread is the staff of life, but in this figure
death is mixed in with life, grows out of life, just as it does in the
child with whom life and death are still one, before death has
become the antagonist who comes from outside (because our
consciousness of it and hence our fear of it has pushed it outside)
when it is still part of life. This thought is carried on in the next
image. A child has eaten an apple—has tested life, perhaps also
knowledge. Now the core remains in its mouth as a foretaste of
death. Thus its mouth is full of death even while it is full of life.
The seeds of the apple, like the bread, contain both life and death.
So does the child. But for a child to hold death:

> the whole of death,—even before life's begun,
> to hold it all so gently, and be good:
> this is beyond description! [125]

den ganzen Tod, noch *vor* dem Leben so
sanft zu enthalten und nicht bös zu sein,
ist unbeschreiblich.[126]

With this sense of wonder at the incredible insight into the
unity of life and death, as exemplified by the child, the *Fourth
Elegy* ends. This insight which "startles us" and is "beyond description" is quite common with the angels who "are often unable
to tell/ whether they move among living or dead." It startles us
because "we make the mistake of drawing too sharp distinctions."
A child does not draw such distinctions because it is unconscious
of death, and everything in its world is alive. Thus an affinity
exists between the angel and the child, and the incredible phenomenon of a child's death is meant to add credibility to the angel.

When he interpreted the *Elegies* Rilke always insisted that their
major theme was "affirmation of life as well as of death!" for "to
admit the one without the other would . . . be a limitation
which would ultimately exclude everything infinite." [127] He did
not say that

> . . . one should love death, rather that one should love life so whole-
> heartedly, so completely without calculation and selection, that in-
> voluntarily one always includes him (the offside of life) and loves him
> too. For only because we have excluded death from our consciousness
> has he more and more become the stranger and because we have alienated
> him has he become an adversary. It is thinkable that he is much closer
> to us than life itself. . . . What do we know of him? . . . I think our
> effort should be to presuppose the unity of life and death so that it
> would gradually become apparent.[128]

Many commentators find these ideas unacceptable. Guardini,
for example, says that, though the images of the *Elegies* are great
and their affirmation powerful, "they deprive death of its real
seriousness. This seriousness is the reason that man cannot affirm
death—I mean death as such. Every affirmation of this kind is
unconvincing." [129] Jung, on the other hand, is of the opinion that
"from the standpoint of psychotherapy it would be desirable to
think of death as only a transition—one part of a life process
whose extent and duration escape our knowledge." [130] This is
obviously a question the reader must decide for himself. If he

believes that there is a poetic truth, inaccessible to rational re-
futation or confirmation, he will not find it hard to accept the
major theme of the *Duino Elegies*. If he does not, no commentator, not even Rilke himself, will convince him.

For almost seven years the concluding words of the *Fourth
Elegy*, "beyond description," were the last words Rilke wrote in
the cycle. There were times when he feared he would never finish
it. Castle Duino had been destroyed in the war, and where in
postwar Germany could he hope to find the right conditions for
a work of such immense concentration? "I am homesick for the
right place," he wrote Princess Taxis in January, 1920, "the place
of the *Elegies* which I am still waiting, longing for: quiet, care
according to my precise needs, nature, solitude, and no people for
half a year. When will this be?" [131]

It was to be two years later in the little Swiss Château Muzot,
situated in the Valais, "an incomparable landscape" where Spain
and Provence are strangely blended and which "offers manifold
equivalents and correspondences to our inner world." [132] Paul
Valéry, who visited him there, was oppressed by the "terrible
solitude" of the little tower and by the gloomy mountains sur-
rounding it. But Rilke, although he ordinarily preferred open
country, felt that the mountains of the Valais created space: "like
a Rodin statue which lives in its own spaciousness and exudes
it." [133] This feeling constituted an important element in his love
for the "magic" of this landscape, for what he was looking for
was an outer equivalent for the space within, the "inner-world-
space":

> One space spreads through all creatures equally—
> inner-world-space. Birds quietly fly and go
> right through us. Oh, I that want to grow,
> I look outside and in me grows the tree.[134]

> Durch alle Wesen reicht der *eine* Raum:
> Weltinnenraum. Die Vögel fliegen still
> durch uns hindurch. O, der ich wachsen will,
> ich seh hinaus, und *in* mir wächst der Baum.[135]

Impressionable as he was, the fact that he had at last found the
place where his inner world and the world around him were in

balance undoubtedly helped him to re-enter into the spirit of the *Elegies*. But that was not the only reason. Before he could complete the cycle he had to find a way out of the impasse he had reached in the *Fourth Elegy*, where in his consequent despair about the human condition he had given up man. Before he could go on he had to bring man back. Somehow he had to justify human existence, had to

> discover some pure, contained,
> narrow, human, own little strip of orchard
> in between river and rock! [136]

> Fänden auch wir ein reines, verhaltenes, schmales
> Menschliches, einen unseren Streifen Fruchtlands
> zwischen Strom und Gestein.[137]

In a world of dolls and angels he had to find a place for man, had to discover a mediate position. Having rejected divine mediation he found the mediator in the realm of poetry. Poetry is transformation. The poet transforms the world into the word. Through the miracle of human speech he reveals the symbolic character of reality and replaces the transitory event by the lasting symbol, hence: "all that remains is the work of poets" (Hölderlin).

> Are we, perhaps, here just for saying: House,
> Bridge, Fountain, Gate, Jug, Olive tree, Window,—
> possibly: Pillar, Tower? . . . .[138]

> Sind wir vielleicht *hier*, um zu sagen: Haus,
> Brücke, Brunnen, Tor, Krug, Obstbaum, Fenster,—
> höchstens: Säule, Turm. . . .[139]

Again the ellipses indicate that he has reached the end of the sayable. Saying is not enough. We must feel what we say so intensely that the word becomes flesh. We must praise the world to the angel—"praising: that's it"—we must tell him things, show him "how happy a thing can be, how guileless and ours." For

> These things that live on departure
> understand when you praise them: fleeting, they look for
> rescue through something in us, the most fleeting of all.[140]

Und diese, von Hingang
lebenden Dinge verstehn, daß du sie rühmst; vergänglich,
traun sie ein Rettendes uns, den Vergänglichsten, zu.[141]

The ability to transform the world of things into the world of symbols, the concrete into the abstract, the visible into invisible vibrations of the heart, is a uniquely human gift. It distinguishes man from all other creatures we know, and it distinguishes the poet from other men, in so far at least as to be a poet means to possess this gift to an unusual degree. The poet is thus the most representative man, "poetry the mother tongue of mankind."

By transforming the visible world into invisible vibrations, the poet obeys an urgent command of nature, for:

> Nature, and the objects of our environment and usage, are but frail, ephemeral things; yet, as long as we are here, they are *our* possession and our friendship, knowing our wretchedness and our joy, just as they were the familiars of our ancestors. Thus it . . . [befits] us not only not to pollute and degrade the Actual, but, precisely because of the transitoriness which it shares with us, we should seize these things and appearances with the most fervent comprehension and transform them. Transform them? Yes, for such is our task: to impress this fragile transient earth so sufferingly, so passionately upon our hearts that its essence shall rise up again, invisible, in us. *We are the bees of the Invisible.*[142]

In these often quoted words to his Polish translator, Rilke stated the second major theme of the *Elegies*: the will-to-transformation. It forms the leitmotiv of the *Seventh* and *Ninth Elegies* and is demonstrated in the *Sonnets*. Lou Salomé thought the *Ninth Elegy* was "the most powerful and, at the same time, the gentlest of all," [143] an opinion shared by Guardini, who comments that, "if one considers the elegies as a whole, one gains the impression that it is the *Ninth* that stands in the happiest inner equilibrium, full of beauty and confidence." [144] The two poles of the rhythmic event that gave rise to the *Elegies* lie at the *Fourth* and and the *Ninth*. Between the lament of the *Fourth* and the praise of the *Ninth* the Duino cycle oscillates. It is quite true that there is more lament than praise in the *Elegies*, but if the *Sonnets* are taken into account as well—and this must be done, since the two

cycles belong together—the total effect of Rilke's major poetry is
affirmation, not despair.

In the aforementioned letter Rilke goes on to say that the
Elegies show "the perpetual transformation of beloved and tangi-
ble things into the invisible vibration and excitability of our
nature." [145] This idea is easy to understand. It becomes more difficult when he talks of "new frequencies" which are thus "introduced into the vibration spheres of the universe" and quite paradoxical when he adds (to be sure only parenthetically) that,
"since the various materials in the cosmos are only the results of
different rates of vibration, we are preparing in this way, not only
intensities of a spiritual kind, but—who knows?—new substances,
metals, nebulae and stars." [146]

Miss Butler rightly points out that this extended concept of
transformation (a better term would be transubstantiation) is
"hardly a consummation devoutly to be wished from [Rilke's]
point of view, but rather a vicious circle, if not a *reductio ad
absurdum*." [147] Simenauer, too, thinks that "apart from being a
magnificent poetic image" it has no validity.

It should be stressed, however, that from the manner in which
he introduced this idea it is clear that Rilke considered it merely
a hypothesis, something that might be taken into account, for
who knows how far our feeling reaches, and:

> who shall calculate
> what in pure space its consequences are,
> where some whit more of lightness or of weight
> can start a system or displace a star? [148]

> Und ists Gefühl: wer weiß, wie weit es reicht
> und was es in dem reinen Raum ergiebt,
> in dem ein kleines Mehr von schwer und leicht
> Welten bewegt und einen Stern verschiebt.[149]

But transubstantiation is not the theme of the *Elegies*. The theme
of the *Elegies* is transformation. It is our task—"whosoever we
are"—to transform the visible world into invisible vibrations of
the heart.

Some commentators have suggested that Rilke's emphasis on
transformation as one of the basic processes in the universe is a

reflection of modern scientific thought, possibly influenced by Rilke's interest in mathematics. Holthusen, for example, finds that "Rilke's ideas are strangely reminiscent of certain theories of modern physics," [150] and Mason says that Rilke *lived* what Einstein *thought*. That there are similarities between Rilke's conception of transformation and certain scientific theories current today is undeniable. In *The Mysterious Universe* Sir James Jeans says that

> . . . if we accept the astronomical evidence of the ages of the stars and the physical evidence of the highly penetrating radiation as jointly establishing that matter can really be annihilated, or rather transformed into radiation, then this transformation becomes one of the fundamental processes of the universe . . . for ever solid matter melts into insubstantial radiation: for ever the tangible changes into the intangible.[151]

However, it would certainly be wrong to assume that Rilke's urgent command "will transformation" was in any way influenced by modern scientific theories. All that can be said is that his intuitive insight into the nature of reality coincided with the most advanced scientific thought of his age. This may be one more reason for the wide appeal of his poetry. Both his psychological insights into the nature of man and his intuitive grasp of the nature of reality satisfy the modern mind.

The theme of transformation stated in the *Duino Elegies* found its most convincing expression in the *Sonnets to Orpheus*. In the god of the double kingdom Rilke saw a symbol of his own existence. And through an act of complete identification symbol and reality became so closely integrated that the incredible happened: the Orphic myth came to life again.

7 Orpheus

Patience, Patience
Patience dans l'azur!
Chaque atome de silence
Est la chance d'un fruit mûr!

Patience, patience
Patience in the blue sky!
Every atom of silence
is the chance of a ripe fruit!
Paul Valéry, *La Palme*

During the final months of Rilke's long search for the source of the *Elegies* two events occurred that had a catalytic effect on him: he came across the poetry of Paul Valéry and he learned about the death of a talented young girl. Although disconnected, these two events (to which may perhaps be added a chance encounter with an engraving of Orpheus in a shop window) fused Rilke's long-pent-up poetic energy and released the Orphic uprush at Muzot in February, 1922.

Valéry's example in particular quickened Rilke's sensibilities and stimulated his creative imagination, so much so that a French Rilke scholar thinks "the key to the Elegies and Sonnets can be found with Valéry." [1] This opinion certainly oversimplifies a complex relationship, but there is no doubt that Rilke owes a great deal to Valéry, whose influence is comparable to J. P. Jacobsen's during Rilke's formative period, or to that of Kierkegaard, Rodin, Baudelaire, and Cézanne at the time of *Malte* and *New Poems*.

On September 8, 1921, Rilke mentioned in a letter to Princess

Taxis that he was reading Valéry, whose "magnificent *Cimetière Marin*" he had shown her; "other things by him that I did not know; he has been silent for about twenty years, occupied with mathematics; only since 1915 are there again poems by him '*en recompense de la longue attente de sa vie.*' " [2] Then he quoted Valéry's lines on patience, or rather misquoted them, for where Valéry says "every atom of silence" Rilke makes him say "every drop of silence." This unconscious slip of the pen goes far to show the difference between the two poets, between the intellectual nature of Valéry's genius and the visual character of Rilke's poetry.

Valéry and Rilke represented diametrically opposite types. Valéry believed in pure intellect (*"je mets le plaisir intellectuel au-dessus du plaisir poétique"*), Rilke in pure feeling. Valéry was contemptuous of every form of enthusiasm (*"l'enthousiasme n'est pas un état d'âme d'écrivain"*); Rilke wrote his greatest poetry in a state of exaltation. Valéry worshiped at the shrine of Apollo. Rilke was a devoted disciple of Dionysus. And yet a deep affinity existed between the Latin intellectualist and the German sensualist, which made them feel that they complemented each other, for, although they started from different premises, their aims were the same: they both believed that art was the principle of order in an otherwise meaningless universe. This common faith caused "an immediate and mutual sympathy" to arise between Valéry and Rilke:

> We were two poets, but as different as we could possibly be and almost inconceivable one to the other—and yet because of this difference, we both miraculously experienced the need to get to know each other so that, through an exchange of friendly admiration, we would in effect understand ourselves better.[3]

One reason for Rilke's admiration for Valéry was undoubtedly the latter's long, self-imposed silence. That a great poet had the patience to wait more than twenty years for his art to mature struck him as an act of pure heroism. He never failed to mention it, for was not Valéry's example proof that genuine art requires severe self-discipline, that patience is the secret of wisdom, and that *"tout peut naître ici bas d'une attente infinie"*?

Thus, during the winter of 1921, while Rilke waited in his

solitary Swiss tower for the reappearance of the Duino angels, Valéry became a symbol for him and a promise of final fulfillment. He read everything the French poet had written, including the two Socratic dialogues just off the press: *Eupalinos ou l'architecte* and *L'âme et la danse*. Through Valéry's lucid prose he became conscious of ideas that had long been germinating and now fell into a pattern. Suddenly he knew he had found what he had been waiting for: "I was alone and waited. My whole work waited. Then, one day, I read Valéry and knew that my waiting was over." [4]

Among Valéry's ideas that aroused Rilke's creative imagination two are of particular importance: that expressed by Socrates in *Eupalinos* concerning the magic power of Orpheus "to build temples of wisdom with words," and that in *L'âme et la danse* about the metamorphic power of dancing.

Dancing is transformation. "Don't you feel," Valéry makes Socrates say, "that it is the pure act of metamorphosis?" [5] The rhythmic event reveals the essence of things. Unlike an actor a dancer *represents* nothing but *is* everything: love and the sea, life itself and thought. Dancing is a dream, but a dream impregnated with symmetry and order. It is controlled ecstasy and gives us deeper insights into the meaning of existence than "hard and upright reason." In the sleep called life over which reason draws its veil of illusion the dance opens vistas onto a higher reality: "Who knows what august Laws may be dreaming here that they have put on clear countenances and are united in a design that will reveal to mortals how reality, unreality, and intellect may be fused and combined by the power of the Muses?" [6]

In the lovely movements of Athitke, Socrates and his companions find the only effective antidote against the disease of ennui, "that weariness created by life itself and having no other cause than the clairvoyance of the living creature." [7] Drugging our senses or escaping into utopian illusions is no cure for this malady. States of intoxication induced by wine, madness, love, or hate necessarily end in disgust, but those "caused by actions that bring our whole body into play conduct us to a strange and admirable state." [8] Although we are then beyond ourselves we are also in closer touch with reality because "our body plays the universality of our soul." In this state the dancer experiences all the mysteries of absence and presence, of being and nonbeing, of darkness and light.

While Rilke was still under the impression these words made on him, a message reached him that lit the fuse and set off the long-delayed poetic explosion. A friend of his, Frau Gertrud Ouckama Knoop, sent him a journal she had kept during the long and fatal illness of her daughter Wera, a "lovely child . . . who began with dancing and excited wonder in all who then saw her through her body's . . . inborn art of motion and transformation." [9] Wera had died of a strange glandular disease at the age of eighteen, and although Rilke had only seen her once or twice, when she was a child, the news of her death came as a profound shock to him. In a flash of revelation he saw that here was the figure in which all his ideas about life and death, art and transformation, converged. A child almost, and yet familiar with the deepest mysteries of life.

> How wonderful [he wrote to Wera's mother], how unique, how incomparable is a human being! Now, suddenly, when everything was allowed to consume itself, there arose what might otherwise have sufficed for a long here(where?)-after, there arose this excess of light in the girl's heart, and within it appear, so infinitely illuminated, the two extreme borders of her pure insight; *this*, that pain is a mistake, an obtuse misunderstanding springing up in the physical, that drives its wedge, its stony wedge, into the unity of heaven and earth—and, on the other hand, this intimate oneness of her universally open heart with this unity of existing and persisting world, this acceptance of life, this joyful, this affectionate, this to the last degree capable appropriation of herself into the here and now—ah, *only* into the here and now?! No (what she could not know in these first attacks of upheaval and parting!)—into the *whole*, into a far more than here. Oh, how, how she loved, how she reached out with the antennae of her heart beyond all that is comprehensible and embraceable here—during those sweet hovering pauses in pain that, full of the dream of recovery, were still granted her. [10]

This letter, written a few weeks before the storm of the *Sonnets* broke, foreshadowed what was to come. It shows the violence of Rilke's emotional response to the news of Wera's death:

The antennae feel the far antennae
and the empty distance bore.[11]

Die Antennen fühlen die Antennen,
und die leere Ferne trug . . .[12]

Finally, on February 7, 1922, his hands still trembling with excitement, Rilke informed Wera's mother that

> . . . in a few thrillingly impassioned days, when I was really thinking of settling down to something else, these *Sonnets* were given me. You will understand at first glance why you must be the first person to possess them. For tenuous though the relationship be [only one *Sonnet*, the penultimate *Twenty-fourth*, summons Wera's own figure into the rhapsody that is dedicated to her], it nevertheless governs and animates the march of the whole sequence and—even if so secretly that I only became aware of it little by little—inspired with its presence this irresistible and convulsive birth.[13]

He called them *Sonnets to Orpheus*, for he felt that, although Wera's youthful figure had inspired them, it was the "singing god" whose mouthpiece he had been. Hence:

We should not try
to find other names. Once and for all,
it's Orpheus when there's song.[14]

Wir sollen uns nicht mühn
um andre Namen. Ein für alle Male
ists Orpheus, wenn es singt.[15]

And yet it took some time before even Rilke understood the true significance of the *Sonnets*. He was inclined to consider them at first as a by-product of the *Elegies*, the overture to the great work. And some of his commentators have expressed the same opinion; MacIntyre, for instance, mentions the "powerful and mystic *Duino Elegies* and their by-product the *Sonnets to Orpheus*." [16] Occasionally Rilke even compared the *Sonnets* to his *Life of Mary*, a group of poems written concurrently with the first *Elegies*, but reflecting a much earlier phase of his poetry. In the jubilant letter to Princess Taxis, written at Muzot on February 11, 1922, in which he announced the completion of the *Elegies*, he failed to mention the *Sonnets* entirely, although in a subsequent letter he told her that during some inspired hours preceding and following the *Elegies* he had written fifty sonnets. In the same casual manner he informed his publisher that, "just as during the writing of the first *Elegies* at Duino in inspired marginal hours the *Life of Mary* resulted, so this time, coincidentally with the uprush of the great poems, a minor collection of emerging work was given me as a natural consequence of abundance." [17] Three months later he still spoke of the *Sonnets* as a "minor work," an "almost involuntary, subsidiary current" that had accompanied the tidal wave of the *Elegies*. However, he was gradually forced to revise that opinion and to admit that "he himself could enter only gradually into the spirit of the message expressed in the *Sonnets*."

His first insight into the true significance of the *Sonnets* came when he read them to Princess Taxis, whom he had invited to Muzot because he wanted her to be the first to hear the completed cycle of the *Elegies*, which he had dedicated to her ten years before. She responded to both cycles with wholehearted admiration and had as much praise for the *Sonnets* as for the *Elegies*. He realized then, for the first time, that he had treated the *Sonnets* rather lightly, "compared with their older and more sublime sisters, the *Elegies*," [18] but that her "marvelous manner of listening" had opened his eyes to their "true significance." To another friend he wrote that he had read the Princess the *Elegies* one day and the *Sonnets* the next, and he added that "only as I listened to them did I sense their inner unity and their connection with the *Elegies* which they parallel magnificently. . . . The Princess was astonished and I, if I may be quite frank, I too was astonished." [19]

He had good reason to be astonished, for the *Sonnets* demonstrated, as nothing before in his work, the truth of his *Umschlag* hypothesis, that sudden and wholly mysterious reversal of woe to beatitude, lament to praise. He had long known that in his work "lamentation had frequently preponderated," but he had also known that "one is only entitled to make such frequent use of the strings of lamentation if one is resolved to play on them, later, the whole of that triumphant jubilation that swells up behind everything hard and painful and endured and without which our voices are incomplete." [20]

The true significance of the *Sonnets to Orpheus* lies not in the fact that they parallel certain movements of the *Elegies*, but that they complete Rilke's world view. For it is difficult to see how he could have finished the *Elegies*, after the impasse he had reached in the *Fourth*, had it not been for the *Sonnets*, which were "like molten lava issuing from the depths of Rilke's mind and ejecting in the process petrified blocks formed during a previous eruption." [21] One may agree or disagree with Mason's opinion: "If the *Duino Elegies* had been Rilke's last word one would be forced to conclude that he was really a thoroughly satanic hero of individualistic arrogance, of negative misanthropic isolation; as such he would have to be placed next to Leopardi, Baudelaire, Flaubert and Nietzsche." [22] But there is no doubt:

> Only in the *Sonnets to Orpheus* do his words of sacrificial love, serving humility, continuous surrender achieve a real meaning, a convincing affirmation. Only here and not in the *Elegies* there happens, almost unnoticed and by the way, what he wanted to experience all his life. The *Sonnets* show what giving virtue means as hardly any work in world poetry.[23]

It is quite true that Rilke always considered the *Elegies* his major work, but as he entered more deeply into the spirit of the *Sonnets* he realized that, while he was struggling with his angel, something very mysterious had happened: the antinomies of his existence had been transformed into a rhythmic event. Orpheus had transcended the angel. "The more we are outwardly severed and cut off from tradition, the more it becomes decisive whether we are able to remain open and receptive for the most secret and oldest traditions of mankind. The *Sonnets to Orpheus* are—thus I understand them more and more—an effort in this deep direction performed in a final obedience." [24]

The ancient enmity between art and existence which he had not succeeded in transcending in the *Elegies*, for "even there, even there, alas even there—the contradiction between life and art somehow exists," [25] is absent in the *Sonnets*. Gone is the tension between outer and inner world, body and soul, life and death. Everything is harmony, rhythmic equilibrium, a pure relation of forces. The act of breathing has become symbolic for the human condition:

> Breathing, invisible poem! That great
> world-space, at each inhalation
> exchanged for this human existence. Counter-weight
> of my rhythmical realization.[26]

> Atmen, du unsichtbares Gedicht!
> Immerfort um das eigne
> Sein rein eingetauschter Weltraum. Gegengewicht,
> in dem ich mich rhythmisch ereigne.[27]

At last Rilke's long quest for the "fundamental equation of life," which had led him to explore such extreme positions as those symbolized by doll and angel, had been answered. In Orpheus, the "singing god" of the double kingdom, he had found the symbol for the continuous transformation of the world into rhythmic vibrations; and in the figure of the dancer, both an illustration of that process and the assurance that at the highest level the dichotomy between art and life is resolved:

> For song, as taught by you, is not desire,
> not wooing of something finally attained;
> Song is existence.[28]

> Gesang, wie du ihn lehrst, ist nicht Begehr,
> nicht Werbung um ein endlich noch Erreichtes;
> Gesang ist Dasein.[29]

By identifying himself with one of the oldest of myths Rilke had found the clue to his life.

> In the transparent radiance of Greek symbolism was to be found the apotheosis of art as a cosmic, creative, transforming force which Rilke had tried to achieve in the God of *The Book of Hours* and the angels of *Duino Elegies*. . . . The functions and the destiny of Orpheus were clearly a mythical counterpart of Rilke's, and therefore of all poets and of poetry itself.[30]

The perceptive reader of these poems is transported into a state of rhythmic equipoise. Through their sound magic and their anti-thetical structure (Holthusen compares it to the form of the fugue) he experiences the flux and counterflux of life and, although constantly reminded of the existence of opposites, is made to feel

> how rested all things are:
> shadow and fall of light,
> blossom and book.[31]

> Alles ist ausgeruht:
> Dunkel und Helligkeit,
> Blume und Buch.[32]

This almost effortless reconciliation of opposites in the "realm of praise" is the secret of what Lou Salomé has called the "strangely helpful, almost healing" power of these poems. It is not without justification that an American Rilke scholar calls the *Sonnets to Orpheus* "the most original contribution to eschatological thought in recent times. Through the role of the 'double kingdom' where life and death impinge, through Orpheus standing on its threshold, intercession is obtained, not through atonement, but through justificatory praise of God's creature world." [33]

The rhythmic event expressed in the *Sonnets* passed through two phases. In the first phase, from February 1 to February 5, Rilke wrote twenty-five *Sonnets* of the first part as well as six related poems. Two days later he sent a copy to Wera's mother, asking her to receive them kindly as a memorial for her daughter. Apart from minor alterations, one substitution, and one addition, the sequence of these sonnets has remained unchanged. The second phase lasted from February 15 to February 18 and resulted in the twenty-nine *Sonnets* of the second part and in fifteen related poems. In grouping them Rilke did a good deal of rearranging; thus the first poem of the second part is actually one of the last he wrote. In general the sequence of the second part is less closely knit than that of the first. Between those two Orphic phases falls the completion of the *Elegies*. The elegiac mood was thus preceded and followed by the Orphic upsurge. During the "hurricane in the spirit" that climaxed Rilke's work, the Orphic predominated. "Not the world seen through the angel but that sung by Orpheus is Rilke's real achievement." [34]

Only in the first part a close connection with the legendary singer exists: "A great arc stretches from the opening to the concluding two *Sonnets:* the arc from the rising of Orpheus to his decline; symmetrically contrasted are the second and the penultimate *Sonnet:* Wera's evocation and the description of her death." [35]

In the second part the motif of the "singing god" has receded. Here the central theme is the will to transformation: "But a great arc stretches across this sequence also, connecting the first and the last *Sonnet* through the common motif of breathing which means the interchange of man and space: the first depicts the human situation as a rhythmic event, the last issues the command to metamorphosis, the will to rhythm." [36]

When Rilke talked about the *Sonnets to Orpheus* he often said that the thirteenth of the second part was the "closest to him and perhaps the most valid of all." Lou Salomé also called it "the most magnificent of the *Sonnets*," and many commentators have referred to it in similar terms. It may therefore serve as an illustration of Rilke's Orphic achievement although, like most of the *Sonnets*, it presents formidable difficulties to the translator:

Forestall all farewells, as though they were behind you
now, like the winter going at last.
For among winters one infinite winter will bind you
so that, out-wintering, your heart will always outlast.

Be ever dead in Eurydice—, mount with more singing
into the pure relation with a more celebrant tongue.
Here, among fleeting, be, in the realm of the vanishing,
Be a vibrating glass that shatters itself in its song.

Be—and yet know non-being's condition
that infinite source of your fervent vibration,
beat, just this once, to the fullest amount.

To the used-up as well as to the muffled and muted
store-rooms of nature, those sums that can't be computed,
count yourself joyfully in and destroy the account.[37]

Sei allem Abschied voran, als wäre er hinter
dir, wie der Winter, der eben geht.

Denn unter Wintern ist einer so endlos Winter,
daß, überwinternd, dein Herz überhaupt übersteht.

Sei immer tot in Eurydike—, singender steige,
preisender steige zurück in den reinen Bezug.
Hier, unter Schwindenden, sei, im Reiche der Neige,
sei ein klingendes Glas, das sich im Klang schon zerschlug.

Sei—und wisse zugleich des Nicht-Seins Bedingung,
den unendlichen Grund deiner innigen Schwingung,
daß du sie völlig vollziehst dieses einzige Mal.

Zu dem gebrauchten sowohl, wie zum dumpfen und stummen
Vorrat der vollen Natur, den unsäglichen Summen,
zähle dich jubelnd hinzu und vernichte die Zahl.[38]

The most striking quality of this *Sonnet* is its exhortative tone: it adjures and entreats. All its statements are evocative gestures summoning the reader to collect himself. In this respect it is typical of the entire cycle. As he enters it the reader is faced with the imperative challenge to change his life, to "will transformation." For the Rilkean *Sonnet* does not merely affirm, it adjures. Again and again the reader is urged to enter into a rhythmic relation, to "turn, if drinking is bitter, into wine," to "dance the orange," to "be a vibrating glass." These urgent commands to metamorphosis are in effect commands to a rebirth from within. Do not be distracted by outer events, Rilke implores the reader, listen to their inner rhythm, descend to "that infinite source of your fervent vibration":

> murmur to the quiet earth: I'm flowing.
> To the flowing water speak: I am.[39]
>
> zu der stillen Erde sag: Ich rinne.
> Zu dem raschen Wasser sprich: Ich bin.[40]

Transformation through the spirit of adjuration: that is the aim of the *Sonnets to Orpheus*.

In the *Elegies* Rilke had lamented the fact that "staying is nowhere," that "we live our lives forever taking leave"; now he exhorts us to "leave our farewells behind us," to anticipate them, for by so doing we transcend them. He reminds us of winter, the season of farewells. Winter is finally going, but it will have served its purpose only if we have accepted it wholeheartedly as a necessary phase in the cycle of seasons; if we have seen in it not an end only, but a beginning as well; if we have entered so fully into it that it has become part of us; then "our out-wintering heart will always outlast." Four times the word "winter" appears in the first quatrain, and the transformation it undergoes is a good illustration of the metamorphic process celebrated in the *Sonnets*.

At its first mention it refers to a concrete event, to the winter of 1921–22 which was nearing its end when Rilke wrote this *Sonnet*. But through the repetition it loses its concreteness. First it becomes more general: "among winters" is a generalization of winter. Then it disappears completely: "an infinite winter" refers to the essence of "wintriness" (in his translation Leishman uses this term), to all that is negative and destructive in life. Last, in an "out-wintering" heart, winter has become a quality of feeling, has been transformed into a vibration of the heart. The threefold repetition of "over" (*über*) in the last line of the first quatrain— "*überwinternd, überhaupt, übersteht*"—adds a sense of triumph to the thought of transcending negation.

This thought is carried on in the second quatrain. Again we are urged to anticipate the end: death, the winter of life, the last farewell—to anticipate it as Orpheus anticipated it when he "died in Eurydice." Her departure, which went through the center of his heart, made him the "singing god," the transformer of death. "To be dead in Eurydice" means to have made one beloved person, whose death was our death, an element of our life; to have impressed our grief so deeply upon our heart that it burst into song. The idea that from supreme suffering music arose Rilke had expressed before, when, at the end of the *First Elegy*, he had asked:

Is the story in vain, how once, in the mourning for Linos,
venturing earliest music pierced barren numbness, and how,
in the horrified space an almost deified youth
suddenly quitted for ever, emptiness first
felt the vibration that now charms us and comforts and helps? [41]

Ist die Sage umsonst, daß einst in der Klage um Linos
wagende erste Musik dürre Erstarrung durchdrang;
daß erst im erschrockenen Raum, dem ein beinah göttlicher Jüngling

plötzlich für immer enttrat, das Leere in jene
Schwingung geriet, die uns jetzt hinreißt und tröstet und hilft.[42]

In the *Sonnets* it is Orpheus, torn to pieces by the Maenads, who
bestowed the gift of poetry on man:

> O you god that has vanished! You infinite track!
> Only because dismembering hatred dispersed you
> are we hearers to-day and a mouth which else Nature would lack.[43]

> O du verlorener Gott! Du unendliche Spur!
> Nur weil dich reißend zuletzt die Feindschaft verteilte,
> sind wir die Hörenden jetzt und ein Mund der Natur.[44]

It is Orpheus who, by dying in Eurydice, proved that if we
anticipate death we complete the cycle of Being. "Once more,"
comments Leishman, "Rilke suggests a new interpretation of some
famous lines:

> So shalt thou feed on death that feeds on man
> and, death once dead, there's no more dying then." [45]

The image of the "vibrating glass that shatters itself in its song"
sums up the Orphic destiny: to be carried across the threshold of
death through the power of music.

The phenomena evoked in the octet —farewell, winter, Eurydice, death —and the passionate plea to take them to our heart so
that all their negation is changed into jubilant affirmation state
the sonnet's theme, which, in the sestet, is restated canonically.
Being and nonbeing are interdependent states. Life exists only
because death exists; by trying to exclude one we impoverish the
other. Hence the command: "Be—and yet know nonbeing's condition," for this knowledge alone enables us to experience the unity
of being. But knowing it is not enough—"praising, that's it"—
like Orpheus we must praise the duo-unity of life and death, "that
infinite source of our fervent vibration," must assume it so pas-
sionately that it will gradually become apparent.

True, as finite beings we can experience it only once. All the
more reason to "beat just this once to the fullest amount," i.e., to
realize completely our unique individuality. For in moments of
intense self-realization we, the most fleeting of all, get a foretaste
of permanence, or, in the words of the *Ninth Elegy:*

> Just once,
> everything, only for once. Once and no more. And we, too,
> once. And never again. But this once,
> having been once on earth—can it ever be cancelled? [46]

> *Ein* Mal
> jedes, nur *ein* Mal. *Ein* Mal und nicht mehr. Und wir auch
> *ein* Mal. Nie wieder. Aber dieses
> *ein* Mal gewesen zu sein, wenn auch nur *ein* Mal:
> *irdisch* gewesen zu sein, scheint nicht widerrufbar.[47]

Again we note that Rilke's adjuratory power transforms the meaning of "once" to its opposite and thus affirms the paradox that the temporary is the permanent. We also note that Rilke preaches not self-surrender, but self-fulfillment; he thinks that we can enter into a true relation not by losing our identity, but by fully achieving it. This shows again that he is not a mystic, either in the Western or in the Eastern sense, although his concern with the nature of being and his insistence on transformation as a means of attaining it have a decidedly Eastern ring. "At times, one feels, he is nearer to the East than to the West." . . .[48] On the other hand, his praise of the uniqueness and value of the individual is an unmistakably Western trait. To experience "pure being" is indeed his aim, as it is the aim of the Eastern mystics, but unlike them he tries to reach it with his senses, not in spite of them. His method is spiritualization, not mortification, of the flesh. He seeks transcendence in immanence. This paradox is beautifully stated in the conclusion of the *Sonnet*, when he exhorts the reader to "count himself joyfully in" to the vast sums of nature and then to "destroy the account."

The figure of the dancer is an illustration of this paradox, for during the ecstasy of the dance the dancer attains both complete self-expression and complete self-surrender. Hence, like Orpheus, the dancer is a mediator: he is an artist who thrusts figures into space and a mystic who experiences pure being. Dancing is both an art and a cult.

In Orpheus and Wera, in the mythical poet-god and in the young dancer whose death went straight to his heart, Rilke found two mediating symbols in which the antinomies of his life could be reconciled. They filled the void left between terrifying angels and lifeless dolls and provided a symbolic center in place of the close, warm, human center that, he knew, was denied him:

> For we truly live our lives in symbol,
> and with tiny paces move our nimble
> clocks beside our real day and night.[49]

> denn wir leben wahrhaft in Figuren.
> Und mit kleinen Schritten gehn die Uhren
> neben unserm eigentlichen Tag.[50]

The Orphic myth showed that life and death are interdependent states, linked by the transforming power of love; the dancer, that through controlled ecstasy we can experience the unity of being. The joyous wonder Rilke felt that these insights had been granted him is reflected in the *Sonnets*. The spirit of reconciliation permeates the whole cycle.

In the first part the dominant figure is Orpheus. When his song, "a tall tree," rises in the ear everything falls silent; even the wild beasts listen, are transformed into hearing. Wera's death becomes a rhythmic event: it causes the poet's soul to vibrate, as a glass vibrates when the right chord is struck. He feels she "sleeps in him." The shock of her death tears away the veil that separates the living from the dead, and lets him see the unity of being. Like Orpheus he wants to enter into it, but then the question arises: Can a mortal poet follow the "singing god"? Man's mind is discord; how can he penetrate the narrow lyre? It is easy for the god to transform his life into song, but is it possible for us who do not even know when we exist? Can we ever become a "mouth of nature"? The answer, given in the *Ninth Sonnet, I,* reads:

> Only who ventured to raise
> shadowed his lyre,
> dare to the infinite praise
> softly aspire.

> Only who tasted their own
> flower with the sleeping
> holds the most fugitive tone
> ever in keeping.

What though the form in the pond
fades without traces:
Know it is there.

Not till raised here and beyond
are all the voices
eternal and fair.[51]

Nur wer die Leier schon hob
auch unter Schatten,
darf das unendliche Lob
ahnend erstatten.

Nur wer mit Toten vom Mohn
aß, von dem ihren,
wird nicht den leisesten Ton
wieder verlieren.

Mag auch die Spieglung im Teich
oft uns verschwimmen:
Wisse das Bild.

Erst in dem Doppelbereich
werden die Stimmen
ewig und mild.[52]

The example of Orpheus, who ventured to visit the dead and thus earned the right to proffer "infinite praise," is recalled in the octet. It is this example which the poet must follow. Like Orpheus he must descend into the underworld of the soul, must plumb the depths of despair. Only if he does that, only after he has conquered negation, will he have gained an indestructible insight, a steady image amidst the changing patterns of life, for:

Change though the world may as fast
as cloud-collections,
home to the changeless at last
fall all perfections.[53]

Wandelt sich rasch auch die Welt
wie Wolkengestalten,
alles Vollendete fällt
heim zum Uralten.[54]

The imperative conclusion of the first tercet—"know the image"—shows that there is no doubt in Rilke's mind: the unity of life and death *can* be known. There is no doubt, either, that only if a poet takes this unity as his basic frame of reference will his utterances attain eternal validity.

It is a sign of the powerful verbal magic that radiates from the *Sonnets* that most readers respond positively to these Rilkean assumptions. And even those who reject them—Miss Butler, for example, says that "no human power can stay or hasten the course of nature's cyclic rhythm. The strongest magic ever brewed, the most dynamic spiritual energy, the divinest poetry are so much waste energy here"—admit that the *Sonnets to Orpheus* "share with the legendary founder of that religion a magical, musical, spell-binding power." [55] The secret of that power lies in the almost perfect fusion of sound and symbol, form and content.

Images and sound patterns abound even in Rilke's early verse, but they are not well integrated, tend to run wild, and hence do not always carry conviction. Even the *Book of Hours* suffers from an uncontrolled abundance of metaphors and metric-musical effects. In *New Poems* a controlling intelligence is clearly at work, so much so that at times one feels it endangers the spontaneity of the spirit. In *Duino Elegies* images and ideas preponderate to the detriment of sound, but "in many of the *Sonnets to Orpheus* and some of the last lyrics, Rilke appears as the supreme craftsman in sound married to image." [56]

David I. Masson, who carried out a close analysis of the complex sound pattern of the *Ninth Sonnet*, concluded that,

> . . . considered from the point of view of the intellectual or spatial images which are derived from the associations of its vowels, the poem starts in the heavy darkness of the "chthonic" underworld, and gradually, modulating from dull A-vowels and deep O's through vowels expressing depth alone to vowels of depth-and-height, expands and frees itself from the restrictions of time and space, until in the last tercet it has reached the *speciem aeternitatis.* Thus Rilke's expression, by images and statements, of the development of the Orpheus-figure, is reinforced, with something which looks like conscious though inspired craftsmanship, by the sensuous pattern of the poem.[57]

The keynote of the whole poem is contained in the "stressed and sound-contrasting word" *Doppelbereich* (double kingdom) in the opening line of the second tercet:

Upon this poetic rising from the dead and ascension up to heaven—
early in the second tercet's delicate-tinted apotheosis of the voices of
life—into the sestet's muted high strings—strikes (the last contrast)
heralded only by the D of DEM, the sombre dumb-bell, the double-
beat of the timpani, DOPPEL-; followed by the short light beat of
the -BE- and the golden opening-out triumphal blast of -REICH: the
twofold domain where the dead and the living are one. There are
parallel effects in Beethoven.[58]

It need hardly be said that not every one of the fifty-five *Sonnets
to Orpheus* attains such a perfect union of sound and image. Rilke
himself felt that some had only served to conduct the poetic current and had remained empty. For that reason he had eliminated
one sonnet originally included in the first part and substituted the
charming spring poem (I, 21). Others pose considerable difficulties
to the understanding, either because they are obscure or because
they shock our moral susceptibilities. The *Sixteenth Sonnet* of the
second part, for example, has the puzzling ending:

> Only the dead dwell
> where they can drink the spring we hear,
> when the god silently beckons them, the dead.
>
> We are offered nothing but noise instead.
> And the lamb's more silent instinct's clear
> when it begs us for its bell.[59]
>
> Nur der Tote trinkt
> aus der hier von uns gehörten Quelle,
> wenn der Gott ihm schweigend winkt, dem Toten.
> *Uns* wird nur das Lärmen angeboten.
>
> Und das Lamm erbittet seine Schelle
> aus dem stilleren Instinkt.[60]

This, Miss Butler comments, is nonsense, albeit "Orphic nonsense"; and she goes on to quote Jane Harrison, according to whom
the attempt of Orphic mystics "to utter the ineffable often verges
on imbecility." [61] Leishman, too, admits that he does not yet
"fully understand" the last two lines, but gives an interesting account of the place of the bell in the lives of animals in certain
regions in Germany where "every sheep and lamb, cow and calf,
had its own particular bell, and would often refuse to go out to

pasture until this bell had been duly fastened on its neck." [62] What significance this custom has in the *Sonnet*, Leishman does not say. Norbert Fürst, on the other hand, has no doubt about the meaning of these lines. The poet, he says, is here speaking of the dead, who in his hierarchy stand nearer to God than we do.

> In such an exposition of his world-view Rilke had to give a place to his beloved animals. That accounts for the strange final tercet, shared by the man and the lamb: *Uns* (we) emphasizes once more the super-ficiality of the living, in contrast to God (1–8), to the dead (9–11), in contrast even to the animal (13–14). The animals with which we are in contact are not noisy enough for us . . . so they let us supply them with the necessary means of noise. [63]

This interpretation still leaves unanswered the question why the lamb should wish to share in the noise of the human world. What does this strange wish imply? Or are we here confronted with another of Rilke's paradoxes: does the lamb beg for noise precisely because it has an instinct for silence? But perhaps this is one of those obscurities which demand "inclination rather than explanation."

A difficulty of another kind arises in connection with the *Eleventh Sonnet* of Part II. Here there is no question of obscurity. The meaning of this *Sonnet* is perfectly clear; it refers to "the man-ner in which, according to ancient hunting custom, in certain districts of the Karst, the peculiarly white rock-doves are scared out of their subterranean dwellings, by means of clothes carefully suspended into their caves and shaken in a particular way, and shot during their terrified escape." [64] Leishman comments that "[this custom] might seem to epitomize all that is most barbarous and brutal in human nature," [65] and yet Rilke says that "even this is right," for:

> *Killing is but one form of our wandering sadness . . .*
> Pure in the spirit serene
> is what happens to us. [66]

> *Töten ist eine Gestalt unseres wandernden Trauerns . . .*
> Rein ist im heiteren Geist,
> was an uns selber geschieht. [67]

This is a hard saying and hard to accept, even if we grant that Rilke saw in life and death not irreconcilable opposites but interdependent states, two phases in the rhythm of being. For, quite apart from the moral issue involved, killing would seem to be a violent interference in this rhythm; an interference coming from outside and letting a man-made death usurp the place of the great death that grows within. Rilke's insistence on praising every aspect of life, no matter how gruesome, and on subjecting it to the process of poetic transformation leads him sometimes to statements that we cannot accept unreservedly. This is the case here. As a poem the *Eleventh Sonnet, II,* is among the most beautiful he wrote. Its climactic line *"killing is but one form of our wandering sadness"* reverberates in our mind like some of the great lines in poetry. And yet, despite its beauty, uneasiness remains. The Keatsian equation "beauty is truth" assumes a dubious validity, and we cannot help wondering whether *that* is indeed all we need to know on earth.

But while this is essentially a question for philosophers to decide, for us,

> . . . living in this age of shifting foundations and looming catastrophes, when quacks are bawling their nostrums from every stall, it is worthwhile to consider very seriously this man who, though he might sometimes be gravely mistaken, spent a lifetime of such passionate insight and imagination *de novissimis,* concerning the last things; who reached frontiers and cross-roads that we too may be approaching and where we too will be compelled to pause and to decide. It is abundantly worthwhile to turn, not with cocky assurance and easy superiority, but with humility and a sincere desire to understand, from Rilke, *On the Heights,* proclaiming that, in what is important and essential, there is no such thing as injustice on the whole earth, to Rilke, *In the Depths,* writing to friends of the agonies of a life that seemed hardly supportable any longer, to Rilke on his death-bed, murmuring *Oh, but the hells. . . .*—to turn, and to try to decide whether, and if so, just where and how, he was wrong.[68]

There are thus enough questions left in the *Sonnets to Orpheus,* despite their jubilantly affirmative tone; there are muted sadness and lament underneath their praise. We are never given the impression that an optimist is speaking. Amidst the joyful acceptance

of all that exists we are constantly reminded of the precariousness
of the human condition:

> Anxiously we hanker for a hold,
> we, too young sometimes for what is old,
> and too old for what has never been.
>
> Only just when we praise with completeness,
> for we are, alas, branch, axe and sweetness
> of a peril ripening unseen.[69]
>
> Bang verlangen wir nach einem Halte,
> wir zu Jungen manchmal für das Alte
> und zu alt für das, was niemals war.
>
> Wir, gerecht nur, wo wir dennoch preisen,
> weil wir, ach, der Ast sind und das Eisen
> und das Süße reifender Gefahr.[70]

And yet, the total impact of these poems is a sense of liberation.
We feel the human spirit rising above doubt and despair; we feel
that for a while fate is in balance. Compared with this total impact
of the cycle the theme of the individual sonnet is almost unimportant. Whatever Rilke's magic conjures up: mirrors, unicorns,
flowers, gardens, roses, fountains, machines, the temple world of
Karnak, a Russian horse, or a nonexisting constellation, the effect
is a rhythmic realization, a vibration of the spirit that "charms us
and comforts and helps."

Like the *Chorus Mysticus* at the end of *Faust*, some of the *Son-
nets to Orpheus* reach into the realm of metaphysical revelation.
A tone of Goethean wisdom is unmistakable in the *Twenty-second,
I*, which, with its short lines, dactylic rhythm, and three-syllabic
rhymes of participial abstracts is surprisingly similar in form to
Goethe's most mature style:

> We wax for waning.
> Count, though, Time's journeying
> as but a little thing
> in the Remaining.
>
> End of unmeasured
> hasting will soon begin;
> only what's leisured
> leads us within.

Boys, don't be drawn too far
into attempts at flight,
into mere swiftness.—Look

how rested all things are:
shadow and fall of light,
blossom and book.[71]

Wir sind die Treibenden.
Aber den Schritt der Zeit,
nehmt ihn als Kleinigkeit
im immer Bleibenden.

Alles das Eilende
wird schon vorüber sein;
denn das Verweilende
erst weiht uns ein.

Knaben, o werft den Mut
nicht in die Schnelligkeit,
nicht in den Flugversuch.

Alles ist ausgeruht:
Dunkel und Helligkeit,
Blume und Buch.[72]

But while in the *Chorus Mysticus* "the indescribable *becomes*
event, with Rilke everything *is* rested, and the sound-curve of his
verses clearly descends from the bright vowels at the beginning to
the dark vowels at the end, whereas Goethe's poem lifts us up-
wards."[73] Goethe thinks of happiness rising; Rilke feels

the emotion
that almost startles
when happiness *falls.*

die Rührung,
die uns beinah bestürzt,
wenn ein Glückliches *fällt.*[74]

8   O Pure Contradiction

> Rose, o pure contradiction, delight
> to be nobody's sleep beneath so many
> eyelids.
>
> Rilke, *Sämtliche Werke*

In his testament, written about a year before he died, Rilke requested that his tombstone be inscribed with the words:

> Rose, oh reiner Widerspruch, Lust
> Niemandes Schlaf zu sein unter soviel
> Lidern.

Rarely has an epitaph aroused so much speculation and stirred so many pens as this exquisite little poem, this "pearl of poetry," which, although "shorter than a Japanese Haiku, is probably one of the greatest and most suggestive inventions that ever occurred to a poet." [1]

In selecting the rose as his parting symbol Rilke gave final form to one of the most persistent images in his poetry. Even in his first poor verses roses had blossomed forth in dreamlike enchantment. In the *Book of Hours* "the great rose of poverty" was one of the many metaphors through which his enraptured soul had tried to express the paradox of God. In *New Poems* the rose symbolized those inner intensities of life compared with which the tumult of the outer world fades into insignificance. Here already, twenty years before it appeared in its final form, the image of the epitaph emerges. The roses in the poem *Rose-Bowl*—"that exquisite piece of preciosity" [2]—are filled to overflowing with the "uttermost being"; they are all inwardness, noiseless life, and, if one of them opens a petal, it is as if an eyelid opened:

and beneath there are nothing but eyelids
closed, as though a tenfold sleep
had to subdue the visionary force within.[3]

und drunter liegen lauter Augenlider,
geschlossene, als ob sie, zehnfach schlafend,
zu dämpfen hätten eines Innern Sehkraft.[4]

These roses, completely occupied with themselves, reflect an
"eminently narcissistic attitude"; they contain only themselves:

if to contain oneself means: to change the world
and wind and rain and the patience of spring
and guilt and unrest and disguised fate
and darkness of the dusky earth
even the changing clouds, gathering and flight,
even the vague influence of distant stars
into a handful of inwardness.[5]

wenn Sich-enthalten heißt: die Welt da draußen
und Wind und Regen und Geduld des Frühlings
und Schuld und Unruh und vermummtes Schicksal
und Dunkelheit der abendlichen Erde
bis auf der Wolken Wandel, Flucht und Anflug,
bis auf den vagen Einfluß ferner Sterne
in eine Hand voll Innres zu verwandeln.[6]

Even at this early stage Rilke thus attributed to the rose trans-
formatory powers. Its intense existence seemed to him exemplary
of life as it should be lived: inwardly. Inwardness does not mean
rejection of the outer world, for even though the rose does not
actively participate in it the world is still there with its fate and
guilt and unrest; it means accepting it, living it, transforming it.
This the rose does simply by its presence. In the *Elegies* and *Sonnets* Rilke would say that the poet does it too: he transforms the
world into the word. Both the rose and Orpheus are symbols of
transformation:

Other flowers embellish the table
which you glorify.

D'autres fleurs ornent la table
que tu transfigures.[7]

The next stage in the development of the rose symbol occurred in the *Sonnets to Orpheus*. Here not only the presence of the rose, but also its absence is celebrated:

> For centuries, name after sweetest name,
> we have heard your fragrance singing:
> suddenly it hangs in the air like fame.[8]

> Seit Jahrhunderten ruft uns dein Duft
> seine süßesten Namen herüber;
> plötzlich liegt er wie Ruhm in der Luft.[9]

A dimension in depth has been added. The rose is no longer admired only for its present beauty; its past is recalled. Filtering down through the ages the sweet perfume of the rose of antiquity hangs like "fame in the air." It is completely ineffable, and yet it moves our memory. In moments of vision we suddenly feel the essence of the rose, see the total rose blooming outside time, unconcerned and self-occupied. Like Orpheus it is at home in both realms, that of the living and that of the dead. Hence no flower is so well suited as the rose to commemorate the "singing god":

> Raise no memorial. Let the rose
> bloom every year just for his sake.
> For this is Orpheus.[10]

> Errichtet keinen Denkstein. Laßt die Rose
> nur jedes Jahr zu seinen Gunsten blühn.
> Denn Orpheus ists.[11]

As Rilke tended the roses in his little garden at Muzot he became more and more convinced that, because of the universal love bestowed upon it and the mysterious qualities with which it has been endowed through the ages, the rose had acquired a magical presence. He relived the wonder the ancients had felt for the simple beauty of the red and yellow eglantine; he understood the rapture of the mystics for the rose as a symbol of the mystic union; and he shared the romantic feeling that the rose was a flower of death. Gradually the rose became the major symbol for that unity of life and death which he celebrated in his poetry. "Every day when I look at these beautiful white roses I ask myself whether they are not the most perfect image of this unity, I would even say this identity, of absence and presence which, perhaps, constitutes the fundamental equation of our life." [12]

To assume the identity of absence and presence, the unity of life and death, the proximity of horror and holiness, is of course paradoxical. But Rilke felt that these paradoxes or, as he preferred to call them, these "pure contradictions" only *seemed* so to us because of our incomplete insight. For "where the Infinite entirely enters (whether as a minus or a plus) the sign, alas, the so human sign, falls away . . . and what remains is being there, Being!" [13] The ultimate purpose of his poetry was to convey such a complete insight; its *telos* is therefore the reconciliation of opposites. In praising life he praised all the contradictory forces of which it consists:

> Time-Of-A-Life-Time Life, that can extend
> from contradiction into contradiction[14]

> O Leben Leben, wunderliche Zeit
> von Widerspruch zu Widerspruche reichend.[15]

He found in the rose the symbol in which all these contradictions were jubilantly affirmed because they were seen to arise from a common source, the primordial unity of being:

> Your innumerable state does it make you discern
> in a mixture where everything blends
> the unutterable harmony of nonbeing and being
> which we ignore?

> Ton innombrable état te fait-il connaître
> dans un mélange où tout se confond,
> cet ineffable accord du néant et de l'être
> que nous ignorons? [16]

It is therefore not surprising that he selected the rose as his parting symbol, although (or perhaps because?) the rose is quite indifferent to man. It blooms for itself alone. It wants to be rose, nothing but rose. It does not want to become involved in our human fate.

> Does the rose withdraw from us with all its petals? Does it
> want to be rose only, nothing-but-rose? Nobody's sleep beneath
> so many eyelids?

Est-ce de toutes ses pétales que la rose s'éloigne de nous?
Veut-elle être rose-seule, rien-que-rose? Sommeil de personne
sous tant de paupières? [17]

The questions in this French version, which probably preceded the
poem on his gravestone, show that for a time he was in doubt if the
rose could assume a role in our lives.

When he finally resolved this doubt and wrote his epitaph he
introduced two additional ideas: the idea that it is a "pure contradiction" for the rose to be so involved in fate and yet to be
fateless, to have so many eyelids and yet to be nobody's sleep; and
the idea that the rose *delights* in precisely that contradiction. It
delights in both being here and not being here, in its presence and
in its absence.

This delight of the rose in its uniqueness seemed to Rilke the
ultimate in self-expression and a perfect representation of his
own delight in his work. For he, too, wanted to get lost behind
his songs, longed for anonymity. Read with this in mind, as
Holthusen suggests, his epitaph fits perfectly. All one has to do is
read *"Liedern"* (songs) for *"Lidern"* (eyelids) to be face to face
with another pure contradiction, standing at Rilke's grave where
nobody now sleeps beneath so many songs. Behind the *persona* of
the poet, the *person* has vanished.

The story of Rilke's epitaph would be imcomplete without a
brief reference to the peculiar circumstances of his death. A year
after he had written his testament, the exotic Egyptian beauty,
Madame Eloui Bey, came to Muzot to pay her respects to the poet
she loved. In accordance with his chivalrous nature Rilke wanted
to present her with a bouquet of roses. As he went into his garden
to cut them he hurt his hand on a thorn. This slight wound led
to a painful, festering infection that revealed the advanced state
of his leukemia. Two months later he was dead. The rose of love
had been a harbinger of death; this paradox climaxed the paradoxes
of Rilke's life:

Life and death—let both of them express
something strangely one for you.[18]

Hier- und Dortsein, dich ergreife beides
seltsam ohne Unterschied.[19]

In Rilke's *Late Poems* the concept of "pure contradiction" occupies the place of the earlier *Umschlag*. He no longer insists that there is a sudden change from woe to beatitude, but that both are one. Life and death, absence and presence, light and darkness, speech and silence: "all these apparent opposites somehow converge in one point, sing the hymn of their union in one place, and this place is, for the time being, our heart." [20]

This theme forms the leitmotiv of some of the most beautiful of his *Late Poems* and reappears, a somewhat fainter echo, in his French verse. Part and counterpart always arise together: *"tout jeu veut son contre-jeu."* We have forgotten, he insists, *"les dieux opposés"* and their ancient rites, and he reminds us that it is not a question of compromise between opposites, nor of conversion, but of obedience to "complementary orders":

> It is not a question of pleasing
> nor of transformation,
> provided that we know to obey
> complementary orders.

> Il ne s'agit pas de plaire,
> ni de se convertir,
> pourvu que l'on sache obéir
> aux ordres complémentaires.[21]

Again and again the culminating point of these poems is the paradox: "Defenselessness is our best defense"; "our possession is loss"; "infinite darkness of light." Through the paradox he succeeds in conveying depth and transparency, darkness and light. Like luminous gems some of these poems radiate sheer delight. Who can resist the feeling of early morning freshness, the pure joy of living that the following sonnet emits, even in translation?

> Who was ever so wake
> as this wakening day?
> Not just brooklet and brake,
> but the roof, too, is gay,

> with its tiles that outstand
> in the blue of the sky,
> as alive as a land,
> and as full of reply.

Breathing thanks are conveyed.
All nocturnal affliction
has vanished with night,

whose darkness was made
—O pure contradiction!—
from legions of light.[22]

Wann war ein Mensch je so wach
wie der Morgen von heut?
Nicht nur Blume und Bach,
auch das Dach ist erfreut.

Selbst sein alternder Rand,
von den Himmeln erhellt,—
wird fühlend: ist Land,
ist Antwort, ist Welt.

Alles atmet und dankt.
O ihr Nöte der Nacht,
wie ihr spurlos versankt.

Aus Scharen von Licht
war ihr Dunkel gemacht,
das sich rein widerspricht.[23]

How simply and convincingly this little poem expresses the
feeling we all have at times that the great arc of life encompasses
the inanimate as well as the animate, that darkness and light are
but different intensities. Poems such as these demonstrate the
healing power of poetry; one cannot live with them for any length
of time without responding joyfully to the joy they exude.

The paradox "darkness . . . made . . . from legions of light"
not only heightens the poetic effect, it is largely responsible for
the shock of recognition we get from this poem: the sudden insight that the antinomies of existence are not irreconcilable but
spring from a common source. To convey such insights is the
function of the paradox. "I am part of that force which always
wills evil and always creates good," Goethe has Mephistopheles
say, and in Blake's *Everlasting Gospel* the "shocking" lines occur:

Thou art a Man: God is no more:
Thy own Humanity learn to adore . . .

"Good and Evil are no more!" [24]

The important role of the paradox in the language of prophecy and revelation is thus not surprising. "He that findeth his life shall lose it," said Christ, and the last line of an ancient Brahmanical hymn runs: "I am the food. I feed on food and on its feeder." [25] Faith in the paradox means faith in the miracle. For every miracle is paradoxical.

The shock effect of the paradox is one way by which all religions try to focus attention to the fact that their ultimate goal is liberation from the domination of opposites and the attainment of a state of pure being, life everlasting. This was Rilke's goal also, but lacking the simple faith of less ambiguous men he was tragically aware that destiny means "being opposite/ and nothing else, and always opposite." [26] This awareness is the cause of the deep anxiety that runs through his poetry. It is also the cause of his desperate efforts to overcome it. His apotheosis of the paradox, the pure contradiction, means that, while he did not find the certainty of faith (for to the true believer all paradoxes come to rest in God), he found a precarious equilibrium between hope and despair and affirmed it so fervently that feelings of faith are aroused in the reader. This, too, is paradoxical for, on the scale of emotions, faith (the quiet certainty of a revealed truth) and fervor (the ardent longing for revelation) stand at opposite poles. However, the inner intensity of a work of art can deceive the beholder into thinking that it aims to inspire faith, or love, or hope. "And this deception between it and forsaken man is similar to all those priestlike deceptions which have advanced the divine from the beginning of time." [27]

With these words Rilke himself joined in the great argument that divides his critics: has his poetry "real religious validity; or is it merely the mysterious expression of a one-man dream?" [28] In the latter case there may indeed be "a danger in living with Rilke. Or at least there may be a misapprehension . . . for in seeming to put life's deepest problems before us he may offer us a subtle withdrawal from them." [29] On the other hand, if his poetry gives genuine spiritual consolation, even though unrelated to any given creed or dogma, then it belongs to those rare documents through which the voice of a universal spirit speaks to us.

To answer this question exhaustively would require a detailed examination of the relationship between poetry and religion. That such a relationship exists is usually assumed. It is pointed out that all the great religious documents: the Old and New Testaments, the Koran, the Vedic Hymns, the sayings of Laotse and Buddha, are essentially poetic. As far as differences of opinion exist, they chiefly concern the question whether religion or poetry is the primary source. Since Rousseau and Herder and the rise of individualism the emphasis has been on poetry. The poetic impulse in man, it is said, has given rise to his religion. "All that remains is the work of poets" (Hölderlin); "poetry is the genuinely absolute and real" (Novalis). There have been exceptions to this view— Kierkegaard, for example, opposed it—but on the whole Rilke expressed a sentiment quite common among modern artists when he wrote in his *Tuscan Diary:* "How other future worlds will ripen to God I do not know, but for us art is the way." [30] Uncommon about this expression was the deep earnestness, the sense of responsibility, which even the young Rilke felt for his calling. Ripening to God was not merely a poetic metaphor with him; he took it quite literally to be his task as a poet. It is this earnestness, this fervent and unremitting effort to find God in his work, which distinguishes Rilke's poetry from that of his contemporaries, even from those who, like Stefan George, sought to make a cult out of poetry. If dedication to poetry is a sign of piety then there can be no doubt that Rilke was one of the most pious men of his age, for he certainly was one of the most dedicated.

However, the well-known English Rilke scholar Eudo C. Mason has challenged the assumption that there is such a relationship between poetry and religion. He says that on the contrary there exists between them "a deep and necessary contradiction" that has been obscured by the genius-ridden individualists of the last two hundred years. He rejects Shelley's claim that "poets are the unacknowledged legislators of the world" and calls the efforts of Hölderlin, Nietzsche, and Rilke to make a religion out of poetry "arrogant self-dramatizations." Religion, he says, exists quite apart from poetry, has nothing to do with it, because it is revealed truth while poetry is a beautiful illusion. Compared with the life and teaching of Christ the life and work of even the greatest poet is insignificant. And to illustrate his point he quotes Charles Lamb's famous remark: "If Shakespeare now entered we would all rise, but if Christ entered we would all kneel." [31] This view reflects the growth of orthodoxy in contemporary thinking. It is directed not only against Rilke but against the entire individualist era. Speaking for the opposite point of view, Holthusen sees in poetry "a kind of creative unrest in the service of the one and only logos, inaudibly related to a possible peace in the Lord," [32] and concludes his Rilke study with Henri Bremond's words, "all poetry must end in prayer."

There is of course a difference between a prayer qua prayer and a prayer as a work of art, and no modern poet has been more painfully aware of that difference than Rilke. There were times when the thought of turning his piety into a poem struck him as blasphemous. For did it not mean that instead of paying undivided attention to God he was secretly looking over his shoulder and trying to catch his own reflection in the mirror? At such times he felt that his art was a temptation of the devil, a form of idolatry, a perversion of nature: "No doubt God never foresaw that any of us would turn inward upon himself in this way which can only be permitted to the saint because he seeks to besiege his God by attacking him from this unexpected and badly defended quarter." [33]

Poet or saint: between these two extremes, these borderline positions of existence, revolves the inner drama of Rilke's life, and much of the tension in his work can be attributed to it. He was a poet, a poet in the most absolute and exclusive sense of the word, but he wanted to get beyond poetry, to the "proof"; he wanted to experience God directly as the saints do. When he found that this was impossible he tried to make his mouthpiece, Malte, into a saint. But he failed in that also. For fervor is not enough: a saint must accept sacrifice. Rilke knew that. In a letter to Lou he quoted with approval a sentence from Kassner's *Narciss*: "The way from fervor to greatness leads through sacrifice." [34] He learned, however, that this way was barred to him because he was an artist, and sacrifice, to the artist, means sacrifice to his work, not to God.

In a real and serious sense the great artist is the great rival of God and "loves Him with his high hatred/ because he cannot reach Him." [35] In that sense Rilke's sacrifice was very real: "If the meaning of sacrifice is that the moment of greatest danger coincides with that when one is saved, then certainly nothing resembles sacrifice more than this terrible will to art." [36] But it did not give him certainty and did not make him a saint: "No, Dottor Serafico, you are no 'saint'—even if you slide on your knees all day and all night. . . . And that is good.—A saint would never have written the Elegies." [37]

When Princess Taxis, in her characteristically direct manner, told Rilke this she showed that she understood both his problem and the nature of his achievement. His problem was to find an outlet for his fervor. Had he lived in a more religious age, or had he been a less ambiguous man, he might have found relief in prayer or in an act of contrition, or indeed "he might have got himself crucified." [38] But he was an artist, he poured his fervor into his art, and that made all the difference. For instead of flowing out into God and finding peace in God he was left crying in the wilderness, alone with his fervent heart and the terrifying images that arose in his soul:

> If somewhere deep within me rises up
> a having-been-a-child I don't yet know,
> perhaps the purest childness of my childhood:
> I refuse to know it. Without looking at it
> or asking about it I'll make an angel out of it
> and hurl that angel into the front rank
> of crying angels that remembrance God.[39]

> Wenn irgendwo ein Kindgewesensein
> tief in mir aufsteigt, das ich noch nicht kenne,
> vielleicht das reinste Kindsein meiner Kindheit:
> ich wills nicht wissen. Einen Engel will
> ich daraus bilden ohne hinzusehn
> und will ihn werfen in die erste Reihe
> schreiender Engel, welche Gott erinnern.[40]

And yet he persisted. Defiantly and fearfully, another Columbus, he continued on his self-charted course, rejecting all offers of help, all close human ties, all divine mediation. Note how earnestly he requested in his testament that no priest be allowed near his deathbed because the idea of a spiritual mediator offended his soul. And yet this obstinate individualist, this genius-ridden mono-maniac who turned his back on people and who, bent over his work, "almost forgot God in the hard task of drawing near Him," wrote poetry that has a definitely religious appeal. One may try to explain it away, as Rilke himself did, when he said that it was not the function of a work of art to console, or as Mason does when he says Rilke cannot give

> . . . the one thing most asked for, the one thing which many people believe to have got from him. . . . : "Certainty about value or value-lessness of existence," "clear directions for the development of hu-manity" (Moevius), "instructions for a good life" (Kretschmar) "a new God" (Kippenberg), "assurances of our share in eternity" (Bäumer), "convincing expression of the piety of modern man" (Joachim Müller). All this Rilke cannot give because he does not have it himself, and be-cause, however much he may long for it, he does not really want to have it, if he could.[41]

This is well said, except that it points to the opposite conclusion, namely, that Rilke (whether he wants to or not) *does* give all this, and to many people.

How can we account for this paradox? How account for the fact that Rilke's troubled mind inspires faith; his despair, hope? If his poetry is merely a "one-man dream," how can we account for the universal phenomenon of the Rilke cult?

I suggest there are three main reasons. First, Rilke did more than write poetry—he lived it. Against the background of a thoroughly prosaic age he projected the ancient figure of the poet. That is his unique achievement; it transcends the sphere of the literary. In his presence even a skeptic is forced to exclaim: *"Ecce poeta!"* If one compares him with other poets one realizes that, "however great they were, they were poets in their minds only," [42] while with Rilke poetry was a way of life. "Living poetry" means inhabiting the realm of primordial images that arise in the sub-conscious, penetrating into those deep strata of the soul where its mirage begins, reaching "the rim of the world." When a poet speaks in primordial images, when he takes us back, as Rilke does, into the world of our childhood, that weird and wonderful world of dolls and demons and angels, strange beasts, blue flowers, houses that talk in their sleep, fountains and parks and trees that suddenly walk away, and stars and the moon reflected in the river at night—when a poet does that "he speaks as with a thousand tongues, he moves and overpowers us, and, at the same time, he lifts the singular and transitory he touches into the sphere of eternal being." [43]

Second, Rilke's poetry reflects the ambiguity of modern man. This does not require elucidation. It is almost trite to say (because it has been said so often) that ours is an age of complexity, anxiety, and paradox, and that the truly representative spokesmen of our age must be complex, ambiguous, and difficult. "Rilke's poetry is ambiguous because Rilke is ambiguous—for that reason it forms a great exception and is meant to do so—on the other hand, since the age is ambiguous, Rilke's *Weltanschauung* represents a typical, universal document, as again it is meant to." [44]

Third, Rilke speaks to us with "the soul of the future." These are the final words in Valéry's homage to Rilke, and they refer to the fact that in Rilke's poetry the diverse strains of the European tradition have merged. Germanic and Romanic, Slavic and Nordic elements mingle in his work. Imperceptibly the recluse of Muzot had become a citizen of Europe. But there is more to it than that. One cannot read Rilke without becoming aware of his affinity to Eastern, particularly to Indian, thought. His insistence on transformation, for example, is entirely in the tradition of Indian philosophy, whose "primary concern—in striking contrast to the interests of the modern philosophers of the West—has always been, not information but transformation, a radical changing of man's nature and, therewith, a renovation of his understanding both of the outer world and of his own existence." [45] Another theme Rilke shared with the Indian sages is concern with the paradoxical character of reality. "Indian philosophy continually emphasizes the contrast between the displayed existence of the individual and the real being of the anonymous actor, concealed, shrouded, veiled in the costumes of the play." [46] Finally, Rilke's longing for "pure being" and his efforts to attain it are in the ancient tradition of the East. The Indian thinker has long been convinced that "only introverted awareness bent and driven to the depth of the subject's own nature reaches that borderline where the transitory super-impositions meet their unchanging source." [47]

To avoid misunderstanding, it should again be stressed that the implication is not that Rilke was influenced by Indian thought, merely that there are areas of close agreement between Rilke's thought and that of the East. It must also be said that in many important respects Rilke was a typically Western artist. He was an "empiricist of the heart" (Mason), a "phenomenologist" (Holthusen), and an experimenter. He was animated by a spirit of adventure, a restless search for new sights and insights. He was always trying again, always beginning. He believed that, "if an angel deigns to appear, it will be because you have convinced him, not by tears but your humble resolve to be always beginning—to be a Beginner." [48]

Rilke has been called a great poet of the declining West, and there are aspects of his work that support this view: the extreme delicacy of his sensibilities; a linguistic virtuosity possible only in the most advanced state of culture; a preference for soft and subdued shades, half tones, nuances, hidden meanings; a somewhat feminine timbre. At the same time there is in Rilke also the promise of a new movement, a blending of East and West, a radical return from the surface to the depth of life, an insistence on the need to understand and accept rather than suppress and deny the irrational forces that shape our destinies. It is this part of him that makes the reading of Rilke's poetry such an exciting and rewarding experience. For whatever else the future may hold, that some day there will be such a synthesis, a blending of East and West, the birth of a new man, a *homo universalis*, is a certainty that persists in our hearts in spite of all the evidence to the contrary. And this certainty gleams through the anxiety of Rilke's verse. For although "all combines to suppress us" we feel it is "partly as shame,/ perhaps, and partly as inexpressible hope."

His example is a powerful reminder that "this rich and varied world with its overflowing and intoxicating life is not purely external, but also exists within," [49] that every end is also a beginning, and that our contradictions are rhythmic events in a continuous process of transformation.

> Poems like these arise from transformations
> you cannot name—: Feel and trust!
> We often see how flames turn into ashes
> In art however: flames burst out of dust.

> Magic is here. Into the realm of charm
> the common word seems lifted high above . . .
> and yet it's real like the cock-bird's call
> for the invisible dove.[50]

> Aus unbeschreiblicher Verwandlung stammen
> solche Gebilde—: Fühl! und glaub!
> Wir leidens oft: zu Asche werden Flammen;
> doch, in der Kunst: zur Flamme wird der Staub.

> Hier ist Magie. In das Bereich des Zaubers
> scheint das gemeine Wort hinaufgestuft . . .
> und ist doch wirklich wie der Ruf des Taubers,
> der nach der unsichtbaren Taube ruft.[51]

Chronology of Rilke's Life
1875 - 1926

1875   Born in Prague on December 4, of German parentage. Rilke's father, Josef Rilke, who had hoped to be an officer in the Austrian army, was an inspector of railroads in Prague. His mother, Sofia (Phia), née Entz, was the daughter of a well-to-do businessman who held the title "Imperial Counselor."

1884   Rilke's parents separated. Phia Rilke became responsible for the boy's education.

1886   Entered the military school at St. Pölten in preparation for a military career. His mother, against her husband's wishes, encouraged Rilke's youthful attempts to write poetry.

1890   Successfully completed his course of studies at St. Pölten; entered the military high school at Mährisch-Weisskirchen.

1891   Left Mährisch-Weisskirchen because of constant illness and intended to take up a business career. Entered the school of commerce at Linz. A Viennese journal published his first poem.

1892   Worked in his uncle's law firm and decided to study law.

1893   Love affair with Valery David-Rhonfeld. Wrote and published a great deal of poetry hoping to convince his relatives that he could earn his living as a writer.

1894   Won a twenty-mark prize in a poetry contest for his poem *Evening*; published his first book of poems, *Life and Songs*, now forgotten.

1895   Studied philosophy, literature, and history of art at the German University of Prague. In December published his book of poems, *An Offering to the Lares*, later included, after much revision, in his collected works.

1896   His publisher Kattentidt offered him the editorship of a newly founded literary journal. Wrote reviews, plays, stories, and poems. His play *Now and in the Hour of Our Dying* was performed in the Deutsches Volkstheater in Prague. Published *Wegwarten* (*Wild Chicory*), "songs given to the people"; and another book of poems, *Crowned with Dreams*, now included in his collected works. Became acquainted with such well-known writers as Ludwig Ganghofer, Detlev von Liliencron, Max Halbe, Wilhelm von Scholz, Theodor Fontane, and others, who encouraged his literary endeavors.

1897   Moved to Munich where he met Lou Andreas-Salomé, fourteen years his senior. They soon became lovers. When Lou moved to Berlin in the fall, Rilke followed her. Lou prepared him for his forthcoming journey to Italy. In December he published *Advent*, a book of poems now included in his collected works.

1898   Journey to Italy: Florence, Arco, Viareggio. In Italy met Stefan George, who criticized him for having published so much. In Viareggio he wrote his *Maiden Songs*. Published a two-act play, *Without the Present*, and a collection of short stories, *At the Edge of Life*. Wrote the first version of *The White Princess*.

1899   Journey to Russia with Lou and her husband from April to June. Made the acquaintance of Pasternak, Tolstoy, and Prince Trubetzkoy. Published *Two Stories of Prague* and a book of poems *In My Honor*. Wrote in "one stormy night" *The Tale of Love and Death of Cornet Christoph Rilke*; wrote in seven successive nights *The Tales of God*; wrote the majority of the poems contained in *The Book of Monkish Life*. Studied Russian.

1900   Second journey to Russia with Lou from May to August: Moscow, Kiev, Tula visit with Tolstoy. Upon return from Russia visited Worpswede where he met the artists Otto Modersohn, Fritz Mackensen, Heinrich Vogeler, Paula Becker, and Clara Westhoff.

1901   In March, married Clara Westhoff. Their daughter Ruth born December 12. The couple lived at Westerwede near Bremen. There, between September 18 and 25, he wrote *The Book of Pilgrimage*. Sent the manuscript of *The Book of Pictures* to his publisher. A performance of his play *Daily Life* in Berlin received bad reviews. Mounting financial worries.

1902   Wrote reviews, newspaper articles, and a monograph, *Worspwede*. Repeated requests for work or money. Unable to support his family as a free lance, he accepted a commission to write a monograph on

Rodin. In August left for Paris. Published *The Last Ones,* three sketches; his play *Daily Life;* and *The Book of Pictures.*

1903   Journey to Italy. In Viareggio between April 13 and 20 wrote *The Book of Poverty and Death.* Returned to Paris where he felt lonely and isolated: "The town is against me." Correspondence with Lou Andreas-Salomé about his Parisian nightmares. Genesis of *Malte Laurids Brigge.* In September left Paris for Rome. Published monograph, *Auguste Rodin.*

1904   Journey to Scandinavia. Upon invitation of Ellen Key, spent June to December in Denmark and Sweden. Published *Stories of God* and first version of *The Tale of Love and Death of Cornet Christoph Rilke.*

1905   After a brief reunion with his family in Oberneuland he fell sick and spent March in a sanatorium near Dresden. Met Countess Luise Schwerin, whose friendship and patronage supported him during these difficult years. Through her he met his other patrons, Baron Uexküll and Karl von der Heydt. In September Rodin invited him to come to Paris. Published *Book of Hours.*

1906–7 Left Paris in July and visited Flanders. Spent winter and spring on Capri as the guest of Mrs. Alice Faehndrich. Upon the latter's suggestion, translated Elizabeth Barrett Browning's *Sonnets from the Portuguese.* Published *New Poems I.* Returned to Paris in May.

1908   Again on Capri in spring. Summer in Paris; continued work on *Malte.* Published *New Poems II.*

1909   In Paris with journeys to Chartres and Province. Published *Early Poems,* revised versions of his first verse.

1910   January to March in Leipzig as guest of his publisher, Kippenberg, putting finishing touches on *Malte Laurids Brigge.* Beginning of his friendship with his great patroness, Princess Mary von Thurn und Taxis, and with André Gide. Late fall journey to North Africa.

1911   January in Egypt: Cairo and Karnak. April in Paris. Winter 1911–12 as guest of Princess Taxis at Castle Duino where he conceived the cycle of the *Duino Elegies.*

1912   May to September in Venice. Frequent meetings with Eleonora Duse. Winter in Spain: Toledo, Córdoba, Seville, Ronda, Madrid.

1913   Spring in Paris. Summer journey through Germany. Late autumn in Paris where he wrote the *Third Duino Elegy.* Friendship with Magda von Hattingberg ("Benvenuta"). Published *First Poems.*

1914   Paris until July 20. Translated Gide's *Return of the Prodigal Son*.
           Left Paris for Munich, not suspecting that he could not return.
           His books, papers, and personal possessions were in Paris at the
           outbreak of the war.

1915   Public sale of Rilke's property in Paris. Feeling that he had reached
           the point of no return, wrote the *Fourth Elegy*, November 21–23,
           in Munich. Drafted; served as a clerk in the archives of the Aus-
           trian War Ministry in Vienna from December to June, 1916.

1916   Discharged from the army upon a petition of his friends. Returned
           to Munich. Translated twenty-four *Sonnets of Louise Labé*.

1917–18   In Munich with an occasional journey to Berlin. Waiting for the
           war to end.

1919   Left Germany for Switzerland on a lecture tour upon invitation
           of Swiss admirers. Readings from his works in Zurich, St. Gall,
           Lucerne, Basel, Bern, and Winterthur. In Winterthur met Hans
           and Werner Reinhart whose friendship lasted for the rest of his life.

1920   Journeys to Venice and Paris. From October again in Switzerland
           where Colonel Ziegler put Castle Berg am Irchel at his disposal.
           Tried, unsuccessfully, to work on *Duino Elegies*.

1921   In the company of his friend Baladine Klossowska ("Merline"),
           discovered the little medieval "Château de Muzot sur Sierre,"
           which Werner Reinhart rented for him and gave him as a perma-
           nent home.

1922   At Muzot in February, completed the cycle of the *Duino Elegies*
           and wrote at the same time fifty-five *Sonnets to Orpheus*.

1923   Mostly at Muzot where his friends visited him: Princess Taxis,
           Kippenberg, Werner Reinhart. Beginning of his illness. Spent the
           end of the year in the Sanatorium Valmont sur Territet.

1924   On April 6 Paul Valéry visited him at Muzot. Rilke's wife Clara,
           whom he had not seen since 1918, and many of his other French,
           German, and Swiss friends also visited. From November 24 to
           January 8, 1925, again at Valmont for treatment of an unknown
           disease. Publication of three of his French poems in Valéry's jour-
           nal *Commerce*.

1925   Paris from January to August. Meetings with André Gide, Charles
           du Bos, Edmond Jaloux, and other French writers. Discussed
           French translation of *Malte* with Maurice Betz. In December
           again at Valmont.

1926   July to August in Ragaz. October to November at Muzot. Published *Vergers suivis de quatrains valaisans*. From November 30 at Valmont where his illness was finally diagnosed as leukemia. Died on December 29 and was buried in the cemetery of Raron on Sunday, January 2, 1927.

Notes

ABBREVIATIONS

RMR S.W. I, II   Rainer Marie Rilke, *Sämtliche Werke* (Wiesbaden: Insel-Verlag; Vol. I, 1955; Vol. II, 1957).

RMR G.W. I–VI   Rainer Maria Rilke, *Gesammelte Werke* (6 vols.; Leipzig: Insel-Verlag, 1927)

RMR P.F.   Rainer Maria Rilke, *Poésies françaises* (Paris: Emile-Paul Frères, 1946).

RMR V.P.   Rainer Maria Rilke, *Verse und Prosa aus dem Nachlass* (Leipzig: Insel-Verlag, 1929).

RMR T.F.   Rainer Maria Rilke, *Tagebücher aus der Frühzeit* (Leipzig: Insel-Verlag, 1942).

RMR Br. T.F.   Rainer Maria Rilke, *Briefe und Tagebücher aus der Frühzeit, 1899–1902* (Leipzig: Insel-Verlag, 1933).

RMR Br. 1902–6   Rainer Maria Rilke, *Briefe aus den Jahren 1902–1906* (Leipzig: Insel-Verlag, 1930).

RMR Br. 1906–7   Rainer Maria Rilke, *Briefe aus den Jahren 1906–1907* (Leipzig: Insel-Verlag, 1930).

RMR Br. 1907–14   Rainer Maria Rilke, *Briefe aus den Jahren 1907–1914* (Leipzig: Insel-Verlag, 1933).

RMR Br. 1914–21   Rainer Maria Rilke, *Briefe aus den Jahren 1914–1921* (Leipzig: Insel-Verlag, 1938).

RMR Br. Muzot   Rainer Maria Rilke, *Briefe aus Muzot, 1921–1926* (Leipzig: Insel-Verlag, 1936).

RMR Br. Verleger   Rainer Maria Rilke, *Briefe an seinen Verleger* (Leipzig: Insel-Verlag, 1936).

RMR Br. 1904–7   Rainer Maria Rilke, *Briefe aus den Jahren 1904–1907* (Leipzig: Insel-Verlag, 1939).

RMR Br. I, II   Rainer Maria Rilke, *Briefe I, 1897–1914; II, 1914–1926* (Wiesbaden: Insel-Verlag, 1950).

RMR Br. Dichter   Rainer Maria Rilke, *Briefe an einen jungen Dichter* (Leipzig: Insel-Verlag, 1929)

RMR Br. Frau   Rainer Maria Rilke, *Briefe an eine junge Frau* (Leipzig: Insel-Verlag, 1930).

RMR Br. Taxis   *Rainer Maria Rilke und Marie von Thurn und Taxis, Briefwechsel* (2 vols.; Zurich: Niehans & Rohitansky; Wiesbaden: Insel-Verlag, 1951).

RMR Br. Lou   *Rainer Maria Rilke–Lou Andreas-Salomé Briefwechsel*, ed. Ernst Pfeiffer (Zurich: Niehans; Wiesbaden: Insel-Verlag, 1952).

RMR Br. Gide   *Rainer Maria Rilke–André Gide, Correspondance 1909–1926*, ed. Renée Lang (Paris: Corréa, 1952).

RMR Br. Merline   *Rainer Maria Rilke et Merline: Correspondance 1920–1926*, ed. Dieter Bassermann (Zurich: Niehans, 1954).

RMR Br. Benvenuta   *Rainer Maria Rilke: Briefwechsel mit Benvenuta*, ed. Magda von Hattingberg (Esslingen: Bechtle, 1954).

Leishman/Requiem   *Rainer Maria Rilke: Requiem and Other Poems*, trans. J. B. Leishman (London: Hogarth Press, 1935).

Leishman/L.P.   *Rainer Maria Rilke: Later Poems*, trans. J. B. Leishman (London: Hogarth Press, 1938).

Leishman/Poems   *Rainer Maria Rilke: Poems*, trans. J. B. Leishman (London: Hogarth Press, 1939).

Leishman/Spender   *Rainer Maria Rilke: Duino Elegies*, German text with English translation, introduction, and commentary by J. B. Leishman and Stephen Spender (New York: W. W. Norton and Co., 1939).

Leishman/Orpheus   *Rainer Maria Rilke: Sonnets to Orpheus*, German text with English translation, introduction, and notes by J. B. Leishman (2nd ed.; London: Hogarth Press, 1946).

Leishman/S.P.   *Rainer Maria Rilke: Selected Poems*, trans. J. B. Leishman (London: Hogarth Press, 1945).

Leishman/P. 1906–26   *Rainer Maria Rilke: Poems 1906–1926*, trans. with introduction by J. B. Leishman (New York: New Directions, 1957)

Linton/Malte   *Rainer Maria Rilke: The Notebooks of Malte Laurids Brigge*, trans. John Linton (London: Hogarth Press, 1930).

Green/Norton/RMR   *Letters of Rainer Maria Rilke*, trans. Jane Bannard Greene and M. D. Herter Norton (2 vols.; New York: W. W. Norton, 1945), Vol. I, *1892–1910*.

Hull/RMR   *Selected Letters of Rainer Maria Rilke 1902–1926*, trans. R. F. C. Hull (London: Macmillan and Co., 1947).

PREFACE

1. Peter Demetz, *René Rilkes Prager Jahre* (Dusseldorf: Diederichs, 1953), p. 5.
2. F. W. van Heerikhuizen, *R. M. Rilke: His Life and Work*, trans. Fernand G. Renier and Anne Cliff (New York: Philosophical Library, 1952), p. x.
3. Maurice Betz, *Rilke in Paris*, trans. Willi Reich (Zurich: Verlag der Arche, 1948), p. 36.
4. Ludwig Lewisohn (trans.), *Thirty-one Poems by Rainer Maria Rilke* (New York: B. Ackermann, 1946), p. 8.
5. D. J. Enright, "Rilke and Hölderlin in Translation," *Scrutiny: A Quarterly Review*, XII (Spring, 1944), 93.
6. RMR Br. 1907–14, p. 96.

CHAPTER 1

1. Randall Jarrell, *Poetry and the Age* (New York: Alfred A. Knopf, 1953), p. 11.
2. *Saturday Review* (August 14, 1954), p. 17.
3. W. H. Auden, *In Time of War*, a sonnet sequence with a verse commentary in *Journey to a War*, by W. H. Auden and Christopher Isherwood (New York: Random House, 1939), p. 259.
4. *Ibid.*, p. 265.
5. *Ibid.*, p. 271.
6. *Ibid.*, p. 279.
7. *Ibid.*, p. 281.
8. RMR S.W. I, 557.
9. Auden, *In Time of War*, p. 283.
10. RMR Br. Muzot, p. 103.
11. W. H. Auden, "Rilke in English," *New Republic*, C (September 6, 1939), 135.
12. Sidney Keyes, *The Collected Poems* (London: Routledge and Kegan Paul, 1945), p. xvii.
13. *Ibid.*, p. 75.
14. Leishman/Spender, p. 57.
15. RMR S.W. I, 706 f.
16. Edward Sackville-West, *New Statesman and Nation*, XXI (June 14, 1941), 608.
17. Stephen Spender, "The Forerunner of a Future Poetry," *Dublin Review*, CCIX (October, 1941), 183.
18. J. L. Trausil, "Fitts and Rilke," *Saturday Review of Literature*, XXIV (November 22, 1941), 13.
19. R. M. Rilke, *Worpswede* (Bielefeld and Leipzig: Velhagen and Klasing, 1903), p. 38.
20. Eudo C. Mason, *Lebenshaltung und Symbolik bei R. M. Rilke* (Weimar: Böhlau, 1939), p. 69.
21. Demetz, *René Rilkes Prager Jahre*, p. 6.
22. Heerikhuizen, *R. M. Rilke: His Life and Work*, p. 35.

23. E. M. Butler, *Rainer Maria Rilke* (Cambridge, Eng.: Cambridge University Press, 1941), p. 418.

24. C. F. MacIntyre, *Rainer Maria Rilke: Fifty Selected Poems with English Translations* (Berkeley: University of California Press, 1947), pp. 1 f.

25. *Ibid.*, p. 2.

26. H. Buxton Forman (ed.), *The Letters of John Keats* (2 vols.; Oxford: Oxford University Press, 1931), II, 466.

27. Erich Heller, *The Disinherited Mind: Essays in Modern German Literature and Thought* (Cambridge, Eng.: Bowes and Bowes, 1952), p. 136.

28. Heerikhuizen, *R. M. Rilke: His Life and Work*, p. x.

29. Karl Jaspers, *Vernunft und Existenz* (Groningen: J. B. Wolters, 1935), p. 5.

30. Edmond Jaloux, in "Reconnaissance à Rilke," *Les Cahiers du Mois*, XXIII–XXIV (Paris, 1926), 13.

31. Marcel Brion, in *Rilke et la France* (Paris: Plon, 1942), p. 148.

32. RMR Br. Gide, p. 43.

33. *Ibid.*, p. 53.

34. St. Hubert, "Rainer Maria Rilke et son dernier livre: Les Cahiers de Malte Laurids Brigge," *La Nouvelle Revue Française*, I (July 1, 1911), 32.

35. *Ibid.*, p. 34.

36. *Ibid.*, p. 34.

37. *Ibid.*, p. 32.

38. RMR Br. Gide, p. 126.

39. Brion, in *Rilke et la France*, p. 146.

40. RMR P.F., p. 129.

41. Brion, in *Rilke et la France*, p. 152.

42. Francis de Miomandre, in "Reconnaissance à Rilke," *Les Cahiers du Mois*, XXIII–XXIV (Paris, 1926), 18.

43. Jean Cassou, in *ibid.*, p. 19.

44. André Berge, in *ibid.*, p. 56.

45. Felix Bertaux, in *ibid.*, p. 39.

46. Cassou, in *ibid.*, p. 23.

47. Paul Valéry, in *Rilke et la France*, p. 197.

48. André Gide, in *ibid.*, p. 195.

49. RMR S.W. I, 697.

50. *Ibid.*, p. 710.

51. Leishman/Requiem, p. 105.

52. RMR S.W. I, 660.

53. RMR Br. Dichter, p. 47; *Letters to a Young Poet*, trans. M. D. Herter Norton (New York: W. W. Norton, 1934), p. 69.

54. RMR S.W. I, 664.

55. E. M. Butler, *Rainer Maria Rilke* (Cambridge, Eng.: Cambridge University Press, 1946), p. 9.

56. Carl Sieber, *René Rilke: Die Jugend Rainer Maria Rilkes* (Leipzig: Insel-Verlag, 1932), p. 137.

57. Friedrich Gundolf, *Rainer Maria Rilke* (Vienna: Verlag Johannes Presse, 1937), p. 9.

58. *Ibid.*, pp. 26 f.

59. RMR Br. Taxis, I, xxi.
60. Walter Ritzer, *Rainer Maria Rilke Bibliographie* (Vienna: O. Kerry, 1951), p. vii.
61. RMR Br. Dichter, p. 18; *Letters to a Young Poet*, p. 27.
62. E. E. Cummings, *Six Nonlectures* (Cambridge, Mass.: Harvard University Press, 1953), p. 7.
63. Jarrell, *Poetry and the Age*, p. 7.
64. Ogden Nash, *New York Times Book Review*, June 7, 1953, p. 1.
65. *Saturday Review*, October 17, 1953, p. 18.
66. Rilke, *Auguste Rodin* (Leipzig: Insel-Verlag, 1930), p. 7.
67. Cassou, in "Reconnaissance à Rilke," *Les Cahiers du Mois*, XXIII–XXIV (Paris, 1926), p. 19.

CHAPTER 2

1. RMR Br. 1904–7, p. 336.
2. Rilke, *Briefe an Gräfin Sizzo* (Wiesbaden: Insel-Verlag, 1950), p. 336.
3. Hans Egon Holthusen, *Rainer Maria Rilke: A Study of His Later Poetry*, trans. J. P. Stern (New Haven, Conn.: Yale University Press, 1952), p. 9.
4. H. W. Belmore, *Rilke's Craftsmanship* (Oxford: Blackwell, 1954), p. 223.
5. Leishman/P. 1906–26, p. 251.
6. RMR S.W. II, 131.
7. Leishman/Spender, p. 29.
8. RMR S.W. I, 689.
9. Gundolf, *Rainer Maria Rilke*, p. 37.
10. Cf. Leishman/L.P., p. 181.
11. RMR S.W. II, 406.
12. Leishman/Requiem, p. 78.
13. RMR S.W. I, 496.
14. Leishman/Requiem, p. 78.
15. RMR S.W. I, 496.
16. RMR Br. T.F., p. 337.
17. Cf. Leishman/L.P., p. 29.
18. RMR S.W. II, 158.
19. Ernst Cassirer, *Language and Myth*, trans. Suzanne Langer (London and New York: Harper and Brothers, 1946), p. 7.
20. Mason, *Lebenshaltung und Symbolik bei R. M. Rilke*, p. 61.
21. RMR Br. 1907–14, p. 221.
22. RMR G.W. V, 127; Linton/Malte, p. 98.
23. RMR G.W. V, 130; Linton/Malte, p. 101.
24. RMR G.W. V, 120; Linton/Malte, p. 93.
25. Friedrich Nietzsche, *Jenseits von Gut und Böse* in *Nietzsches Werke*, *Taschenausgabe*, Vol. VIII (Leipzig: Alfred Kröner Verlag, 1927), p. 61.
26. RMR Br. Muzot, p. 154.
27. Ernst Bertram, *Nietzsche: Versuch einer Mythologie* (Berlin: G. Bondi, 1929), p. 177.

28. *The Letters of John Keats*, I, 245.

29. C. G. Jung, *Psychological Types or the Psychology of Individuation* (New York: Harcourt, Brace and Co., 1923), p. 129.

30. *Ibid.*, p. 130.

31. Rilke, *Ausgewählte Werke*, II, 264.

32. *Ibid.*, p. 267.

33. *Ibid.*

34. *Ibid.*, p. 268.

35. J. B. Leishman, *From the Remains of Count C. W.*, German text with English translation (London: Hogarth Press, 1952), p. 9.

36. J. R. von Salis, *Rainer Maria Rilkes Schweizer Jahre* (Frauenfeld-Leipzig: Huber and Co., 1938), p. 56.

37. Leishman/Spender, p. 43.

38. RMR S.W. I, 698 f.

39. *Ibid.*, p. 758.

40. RMR Br. Muzot, p. 19.

41. Rudolf Kassner, *Narciss oder Mythos und Einbildungskraft* (Leipzig: Insel-Verlag, 1928), p. 135.

42. Lou Andreas-Salomé, *Rainer Maria Rilke* (Leipzig: Insel-Verlag, 1928), p. 85.

43. Leishman/P. 1906–26, p. 258.

44. RMR S.W. II, 249.

45. RMR G.W. V, 269; Linton/Malte, p. 217.

46. Cf. Leishman/L.P., p. 97.

47. RMR S.W. II, 79.

48. RMR G.W. V, 140 f.; Linton/Malte, p. 109.

49. RMR G.W. V, 141.

50. Otto Friedrich Bollnow, *Rilke* (Stuttgart: W. Kohlhammer, 1951), p. 272.

51. Kassner, *Narciss oder Mythos und Einbildungskraft*, p. 31.

52. Cummings, *Six Nonlectures*, p. 64.

53. Erich Simenauer, *Rainer Maria Rilke: Legende und Mythos* (Bern: Haupt, 1953), p. 294.

54. RMR Br. Muzot, p. 332

55. RMR S.W. II, 255 f.

56. *Ibid.*

57. RMR G.W. V, 112; Linton/Malte, pp. 86 f.

58. RMR S.W. I, 539 f.

59. *Ibid.*

60. RMR Br. Taxis, I, 155.

61. RMR G.W. V, 153; Linton/Malte, p. 119.

62. RMR Br. Lou, p. 19.

63. RMR Br. Taxis, I, 279 f.

64. Butler, *Rainer Maria Rilke*, p. 245.

65. Leishman/Spender, p. 37.

66. RMR S.W. I, 694.

67. Leishman/P. 1906–26, p. 185.

68. RMR S.W. II, 85.

69. Magda von Hattingberg, *Rilke and Benvenuta*, trans. Cyrus Brooks (New York: W. W. Norton, 1949), p. 67.

70. *Ibid.*, p. 133.

71. Demetz, *René Rilkes Prager Jahre*, p. 107.

72. Edwin Muir, *The Great Wall of China by Franz Kafka* (New York: Schocken Books, 1946), p. xv.

73. RMR Br. 1914–21, p. 399.

74. RMR T.F., p. 135.

75. Demetz, *René Rilkes Prager Jahre*, p. 109.

76. *Ibid.*

77. *Ibid.*, p. 202.

78. Thomas Mann, *Tonio Kröger* (Berlin: S. Fischer, 1921), p. 43.

CHAPTER 3

1. Heerikhuizen, R. M. *Rilke, His Life and Work*, p. 247.

2. *Ibid.*, p. 79.

3. RMR S.W. I, 196.

4. *Ibid.*

5. *Ibid.*, p. 164.

6. *Ibid.*

7. *Ibid.*, p. 195.

8. *Ibid.*

9. *Ibid.*, p. 172.

10. *Ibid.*

11. Demetz, *René Rilkes Prager Jahre*, p. 205.

12. Spender, "The Forerunner of a Future Poetry," *Dublin Review*, CCIX (October, 1941), 188.

13. Heller, *The Disinherited Mind*, p. 137.

14. RMR S.W. I, 257.

15. *Ibid.*

16. RMR Br. T.F., p. 419.

17. RMR Br. 1914–21, p. 292.

18. RMR Br. Taxis, II, 612.

19. RMR Br. 1914–21, pp. 354 f.

20. Lou Andreas-Salomé, *Lebensrückblick: Grundriss einiger Lebenserinnerungen* (Zurich: Niehaus; Wiesbaden: Insel-Verlag, 1951), p. 150.

21. RMR Br. Lou, p. 119.

22. RMR S.W. I, 283.

23. *Ibid.*

24. *Ibid.*

25. *Ibid.*, p. 253.

26. *Ibid.*

27. Andreas-Salomé, *Lebensrückblick*, p. 26.

28. RMR T.F., p. 140.

29. *Ibid.*, p. 110.

30. Walter Rehm, *Orpheus: Der Dichter und die Toten* (Dusseldorf: Schwann, 1950), p. 393.

31. Butler, *Rainer Maria Rilke*, p. 418.
32. RMR V.P., pp. 41 f.
33. RMR Br. Dichter, p. 11; *Letters to a Young Poet*, p. 18.
34. Babette Deutsch (trans.), *Poems from the Book of Hours: Rainer Maria Rilke*, (Norfolk, Conn.: New Directions, 1941), p. 29.
35. RMR S.W. I, 275 f.
36. Angelus Silesius, *Der cherubinische Wandersmann*, I, 8.
37. RMR S.W. I, 351.
38. *Ibid.*
39. Andreas-Salomé, *Lebensrückblick*, p. 152.
40. *Ibid.*, p. 152.
41. *Ibid.*, p. 153.
42. *Ibid.*, p. 154.
43. *Ibid.*, pp. 154 f.
44. *Ibid.*, p. 155.
45. Deutsch, *Poems from the Book of Hours*, p. 35.
46. RMR S.W. I, 313.
47. Leishman/Spender, p. 85.
48. RMR S.W. I, 726.
49. Deutsch, *Poems from the Book of Hours*, p. 37.
50. RMR S.W. I, 327.
51. *Ibid.*, pp. 350 f.
52. *Ibid.*
53. RMR Br. Dichter, p. 46; *Letters to a Young Poet*, p. 67.
54. RMR Br. 1914–21, pp. 89 f.; Hull/RMR, pp. 265 f.
55. Hans Egon Holthusen, *Der unbehauste Mensch* (Munich: R. Piper and Co., 1951), p. 55.
56. Heller, *The Disinherited Mind*, p. 125.
57. *Ibid.*
58. D. H. Lawrence, *The Boy in the Bush* (New York: T. Seltzer, 1924), p. 312.

CHAPTER 4

1. RMR Br. 1907–14, p. 63.
2. RMR Br. Lou, p. 41.
3. *Ibid.*, p. 43.
4. *Ibid.*, pp. 45 f.
5. *Ibid.*, p. 46.
6. *Ibid.*, pp. 46 f.
7. *Ibid.*, p. 55
8. *Ibid.*
9. *Ibid.*, p. 56.
10. *Ibid.*, p. 58.
11. *Ibid.*, p. 63.
12. *Ibid.*, p. 64.
13. *Ibid.*, pp. 65 f.

14. *Ibid.*, p. 90.
15. RMR G.W. V, 195; Linton/Malte, p. 156.
16. RMR G.W. V, 7.
17. RMR G.W. V, 14; Linton/Malte, p. 9.
18. RMR G.W. V, 25; Linton/Malte, p. 18.
19. RMR G.W. V, 29; Linton/Malte, pp. 21 f.
20. RMR G.W. V, 29; Linton/Malte, p. 22.
21. RMR G.W. V, 31; Linton/Malte, pp. 23 f.
22. RMR Br. Lou, p. 246.
23. *Ibid.*, p. 142.
24. *Ibid.*, pp. 142 f.
25. *Ibid.*, p. 150.
26. *Ibid.*, p. 143.
27. Leishman/Spender, pp. 41 f.
28. RMR S.W. I, 697.
29. Mason, *Lebenshaltung und Symbolik bei R. M. Rilke*, p. 4.
30. RMR Br. Lou, p. 92.
31. RMR G.W. IV, 313.
32. RMR G.W. V, 66; Linton/Malte, p. 50.
33. RMR Br. Lou, p. 155.
34. *Ibid.*, p. 156.
35. *Ibid.*, p. 153.
36. *Ibid.*, p. 160.
37. *Ibid.*, p. 180.
38. *Ibid.*, pp. 181 f.
39. *Ibid.*, p. 197.
40. *Ibid.*, p. 246.
41. T. S. Eliot, *Selected Essays, 1917–1932* (New York: Harcourt, Brace and Co., 1932), p. 126.
42. RMR Br. Taxis, I, xviii.
43. Sieber, *René Rilke: Die Jugend Rainer Maria Rilkes*, p. 137.
44. RMR G.W. V, 92; Linton/Malte, p. 71.
45. RMR Br. 1904–7, p. 62.
46. RMR Br. Lou, p. 199.
47. *Ibid.*, p. 202.
48. RMR Br. 1904–7, p. 166; Greene/Norton/RMR, p. 225.
49. RMR Br. 1904–7, p. 328; Hull/RMR, p. 133.
50. Betz, *Rilke in Paris*, pp. 78 f.
51. RMR G.W. V, 249; Linton/Malte, p. 200.
52. RMR Br. 1904–7, pp. 432 f.
53. RMR Br. 1904–7, p. 196; Hull/RMR, p. 209.
54. T. S. Eliot, *Collected Poems, 1909–1935* (London: Faber & Faber, 1936), p. 117.
55. RMR Br. 1907–14, pp. 42 f.; Hull/RMR, p. 171.
56. RMR G.W. V, 246; Linton/Malte, p. 198.
57. RMR G.W. V, 153; Linton/Malte, p. 119.
58. RMR G.W. V, 283 f.; Linton/Malte, p. 229.
59. RMR G.W. V, 241 f.; Linton/Malte, p. 194.

60. Goethe to Eckermann, July 5, 1827.
61. André Gide, *Retour de l'enfant prodigue* (Paris: Gallimard, n.d.), p. 235.
62. RMR G.W. V, 291; Linton/Malte, p. 235.
63. RMR G.W. V, 269; Linton/Malte, p. 217.
64. RMR G.W. V, 293; Linton/Malte, p. 237.
65. RMR G.W. V, 293; Linton/Malte, p. 237.
66. RMR G.W. V, 294; Linton/Malte, p. 238.
67. RMR G.W. V, 296; Linton/Malte, p. 239.
68. RMR G.W. V, 299; Linton/Malte, p. 241.
69. RMR G.W. V, 299; Linton/Malte, p. 242.
70. Job 30: 15, 16, 20.

CHAPTER 5

1. Felix Braun, "Rilkes neue Gedichte," *Süddeutsche Monatshefte,* VI (1909), 286.
2. Stefan Zweig, "Rilkes neue Gedichte," *Das literarische Echo,* XI (1908–9), 415.
3. *Ibid.,* p. 418.
4. *Ibid.*
5. Butler, *Rainer Maria Rilke,* p. 195.
6. RMR Br. Lou, p. 233.
7. RMR Br. 1907–14, p. 73; Greene/Norton/RMR, p. 347.
8. RMR G.W. V, 25; Linton/Malte, p. 19.
9. Eliot, *Selected Essays, 1917–1932,* p. 115.
10. Von Salis, *Rainer Maria Rilkes Schweizer Jahre,* p. 140.
11. RMR Br. 1907–14, p. 74; Greene/Norton/RMR, p. 347.
12. RMR G.W. IV, 376 f.
13. Leishman/Spender, p. 75.
14. RMR S.W. I, 718.
15. RMR Br. Muzot, p. 17.
16. RMR Br. 1902–6, p. 111.
17. RMR Br. Lou, p. 83.
18. RMR Br. 1904–7, p. 339.
19. RMR Br. Taxis, I, 26 f.
20. Leishman/Spender, p. 43.
21. RMR S.W. I, 698.
22. Elisabeth von Schmidt-Pauli, *Rainer Marie Rilke: Ein Gedenkbuch* (Stuttgart: Bürger-Verlag, 1946), p. 20.
23. Andreas-Salomé, *Lebensrückblick,* p. 163.
24. Louise Bogan, "Rilke in His Age," *Poetry: A Magazine of Verse,* L (1937), 34.
25. Heerikhuizen, *R. M. Rilke: His Life and Work,* p. 278.
26. RMR Br. 1904–7, p. 432.
27. RMR Br. II, 406.
28. Cf. Leishman/Requiem, p. 82.
29. RMR S.W. I, 505.

30. Leishman/Spender, p. 67.
31. Butler, *Rainer Maria Rilke*, p. 195.
32. Herman J. Weigand, "Das Wunder im Werke Rainer M. Rilkes," *Monatshefte*, XXXI (January, 1939), 1.
33. Leishman/Requiem, p. 59.
34. *Ibid.*, p. 83.
35. RMR S.W. I, 508.
36. Weigand, "Das Wunder im Werke Rainer M. Rilkes," p. 6.
37. RMR S.W. II, 277.
38. *Ibid.*
39. RMR Br. Muzot, p. 223.
40. Leishman/Poems, p. 40.
41. RMR S.W. I, 636.
42. RMR Br. Verlager, p. 39.
43. Leishman/Orpheus, p. 141.
44. Rudolf Kassner, "R. M. Rilke: Zum Gedächtnis seine Geburtstages," *Frankfurter Zeitung*, December 4, 1935, p. 619.
45. Butler, *Rainer Maria Rilke*, pp. 195 f.
46. RMR S.W. II, 27; Leishman/L.P., p. 43.
47. Leishman/L.P., p. 44.
48. RMR, S.W. II, 150.
49. Leishman/S.P., p. 26.
50. RMR S.W. I, 520.
51. Simenauer, *Rainer Maria Rilke: Legende und Mythos*, p. 404.
52. *Ibid.*, p. 413.
53. *Ibid.*, p. 411.
54. RMR Br. Taxis I, xxii.
55. RMR S.W. I, 609; Holthusen, *Rainer Maria Rilke: A Study of His Later Poetry*, p. 10.
56. RMR S.W. I, 609.
57. RMR Br. 1907–14, pp. 25 f.; Greene/Norton/RMR, p. 329.
58. RMR G.W. V, 283; Linton/Malte, p. 229.
59. Mason, *Lebenshaltung und Symbolik bei R. M. Rilke*, p. 96.
60. RMR Br. Lou, p. 465; Hull/RMR, p. 354.
61. Ernst Rose, "R. M. Rilke's Spätherbst in Venedig: An Interpretation," *Germanic Review*, XVI (February, 1941), 70 f.
62. Leishman/P. 1906–26, p. 176.
63. RMR S.W. II, 411.
64. RMR Br. Lou, p. 248; Hull/RMR, p. 186.
65. *Ibid.*, p. 249.
66. Heerikhuizen, *R. M. Rilke: His Life and Work*, p. 218.
67. RMR Br. Lou, p. 284.
68. *Ibid.*, pp. 284 f.
69. Cf. Leishman/L.P., p. 62.
70. RMR S.W. II, 83 f.
71. Butler, *Rainer Maria Rilke*, p. 196.
72. Leishman/Requiem, p. 87.
73. RMR S.W. I, 557.

CHAPTER 6

1. Leishman/Spender, p. 45.
2. Butler, *Rainer Marie Rilke*, p. 424.
3. Heerikhuizen, *R. M. Rilke: His Life and Work*, p. 247.
4. RMR Br. Muzot, p. 195.
5. Leishman/Orpheus, p. 11.
6. Jung, *Psychological Types or the Psychology of Individuation*, p. 113.
7. *Ibid.*, p. 211.
8. Geoffrey Keynes (ed.), *The Writings of William Blake* (3 vols.; London: Nonesuch Press, 1925), III, 89.
9. *Faust I*, lines 1607 ff.
10. *Ibid.*
11. Leishman/Spender, p. 77.
12. RMR S.W. I, 720.
13. Werner Bergengruen, *Die heile Welt* (Munich: Nymphenburger Verlagshandlung, 1950), p. 25.
14. RMR Br. Muzot, p. 338; Hull/RMR, p. 396.
15. RMR Br. Taxis, I, xxxv.
16. RMR S.W. II, 259.
17. Leishman/Spender, p. 31.
18. RMR S.W. I, 691.
19. RMR Br. Taxis I, xxxv.
20. RMR Br. 1907–14, p. 165; Hull/RMR, p. 195.
21. RMR Br. Taxis I, 27; Hull/RMR, p. 181
22. RMR Br. Lou, p. 248; Hull/RMR, p. 186.
23. RMR Br. Taxis I, 42.
24. RMR Br. Lou, p. 252; Hull/RMR, p. 188.
25. RMR Br. 1907–14, p. 168.
26. RMR Br. 1907–14, p. 170; Hull/RMR, p. 197.
27. RMR Br. I, 318.
28. Leishman/Spender, p. 21.
29. RMR S.W. I, 685.
30. RMR Br. Muzot, p. 337; Hull/RMR, p. 395.
31. Werner Günther, *Weltinnenraum: Die Dichtung Rainer Maria Rilkes* (Bern-Leipzig: Haupt, 1943), p. 224.
32. RMR Br. 1907–14, p. 178; Hull/RMR, pp. 202 f.
33. RMR Br. Taxis I, 27.
34. Hans Carossa, "Führung und Geleit: Ein Lebensgedenkbuch," *Gesammelte Werke* (2 vols.; Wiesbaden: Insel-Verlag, 1949), I, 650.
35. RMR Br. 1907–14, p. 196.
36. Cf. Leishman/L.P., p. 51.
37. RMR S.W. II, 49.
38. Leishman/Spender, p. 67.
39. RMR S.W. I, 714.
40. Leishman/Spender, p. 61.

41. RMR S.W. I, 710.
42. Leishman/Spender, p. 73.
43. RMR S.W. I, 717.
44. Jung, *Psychological Types or the Psychology of Individuation*, p. 61.
45. RMR Br. 1914–21, p. 80.
46. RMR Br. Taxis I, 27; Hull/RMR, p. 181.
47. RMR Br. 1907–14, p. 275.
48. Leishman/Spender, p. 23.
49. RMR S.W. I, 686.
50. RMR Br. Lou, p. 290.
51. Mason, *Lebenshaltung und Symbolik bei R. M. Rilke*, p. 24.
52. RMR Br. Lou, p. 317.
53. RMR, *Ausgewählte Werke*, II, 279.
54. Leishman/Spender, p. 45.
55. RMR S.W. I, 699.
56. RMR Br. 1914–21, pp. 380 f.; Hull/RMR, pp. 315 f.
57. RMR Br. Lou, pp. 100 f.
58. RMR Br. 1907–14, pp. 182 f.; Hull/RMR, pp. 204 f.
59. Cf. Leishman/Spender, p. 77.
60. RMR S.W. I, 720.
61. RMR Br. Muzot, p. 347.
62. Butler, *Rainer Maria Rilke*, p. 330.
63. E. L. Stahl, "The Duineser Elegien," in *R. M. Rilke: Aspects of His Mind and Poetry*, ed. William Rose and G. C. Houston with an introduction by Stefan Zweig (London: Sidgewick and Jackson, 1938), p. 143.
64. Mason, *Lebenshaltung und Symbolik bei R. M. Rilke*, p. 119.
65. Romano Guardini, *Rainer Maria Rilkes Deutung des Daseins* (Munich: Kösel Verlag, 1953), p. 165.
66. RMR S.W. I, 685.
67. Leishman/Spender, p. 35.
68. RMR S.W. I, 693.
69. Leishman/Spender, p. 37.
70. RMR S.W. I, 695.
71. Leishman/Spender, p. 21.
72. RMR S.W. I, 685.
73. Butler, *Rainer Maria Rilke*, p. 246.
74. Von Hattingberg, *Rilke and Benvenuta*, p. 2.
75. *Ibid.*, p. 190.
76. *Ibid.*, pp. 8 f.
77. *Ibid.*, pp. 9 f.
78. *Ibid.*, p. 9.
79. *Ibid.*, p. 24.
80. RMR S.W. II, 216.
81. Von Hattingberg, *Rilke and Benvenuta*, pp. 93 f.
82. *Ibid.*, p. 98.
83. *Ibid.*, p. 127.
84. *Ibid.*, pp. 127 f.
85. *Ibid.*, p. 131.

86. *Ibid.*
87. Von Salis, *Rainer Maria Rilkes Schweizer Jahre,* p. 200.
88. Cf. Leishman/L.P., p. 73.
89. RMR S.W. II, 84.
90. Leishman/L.P., p. 67.
91. RMR S.W. II, 89.
92. RMR Br. 1914–21, p. 74.
93. *Ibid.,* p. 78.
94. Katharina Kippenberg, *Rainer Maria Rilke: Ein Beitrag* (Leipzig: Insel-Verlag, 1938), p. 231.
95. RMR Br. Lou, p. 268.
96. Leishman/Spender, p. 41.
97. RMR S.W. I, 697.
98. Leishman/Spender, p. 41.
99. RMR S.W. I, 697.
100. Leishman/Spender, p. 41.
101. RMR S.W. I, 697.
102. Leishman/Spender, pp. 41 f.
103. RMR S.W. I, 697.
104. Günther, *Weltinnenraum,* p. 180.
105. Leishman/Spender, p. 43.
106. RMR S.W. I, 697 f.
107. Leishman/Spender, p. 43.
108. RMR S.W. I, 698.
109. Leishman/L.P., p. 72.
110. RMR S.W. II, 104.
111. RMR Br. Lou, p. 269.
112. Leishman/Spender, p. 43.
113. RMR S.W. I, 698.
114. Leishman/Spender, p. 43.
115. RMR S.W. I, 698.
116. Leishman/Spender, pp. 43 f.
117. RMR S.W. I, 698 f.
118. Guardini, *Rainer Maria Rilkes Deutung des Daseins,* p. 165.
119. RMR Br. Taxis, II, 698; Hull/RMR, p. 352.
120. Leishman/Spender, p. 45.
121. RMR S.W. I, 699.
122. Friedrich Nietzsche, *Ecce Homo,* in *Nietzsches Werke, Taschenausgabe,* Vol. XI (Leipzig: Alfred Kröner, 1923), p. 350.
123. Leishman/Spender, p. 45.
124. RMR S.W. I, 699.
125. Leishman/Spender, p. 45.
126. RMR S.W. I, 700.
127. RMR Br. Muzot, p. 332; Hull/RMR, pp. 392 f.
128. RMR Br. II, 381 f.
129. Guardini, *Rainer Maria Rilkes Deutung des Daseins,* p. 414.
130. C. G. Jung, *Modern Man in Search of a Soul* (London: K. Paul, Trench, Trubner and Co., 1933), p. 129.

131. RMR Br. Taxis, II, 588.
132. RMR Br. Muzot, p. 109.
133. *Ibid.*
134. Cf. Leishman/L.P., p. 128.
135. RMR S.W. II, 93.
136. Leishman/Spender, p. 33.
137. RMR S.W. I, 692.
138. Leishman/Spender, p. 75.
139. RMR S.W. I, 718.
140. Leishman/Spender, p. 77.
141. RMR S.W. I, 719.
142. RMR Br. Muzot, p. 334; Hull/RMR, p. 394.
143. RMR Br. Lou, p. 474.
144. Guardini, *Rainer Maria Rilkes Deutung des Daseins*, p. 334.
145. RMR Br. Muzot, p. 335; Hull/RMR, p. 394.
146. RMR Br. Muzot, p. 335.
147. Butler, *Rainer Maria Rilke*, p. 390.
148. Leishman/P. 1906–26, p. 330.
149. RMR S.W. II, 265.
150. Holthusen, *Der unbehauste Mensch*, p. 63.
151. Sir James Jeans, *The Mysterious Universe* (London: Pelican Books, 1937), p. 96.

CHAPTER 7

1. M. Bemol, "Rilke et les influences," *Revue de la littérature comparée* (April–June, 1953), p. 174.
2. RMR Br. Taxis, II, 686.
3. Paul Valéry, *Lettres à quelques-uns* (Paris: Gallimard, 1952), pp. 238 f.
4. Monique Saint-Helier, *A Rilke pour Noël* (Bern: Ed. du Chandelier, 1927), p. 16.
5. Paul Valéry, *L'âme et la danse* (Paris: Gallimard, 1924), p. 46.
6. *Ibid.*, p. 25.
7. *Ibid.*, p. 52.
8. *Ibid.*, p. 56.
9. RMR Br. II, 408; Leishman/Orpheus, p. 12.
10. RMR Br. Muzot, pp. 83 f.; Leishman/Orpheus, p. 12.
11. Cf. Leishman/Orpheus, p. 57.
12. RMR S.W. I, 738.
13. RMR Br. Muzot, p. 98.
14. Cf. Leishman/Orpheus, p. 43.
15. RMR S.W. I, 733.
16. C. F. MacIntyre, *Rainer Maria Rilke: The Life of the Virgin Mary* (Berkeley and Los Angeles: University of California Press, 1947), p. viii.
17. RMR Br. Verleger, p. 360.
18. RMR Br. Taxis, II, 716.
19. RMR Br. Muzot, p. 142.

20. RMR Br. 1907–14, p. 254.
21. Butler, *Rainer Maria Rilke*, p. 340.
22. Mason, *Lebenshaltung und Symbolik bei R. M. Rilke*, p. 200.
23. *Ibid.*, p. 206.
24. RMR Br. II, 419.
25. *Ibid.*, p. 337.
26. Leishman/Orpheus, p. 89.
27. RMR S.W. I, 751.
28. Leishman/Orpheus, p. 39.
29. RMR S.W. I, 732.
30. Butler, *Rainer Maria Rilke*, pp. 344 f.
31. Leishman/Orpheus, p. 77.
32. RMR S.W. I, 745.
33. Frank Wood, "Rilke and D. H. Lawrence," *Germanic Review*, XV (October, 1940), 217.
34. Rehm, *Orpheus: Der Dichter und die Toten*, p. 511.
35. H. E. Holthusen, *Rilkes Sonette an Orpheus* (Munich: Neuer Filser Verlag), p. 44.
36. *Ibid.*, pp. 44 f.
37. Cf. Leishman/Orpheus, p. 113.
38. RMR S.W. I, 759 f.
39. Cf. Leishman/Orpheus, p. 145.
40. RMR S.W. I, 771.
41. Leishman/Spender, p. 27.
42. RMR S.W. I, 688.
43. Leishman/Orpheus, p. 85.
44. RMR S.W. I, 748.
45. J. B. Leishman, *Rainer Maria Rilke: Sonnets to Orpheus* (1st ed.; London: Hogarth Press, 1936), p. 181.
46. Leishman/Spender, p. 73.
47. RMR S.W. I, 717.
48. Leishman/Orpheus, p. 26.
49. *Ibid.*, p. 57.
50. RMR S.W. I, 738.
51. Cf. Leishman/Orpheus, p. 51.
52. RMR S.W. I, 736.
53. Leishman/Orpheus, p. 71.
54. RMR S.W. I, 743.
55. Butler, *Rainer Maria Rilke*, p. 358.
56. David I. Masson, "Patterns of Vowel and Consonant in a Rilkean Sonnet," *Modern Language Review*, XLVI (July–October, 1951), 419.
57. *Ibid.*, p. 421.
58. *Ibid.*, p. 429.
59. Cf. Leishman/Orpheus, p. 119.
60. RMR S.W. I, 761 f.
61. Butler, *Rainer Maria Rilke*, p. 357.
62. Leishman/Orpheus, p. 170.

63. Norbert Fürst, "A Silly Sonnet to Orpheus," *Modern Language Notes,* LIX (December, 1944), 558.

64. Leishman/Orpheus, p. 166; RMR S.W. I, 773.

65. Leishman/Orpheus, p. 167.

66. Cf. *ibid.,* p. 109.

67. RMR S.W. I, 758.

68. Leishman/Orpheus (1st ed.), p. 179.

69. Cf. Leishman/Orpheus, p. 133.

70. RMR S.W. I, 766 f.

71. Leishman/Orpheus, p. 77.

72. RMR S.W. I, 745.

73. Ernst Rose, "Goethes 'Chorus Mysticus' als Anregung für Nietzsche und Rilke," *Germanic Review,* XVIII (February, 1942), 46.

74. RMR S.W. I, 726.

CHAPTER 8

1. Holthusen, *Der unbehauste Mensch,* p. 65.

2. Butler, *Rainer Maria Rilke,* p. 183.

3. RMR S.W. I, 553.

4. *Ibid.*

5. *Ibid.,* p. 554.

6. *Ibid.*

7. RMR P.F., p. 96.

8. Leishman/Orpheus, p. 99.

9. RMR S.W. I, 754.

10. Cf. Leishman/Orpheus, p. 43.

11. RMR S.W. I, 733.

12. RMR Br. II, 374.

13. RMR Br. Muzot, p. 128; Leishman/Orpheus, p. 16.

14. Leishman/P. 1906–26, p. 175.

15. RMR S.W. II, 411.

16. RMR P.F., p. 100.

17. *Ibid.,* p. 128.

18. Cf. Leishman/L.P., p. 174.

19. RMR S.W. II, 467.

20. RMR *Die Briefe an Gräfin Margot Sizzo* (Wiesbaden: Insel-Verlag, 1950), pp. 38 f.

21. RMR P.F., p. 21.

22. Leishman/P. 1906–26, p. 267.

23. RMR S.W. II, 470.

24. John Sampson (ed.), *The Poems of William Blake* (London: Florence Press, Chatto and Windus, 1926), p. 303.

25. Heinrich Zimmer, *Philosophies of India* (New York: Pantheon Books, 1951), p. 345.

26. RMR S.W. I, 715; Leishman/Spender, p. 69.

27. RMR Br. Frau, p. 7.

28. Butler, *Rainer Maria Rilke*, p. 4.

29. Barker Fairley, "R. M. Rilke: An Estimate," *University of Toronto Quarterly*, XI (October, 1941), 14

30. RMR T.F., p. 140.

31. Eudo C. Mason, *Der Zopf des Münchhausen* (Einsiedeln: Johannes Verlag, 1949), p. 244.

32. Holthusen, *Rilkes Sonette an Orpheus*, p. 192.

33. RMR Br. Merline, p. 92; cf. RMR *Letters to Merline*, trans. Violet Macdonald (London: Methuen and Co., 1951), p. 48.

34. Kassner, *Narciss oder Mythos und Einbildungskraft*, p. 128.

35. RMR S.W. I, 271.

36. RMR Br. Merline, p. 93; cf. RMR *Letters to Merline*, trans. Macdonald, p. 48.

37. RMR Br. Taxis, I, 254.

38. Fairley, "R. M. Rilke: An Estimate," p. 12.

39. Leishman/Requiem, p. 101.

40. RMR S.W. I, 653 f.

41. Mason, *Lebenshaltung und Symbolik bei R. M. Rilke*, p. 21.

42. Jaloux, in "Reconnaissance à Rilke," *Les Cahiers du Mois*, XXIII–XXIV (Paris, 1926), p. 13.

43. C. G. Jung, *Seelenprobleme der Gegenwart* (Zurich: Rasher and Co., 1931), p. 70.

44. Mason, *Lebenshaltung und Symbolik bei R. M. Rilke*, pp. 28 f.

45. Zimmer, *Philosophies of India*, p. 4.

46. *Ibid.*, p. 237.

47. *Ibid.*, p. 12.

48. RMR Br. Merline, p. 92; cf. RMR *Letters to Merline*, trans. Macdonald, p. 48.

49. Jung, *Psychological Types or the Psychology of Individuation*, p. 512.

50. RMR S.W. II, 174 f.

51. *Ibid.*

Selective Bibliography

In writing this book I found the following titles from among the large body of Rilke literature particularly helpful and suggestive.

Belmore, H. W. *Rilke's Craftsmanship: An Analysis of His Poetic Style*. Oxford: Blackwell, 1954. A close study of Rilke's poetic technique.

Butler, E. M. *Rainer Maria Rilke*. Cambridge, Eng.: Cambridge University Press, 1941. Provocative, but still one of the most important books in English on Rilke.

Demetz, Peter. *René Rilkes Prager Jahre*. Düsseldorf: Diederichs, 1953. Attempts to destroy the legend of Rilke's "hard childhood."

Guardini, Romano. *Rainer Maria Rilkes Deutung des Daseins*. Munich: Kösel Verlag, 1953. An examination of the validity of Rilke's world view by the eminent Catholic theologian and literary critic.

Heller, Erich. *The Disinherited Mind: Essays in Modern German Literature and Thought*. Cambridge, Eng.: Bowes and Bowes, 1952.

Heerikhuizen, F. W. van. *R. M. Rilke: His Life and Work*, trans. Fernand G. Renier and Anne Cliff. New York: Philosophical Library, 1952.

Holthusen, Hans Egon. *Rainer Maria Rilke: A Study of His Later Poetry*, trans. J. P. Stern. New Haven, Conn.: Yale University Press, 1952.

Kraemer, Richard. *Der sensitive Mensch: Versuch einer Darstellung am Bilde des Dichters Rainer Maria Rilke*. Wiesbaden: Verlag der Akademie der Wissenschaften und der Literatur in Mainz, Franz Steiner, 1954. A medical report on the man Rilke.

Mises, Richard von. *Rilke in English: A Tentative Bibliography*. Cambridge, Mass.: Cosmos Press, 1947. Lists some 227 titles of books, articles, and translations in English that appeared up to 1946. Needs to be brought up to date.

Ritzer, Walter. *Rainer Marie Rilke Bibliographie*. Vienna: O. Kerry, 1951. This is the most complete Rilke bibliography extant. It lists 1,600 Rilke scholars, many with more than one entry, and is an indispensable tool for the serious student. But it must be supplemented by publications that have appeared since 1950.

Simenauer, Erich. *Rainer Maria Rilke: Legende und Mythos*. Bern: Haupt, 1953. A detailed 759-page psychoanalytical study of the relationship between Rilke's neuroses and his poetry.

Index

RILKE'S WORKS

English Titles

German and French Titles